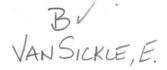

THE IRON GATES OF SANTO TOMÁS

The Firsthand Account of an
American Couple Interned by the Japanese
in Manila, 1942-45

THE IRON GATES OF SANTO TOMÁS

The Firsthand Account of an
American Couple Interned by the Japanese
in Manila, 1942-45

Emily Van Sickle

Academy
Chicago
Publishers

Published in 1992 by
Academy Chicago Publishers
213 West Institute Place
Chicago, Illinois 60610

Printed and bound in the USA

Library of Congress Cataloging-in-Publication Data

Van Sickle, Emily.
        The iron gates of Santo Tomás: imprisonment in Manila, 1942-45/
        by Emily Van Sickle.
                p.   cm.
        ISBN 0-89733-379-9: $25.00
        1. Van Sickle, Emily. 2. Van Sickle, Charles. 3. Santo Tomás
        Internment Camp (Manila, Philippines) 4. World War, 1939-1945--
        Prisoners and prisons, Japanese. 5. World War, 1939-1945--
        Personal narratives, American. 6. Americans—Philippines—Manila—
        Biography. I. Title.
        D805.P6V36 1992
        940.53'17'59916092—dc20
        [B]   92-22991
                                                               CIP

CONTENTS

Photographs and maps following
page 196.

THE IRON GATES OF SANTO TOMÁS

The Firsthand Account of an
American Couple Interned by the Japanese
in Manila, 1942-45

PREFACE

It is one thing to be a student at a university famed as the old-est under the American flag, and quite another to be arbitrarily detained in that illustrious institution for an indefinite period as a civilian prisoner of war. My husband and I were among several thousand American and European civilians to be trapped by war in the Philippines. When Manila fell in January, 1942, the victorious Japanese escorted us to the campus of Santo Tomás University, where we remained unwilling 'guests' for more than three years. There, we learned many things, some funny, some tragic, that are no part of a normal college curricu-lum. At the time of this singular postgraduate course, I was thirty-one; Van's forty-third birthday occurred the following month.

Since no other spot in Manila was large enough to contain thousands of civilian prisoners, the University's Dominican priests, successors to the Spanish padres who had founded Santo Tomás in 1619, offered their forty-eight-acre campus for our internment. Many times during the years that followed, these brave and generous priests interceded with the Japanese on our behalf; sometimes their pleas were heeded.

The university grounds, enclosed on three sides by high concrete walls and along the front by concrete-embedded iron bars, provided a made-to-order concentration camp. For us, our prison offered the advantages of attractive landscaping, central location and comparative spaciousness; on the debit side, there

1

were few washing and toilet facilities, no sleeping quarters — only classrooms equipped with desks and chairs — and, in the beginning, no food except what we had been able to bring with us.

As the iron gates of Santo Tomás swung closed behind us, we, like others before and since, might well have wondered how we had ever become ensnared in this calamitous mesh of circumstances that now shut out the light of liberty which we had always accepted as our inalienable American birthright.

This, in brief, is the train of events which led Van and me to our incarceration: in 1935, I accompanied my parents to Manila, where my father (then Major Myron C. Crammer, U.S. Army) was stationed as Judge Advocate General for the Philippine Department; and there I met Van, who at that time managed the motor trucks division of International Harvester Company of the Philippines. Two years later, we were married in Washington, D.C.

A few months after our return to Manila, Van was transferred to China as sole representative for International Harvester Company, a change which pleased us not only because it was a promotion but because China's climate freed Van from severe attacks of asthma, which had plagued him in the Philippines. During the next two years our headquarters were in Hong Kong, where we lived at the Repulse Bay Hotel. Van made frequent trips to Shanghai, Chungking, North China, Indo-China, and later to Burma. As often as possible, I traveled with him.

By the summer of 1940, however, echoes of the European war were resounding across Asia, and the Japanese stood waiting at the very border to spring on British Kowloon, across the bay from Hong Kong. Strange uneasiness pervaded our island city: like whistlers in the dark, men spoke bravely of their training in the Volunteers; by military order, British women were evacuated; beaches were strung with barbed wire, while overhead three tiny planes, Hong Kong's sole air defense, circled the Crown Colony like futile sparrows defying an unseen swarm of hawks.

Van decided that the time had come to go home, and in

September, 1940 we sailed on the *President Coolidge*, never intending to return again to the Far East. Almost a year later, however, he volunteered, because of personnel difficulties in Burma, to go back for a few months, providing that he could take me. I remember with amused exasperation that the State Department refused me permission to go anywhere except Manila, which, they claimed, was "the only safe place in the Orient."

Upon our arrival there toward the end of August, Van left me at the Bay View Hotel and flew to Rangoon, then to Hong Kong, returning to Manila December 3 on what proved to be the clipper from the island. We had plans for sailing homeward in January.

But now, an end had come to our life of carefree adventuring; we were locked securely away from the world we had known and relished. We were prisoners in a concentration camp.

In a world where many have been deprived of freedom — whether in detention camps or behind Iron and Bamboo Curtains — our experience was by no means unique. Like prisoners everywhere, we left the day behind us and entered a world of twilight — a drab, grey world, only half-real, like nightmares that haunt our souls in sleep.

There are those who have entered such a twilight world never again to return to the light, who have been doomed to the horror of unending night. I would not compare our privations and sufferings with theirs; rather, I would describe the actions and reactions of human beings in whom the sense of freedom has been supplanted by fear — because our world today holds uncounted numbers of such human beings.

When the twilight of imprisonment closed around us, we yearned for the light, and when it shone for us again, we rejoiced: not for ourselves alone, but for innocent prisoners everywhere, for we hoped then that war's end would rid the world of this evil perpetrated against helpless civilians. But the evil did not die with termination of hostilities; and, if war comes again, the territories involved will be so vast that no man, woman or child will be safe from the gigantic net spread out by enemy conquerors to "neutralize" civilian citizens of a defeated land.

I have a letter, postmarked June 2nd, 1945, from Corporal Robert M. Cartwright, a crew member of the plane that flew us after the liberation from Manila to Leyte, to whom I had written when we were safely home. He wrote, "I see by your letter that you remember well the day you climbed on our plane. I guess that will stand out as the day life began again."

I do remember that day well, and the many events that preceded that day. On our ship going home in March, 1945, we heard for the first time a popular song, "Don't Fence Me In," which seemed to have been written especially for ex-internees, now called "repatriates," who had been so long fenced in behind the walls of Santo Tomás.

Van announced, "When I get home, I'm going to sit on the banks of the Ohio and watch that river till it stops flowing." His statement reflected the universal internee sentiment: give us the great open spaces, the green fields, the rivers flowing down to the sea. . . .

In actuality, the open spaces are mere symbols of the freedom we cherish, the freedom we take for granted until we lose it. Freedom means justice, and order imposed by the will of the people rather than by force; it means the right to choose one's job within the limitations of ability, the right to select one's governing officials, the right to worship as one chooses, to speak one's convictions and to seek legal protection against fraud, injury or intimidation, the right of a property owner to fence in whatever part of those great open spaces he may have acquired fairly and legally for himself.

Freedom is the rightful heritage of every human being, one so precious that it must be zealously guarded, as we should have learned by watching its disappearance from so vast a part of the world. Those of us who have been even briefly depriv-

4

ed of this precious heritage perhaps treasure it more than o-thers who have always enjoyed the protection of a nation that was born fighting for freedom. I hope that the story of our pris-on life may arouse in the apathetic an awareness of how ut-terly helpless one becomes with the loss of liberty — that they may be always alert in resisting forces, both from within and without, that would deprive human beings unjustly of their greatest privilege and God-given right: to live as free men, equal among ourselves as we are equal in His sight.

PART I: INTO THE SHADOWS

Chapter One

War struck like the proverbial thunderbolt a few months after our return to the Far East on what was to have been a brief mission. The time: December 8, a Monday morning — Pearl Harbor Day in Manila.

Only the night before we had dined with an old friend, Jack Littig, at the home of his wife's parents, longtime Manila residents Walter and Bettie Stevenson. At about ten o'clock Jack, just back from the States wearing a new U.S.N.R. Commander's uniform, had telephoned his wife, whom he had been forced to leave behind with their two-year-old son in San Francisco. All had appeared that night to be well in our relatively normal and secure world; no warning sign prognosticated the cataclysm to engulf us.

It was nine-thirty on Monday morning before I picked up the paper and stared dazedly at the headlines: "HONOLULU BOMBED!" I could not grasp it at first; then I thought, "Thank God Van got back!" What a narrow escape, to have returned only five days earlier from Hong Kong, where I was not allowed to go!

Van was sleeping. When I wakened him, he glanced at the paper, said, "I don't believe it" — then turned over and calmly went back to sleep. Incredibly stupid though it sounds now, such torpid disbelief mirrored accurately the mental and emotional confusion of most Manilans at that time, although I doubt that others expressed their reaction so graphically. During the weeks since our return, the city had glittered with a restless gaiety, an almost defiant bravado, as it awaited outbreak of an inevitable war vaguely anticipated some four to six months later. Few indeed were those who had envisioned the possibility of a swift, treacherous assault while Japanese diplomats were still talking compromise in Washington.

However, no one could long doubt that just such an improbable catastrophe had befallen us. By noon, extra papers headlined bombings at Baguio, in the hills north of Manila; then at Clark Field, where Japanese planes demolished on the ground our handful of Flying Fortresses. That night, there was a small raid over Manila. When the alarm sounded, we grabbed our clothes and scurried downstairs with the rest of the bewildered guests at Manila's modern, attractive Bay View Hotel. Two or three bombs fell on Nichols Field, the Army airport on the outskirts of the city.

From midday on Wednesday, when the Japanese staged their first big raid, it should have been evident that the enemy held unquestioned air supremacy, for their planes, swarming over us twenty-seven to a group, were unchallenged by a single American fighter. Navy anti-aircraft guns, flak-flakking ineffectually from ships in the harbor, succeeded only in driving them higher. Enemy wings flashed silver in the sunlight as we watched, horrified and helpless, from a sandbagged hotel entrance. Whenever they glided directly over us, our stomachs began to flutter sickeningly, and we scuttered inside like rabbits diving underground to escape a pack of hounds.

However, the Japanese conserved their bombs for Nichols Field and Cavite, the Naval station farther along the bay, which they blasted mercilessly. Thereafter, unhampered by any effective opposition, the planes attacked our military defenses almost daily.

Although Manila fell with breathtaking swiftness, few of us even now foresaw the inevitable outcome. Between air raids and futile bandage rolling, we often walked along the bay-front up Dewey Boulevard, where in peaceful bygone days we had enjoyed magnificent sunsets painted on sky and water. Now, against the backdrop of nature's rich colors at eventide, tall columns of smoke from Nichols Field and Cavite spoke mutely of the day's destruction. Yet our own lack of planes to forestall the enemy's striking power did not worry us unduly, because we believed President Roosevelt's promise that "help is on the way" — never dreaming how long that help would take to reach us.

Disturbed though we were by stories of enemy landings, we did not yet know enough about war to realize what those land-ings meant. At night, by the dull glimmer of blackout lights which served only to deepen the gloom, our spirits sometimes quailed, and we asked one another why our Army did nothing to stop the Japanese; yet most of us concurred readily enough in the naïve suggestion that our troops probably wanted to lure them inland where they would cut off supplies from their beachheads and trap them en masse.

Ignorance of Manila's pitiful vulnerability, however, did not deter some of us from trying to escape the bomb-blasted city, only to discover that, for the time being at least, all avenues of escape were barred to us. By military order, passengers and crews from ships en route to other ports were brought ashore, and their ships left anchored in the bay to be sunk by Japanese bombs. Only two ships that I know of, and a few privately owned small craft, managed to sneak away form the port.

Not until the High Commissioner and part of his staff had moved to Corregidor on Christmas Eve did we realize at last that Manila, "Pearl of the Orient," was about to fall into grasping Japanese hands. By that time, it had become a city of confusion, its populace surging distractedly from one section of town to another in a frantic search for the elusive "safest spot"— mean-ing, of course, the spot least likely to be bombed. Many sought refuge at the Bay View.

With the designation of Manila as an "Open City," confusion rapidly degenerated to utter chaos as thousands of Filipinos ransacked abandoned warehouses which the Army had thrown open to the public. After stripping them bare of food, cigarettes, clothing, even office equipment, scavengers returned to loot private stores. From our hotel windows we watched them stream along Dewey Boulevard like endless columns of ants, some hauling away plunder in cars and trucks, others on bicycles, pushcarts, shoulder poles or even by hand. The Philippine Police merely looked on, hopelessly inadequate to cope with such widespread vandalism.

A daily rain of bombs thundered down on the harbor district as the Japanese sank every ship still afloat in the bay and in the sluggish Pasig River. Black smoke, billowing up from oil dumps burned by our retreating forces, blanketed the sky for days in a dismal, depressing murk.

One lone episode brightened that grim Christmas week: on December 29, the Naval Intelligence officer in charge of communications, who happened to be our Pearl Harbor Eve companion, Jack Littig, advised us that telephone wires to the States would be briefly opened for private calls. Although we could mention no dates or places, I conveyed our whereabouts by telling my mother that we still lived at the Bay View. To her, the conversation was one of mingled relief and anguish: relief that we were alive, anguish that we had not somehow escaped to safety. Jack Littig put through a final call to his wife before cutting the wires, a job he had been expressly left behind to execute; then he followed precariously in the wake of truck convoys which had rumbled away to Bataan.

On New Year's Eve, last-minute dynamiting of military installations and matériel transformed Manila into a veritable inferno as torches of burning oil, drifting down the Pasig into the bay, touched off fresh blazes along the river banks. A death-like hush had fallen over the city, punctuated now and again by the crackle of flames and an intermittent roar of nearby explosions. Mutely, we watched the dance of fire and flickering shadow across walls of high buildings which for an instant glowed evilly red against the darkness, only to be swallowed up again in the hellish jaws of night.

Next day, the first of an unpromising New Year, we prepared ourselves as best we could to face the Japanese, who had announced that they would enter Manila on the 2nd. Ignoring optimistic speculations that the conqueror might allow enemy aliens to roam freely, or might concentrate men and women together, Van and I packed separate suitcases to meet any eventuality. Then we destroyed papers which might harm us or help the Japanese: International Harvester code books, copies of contracts with the Chinese government, clippings about my father's recent appointment as the Judge Advocate General of the Army. Meanwhile, the hotel staff was busily engaged in dumping liquor down the drain.

When jubilant Japanese soldiers finally clattered down Dewey Boulevard in their tinny cars and putt-putt motorcycles, we gasped dumbfounded, wondering incredulously whether the weapons which they had wielded to vanquish our brave Americans could have been of the same inferior quality as their motor vehicles. Our rudely jolted national pride was more deeply wounded as we watched the Japanese hoist their flag of the Rising Sun over the High Commissioner's mansion across the boulevard, on the flagpole where only a few days before our own Stars and Stripes had waved so majestically.

Allowed to remain in our rooms, we amused ourselves for the next three days by observing the antics of car-happy Japanese soldiers, to whom every handsome American automobile was now a legitimate prize and plaything. Whooping and hollering, they careened gaily in all directions, over curbs, parking strips, sidewalks, lawns and flower beds. The blare of horns and the sickening screech of stripped gears provided appropriately nerve-shattering background music.

On the morning of January 5th, the Japanese informed us

11

that we were to be taken away for "registration" with what luggage we could carry. As to where we were going, we could elicit no reply, but in response to queries concerning the length of time we might be held, a Japanese officer enlightened us thus: "I do not know. After we have captured all the Americans, we will decide what to do with them." Exchanging sardonic glances, Van and I gazed thoughtfully at some of the "captives": unarmed civilians, men, women and children, nervously waiting with us in the hallway for baggage inspection.

After checking each article and removing radios, cameras, large knives and sometimes scissors and flashlights, the Japanese ordered us to carry our luggage outside. The sidewalk near the Bay View entrance swarmed with people, not only hotel guests but numbers of Filipinos and Spaniards, some led there by curiosity, others searching for friends. Among the latter we discovered Eduardo Roxas, a Spanish friend to whom we had recently entrusted our money and jewelry. Not wishing to attract Japanese attention, we paused only long enough to tell Edu that our destination was still unknown to us. He promised to find us and to help in any way possible.

We crossed the street to join British friends who had moved to the Bay View during the bombings: Helen and Edwin Cogan and their seven-year-old daughter, Isabel. We had known the Cogans for many years, as Edwin was a staff member of International Harvester of the Philippines.

All day long with hundreds of others, we waited our turn to be hauled away. A dry, dust-laden wind parched our lips and stung our eyes, bloodshot and smarting already from smoke that still obscured the sun in an unnatural dusk. Our spirits matched the look of the skies as we watched line after line of busses and trucks, jammed with "enemy a-liens," drive off into the unknown. At length, our turn came. Sentries loaded a score of us, some tensely silent, others chattering hysterically, onto a bus which bore us to a destination no longer unknown, one which soon became all too familiar to us as Santo Tomás Internment Camp, prison for civilian enemies of the Japanese.

Chapter Two

Fearing the worst as we passed through the gates that were to shut out the world for an indeterminate period, we were mildly heartened by the sight of other Americans and Europeans thronging the broad campus lawn. Possibly there was comfort in the thought that we would not have to suffer alone whatever fate lay ahead of us: common burdens and sorrows are somehow less terrifying than persecution in lonely solitude.

There was relief, too, in discovering friends and acquaintances whose whereabouts we had not known during the hectic weeks of bombing. From our bus windows we scanned each group of prisoners along the driveway and lawn as we approached the university buildings.

Our bus swung left across a wide, paved plaza and stopped midway at the main building entrance. Scrambling to gather together our meager luggage, we observed only that this building, four stories high, was solidly built of grey concrete blocks surmounted by the cross. To the left, across a road bordering the east side, stood a small restaurant on the corner, and next to it a three-story stucco building which overlooked the front lawn. The latter, we learned, was called the Education building.

A road on the west of the main building bounded a hedged-in plot of grass, trees and flowers known as the Father's Garden. We perceived through the trees a church-like edifice which was actually a seminary housing the university's Dominican priests. Directly opposite the front of the main building, a narrow park of blossoming trees and hibiscus bushes, flanked on either side by roads to the entrance gates, extended from the plaza to an iron-barred fence that marked our front barrier, a distance of a short city block.

Dragging inside the few possessions we had been allowed to bring with us, the Cogans, Van and I made our way slowly through the sea of humanity which flooded the lobby and overflowed onto the first floor hallway. Since we could gain no intelligible direction from this bedlam engulfing us, we trudged upstairs to the second, then to the third floor, where finally we took possession of a small, unoccupied room containing several desks. Such a thing as a bed was not to be found at Santo Tomás, a university for day students only.

Weary, dejected and perspiring, we sat for a moment in glum silence on our suitcases and boxes. Then all of a sudden we realized that we were very hungry, having eaten nothing since early morning. Helen Cogan unpacked and opened a five-pound tin of Spam and a box of crackers, and began to make sandwiches. Since we had no food of our own, the Cogans shared theirs with us, an act of magnificent generosity at a time when no one knew whether personal food supplies, or lack of them, might swing the balance between life and death.

As we were devouring our supper, Van's face turned a clammy grey color and he collapsed so quickly that Edwin and I barely managed to catch him as he fell. Edwin's instant thought was heart attack.

Leaving Helen with Van, Edwin hastened to look for a doctor while I, agonized, helpless and very frightened, dashed off in the opposite direction down the teeming hallway. Almost immediately, by amazing luck, I found a nurse who, calmly efficient, procured a bottle of smelling salts and administered first aid. After a few moments, Van opened his eyes and exclaimed, "What a helluva time to pull a stunt like this!"

Just then, some Japanese soldiers shuffled up to our door, poked their heads in and grunted "Ugh!" I could feel the gooseflesh rising on my arms — but they departed without further comment. However, their appearance suggested the probability that we would not be long allowed to remain in the privacy of our little classroom. Van, still shaky from his attack, decided to look for space in a men's sleeping room, and he urged me to move to a room for women; but, since the Cogans had made up their minds to stick it out together, I elected to stay with them as long as possible before seeking refuge among strangers.

While Edwin helped Van to find a place on the second floor, I discovered a washroom of sorts: four toilets and a basin with a single cold water tap. Without soap, my lavatory efforts removed little dirt, but the cool water was refreshing.

After Edwin returned, we pushed desks together and hung up our mosquito nets, the only hotel equipment we had had the foresight to take. For sleeping togs, I wore an old, shrunken slack suit and a Japanese coolie coat, the latter for modesty, as my slack suit gaped in the middle. We turned out the light and tucked ourselves in. Scarcely had we closed our eyes when a group of soldiers snapped on the light again. Their interpreter smiled toothily and announced, "We make count."

The soldiers peered at each of us in turn. Much conversation between soldiers and interpreters, then the latter turned to us: "One, two, three, four; one man, two women, one child. No. Not right."

"Yes, that *is* right," encouraged Edwin.

"No, not right," the interpreter insisted.

More Japanese chit-chat; finally a question from the interpreter: "What nationality?"

"British," Edwin responded promptly.

"All British?"

"No, I'm an American," I volunteered. It was the wrong thing to say; I hope that some day I may learn when silence is wisdom.

More perplexed than ever, the interpreter varied his chant: "One, two, three, four. One American, three British. No. Not

17

right."

Variety and repetition added no potency to the formula. The Japanese were stumped; they scratched their heads and giggled. Finally I became annoyed with them for keeping the light on when we wanted to sleep. Flinging aside the torn blanket I had that morning ripped from my ironing board, I sat upright and glared at our tormentors. The interpreter bemusedly stared back — then, struck by a flash of inspiration, he dashed to my side and fixed his eyes on my coolie coat.

"Where you buy?" he asked eagerly.

I did not understand — not only because I was angry and sleepy, but because I am naturally slow-thinking. He pointed to the coat. "Japanese," he said.

At last I realized what he was talking about. "Yes, Japanese."

"Where you buy?"

"It was a gift. Osaka, perhaps."

"Ah." The interpreter jabbered excitedly to the soldiers, who gathered around to inspect the coat. Many smiles. Much Japanese talk. I felt a trifle embarrassed, wondering whether the Japanese characters printed on my coat said something rude.

Again the interpreter quizzed me. "How much you pay?"

"I don't know. It was a gift."

"You go Japan?"

"Yes, I've been there."

"Ah."

More smiling Japanese conversation, and then, praise Allah, they flicked off the light and departed. No more counting, for the moment.

An hour later, the interpreter returned with a different group of soldiers, and thereafter he inspected us regularly about once an hour, each time bringing new recruits. He made short work of the confusing count, at which the soldiers only shook their heads blankly. Then — great moment — he would spring my coat on them. It worked every time. Much merriment, Japanese chatter, and good-natured departure with no decision on the sex-nationality problem.

Finally at two a.m. the first lot of soldiers came back and ordered us to move. I suspect that the interpreter, having run through his entire roster, was forced at last to end his little game. They took Edwin to a room for British men. Helen, Isabel and I were escorted to a room for British women, where we tried to compose ourselves for sleep on three large desks of the hardest wood imaginable. The following morning I was transferred to a room around the corner for American women, room 44. Separation of nationalities appeared to be a whim of third floor sentries, as no attempt was ever made on the first and second floors to unscramble them.

Van, who had slept all night on the concrete floor, nevertheless had rested well and felt much better. After a bite of breakfast with the Cogans, we set out to explore our new surroundings and, if possible, to get in touch with friends outside who had promised to send us food and other necessities.

That we were caught without food was largely my own fault, for, even though we had no home in Manila, I could have laid in ample supplies while stores were still open. Instead, while others were buying in quantity for a long siege, I, having no thought of remaining in Manila, had purchased only a few snacks to supplement the Bay View Hotel's meager wartime rations. Van liked to tease me about bringing home only caviar and champagne, and I must confess that in spirit he was quite right. Few could have started three years of internment with less.

We wandered out toward the front fence where, it seemed, most of our 3000-odd[1] companions in misery had already clustered for a glimpse through the bars of that relatively "free" world outside. As we joined their ranks, Van recalled a current story about a bedraggled sparrow who told his feathered friends that he had been imitating dive bombers until he "dove into the

[1] Our total grew at one time to almost 5,000; in the end, about 3800 internees were liberated from Santo Tomás.

damnedest badminton game you ever saw!"

"What a helluva badminton game we dove into!" Van remarked. The comparison was all too apt: not only were we bedraggled, but most of us, I am sure, were as startled and upset by the fate that had befallen us as that luckless sparrow.

Outside the bars, hundreds of Filipinos, Spaniards, Swiss and other neutrals were elbowing their way as close to the fence as possible, while we, like caged animals, scrambled frenziedly back and forth searching for friends. Ordered by the Japanese to stand four feet behind the barrier, we were forced to shout ourselves hoarse to be heard above the hubbub. Our resemblance to wild creatures in a zoo bore in the more deeply when Japanese guards began snapping pictures; long confident of our superiority as masters in the Far East, we suddenly found ourselves allotted the status of captive beasts performing for the entertainment of our Oriental gaolers.

Van spotted several friends in the crowd outside, among them Edu Roxas, who managed somehow to disentangle from the deafening babel our request for five beds with the necessary bedding. A Chinese dealer popped up from nowhere. "Can do," he called to Edu; then he vanished in the human anthill. Twenty minutes later he was back with full equipment.

While Van, Edwin Cogan and I were hauling away our prized acquisitions, the enterprising Chinese merchant returned with more beds for internees who had bargained with him after the first trip. Japanese sentries at the gate passed a few, then, with typical capriciousness, they arbitrarily turned back the remainder.

At least, a few of us slept in beds on our second night at Santo Tomás. Their springless rattan bottoms lacked something in beauty-rest comfort, especially as we had lent mattresses to less fortunate friends. But they were a definite improvement over the concrete floor and wooden desks of our first night.

Chapter Three

By and large, the Japanese left internees pretty much on their own to organize camp functions and facilities. After laying down a few general rules, such as roll call at seven-thirty p.m., they appointed room monitors whose responsibility it was to turn in roll call reports and to enforce all other regulations. As head man of our internal government, the Japanese selected at random an internee named Earl Carroll, who had only recently returned to Manila on business, leaving his family in the States.

Short, blond, bespectacled and boyish-looking for his thirty-five years, Earl Carroll was not the type one would have chosen by appearance to cope with the wily Japanese, or to weld together into a functioning community our disorganized and disparate population. However, he soon proved himself a reasonably good organizer and an exceptionally able mediator.

By nationality, we were approximately three-fourths American, nearly one-fourth British (including Canadians and Australians) and the remainder Dutch, with a sprinkling of Poles, Norwegians, Free French and others. Among the American and British were women from Hong Kong and Shanghai whose husbands had sent them months before to Manila for safety.

American and British classifications covered a variety of mixtures, principally Spanish, Filipino (called Mestizo) and Eurasian; as well as a small number of American Negroes and American-born Chinese. Our group included foreign-born wives of "enemy alien" nationals: White Russians, Orientals,

21

Germans, Europeans of non-belligerent nations, and a few Filipinos — although in general the Japanese did not permit the internment of Filipina wives, allegedly for lack of space. Not only by nationality were we a heterogeneous aggregation, but by occupation and background as well. Rich mining men and landowners now stood in line with seamen and shoemakers; executives from large American firms took their chances with waiters, beachcombers and "oldtimers" from Spanish-American War days; society women, missionaries (of the female sex) and prostitutes slept side by side. Some of us were well-known in camp and outside; some who were transients had not a single friend on either side of the fence. Our common denominator, the galling classification of "enemy alien," served not so much to bind as to lump us together.

Circumstances had indiscriminately packed us into the class-rooms of Santo Tomás, twenty-five to seventy per room. There, rich and poor alike, we found ourselves with little or no food, grossly inadequate sanitation and no privacy whatsoever, sleeping in rooms that were infested with bedbugs and other vermin.

It is a measure of Earl Carroll's intelligence and drive that he was able to quickly create a semblance of order from such chaos. Food, obviously, was our most pressing need, and the one to which he first turned his attention. Although it was six months before the Japanese gave us even a meager food allowance (twenty-five cents a day per adult, half that amount for children up to twelve years old), Earl persuaded them to permit Manila's International Red Cross representative, a fellow internee named Tommy Wolff, to bring in Red Cross supplies stored in the city.

On our third morning in camp, we drank coffee prepared and served by internee volunteers. A few days later, we could avail ourselves of a nourishing breakfast of cracked wheat mush with brown sugar and canned milk. Soon an evening meal of sorts was added, generally corned beef or sardines with some local vegetable such as string beans or pechay (a kind of coarse spinach with celery-like stalks which are eaten along with the leaves).

As time went on, our haphazard dinners were amplified by a variety of local meats and vegetables, paid for with funds borrowed by the Red Cross under Tommy Wolff's signature, and purchased by internee buyers to whom the Japanese issued daily passes to leave camp. When Earl Carroll persuaded them to agree to such an arrangement, he proved conclusively his fitness to handle "diplomatic" relations with the enemy.

Second in importance to food, and closely associated with the general problem of sustenance for a majority of internees, was maintaining contact with friends outside. The Japanese soon shut off our view and fragmentary verbal concourse with neutrals by covering the front fence with sawali, a material woven from flat, fibrous strips, often used for the walls of Filipino houses. Much as we disliked our complete isolation, we could only admit that the Japanese action was a logical one, not only to maintain order in camp, but to discourage Filipinos from tossing us fruit and loaves of bread, which they did each day. It was unfortunate for us, but not unnatural that the Japanese should resent manifestations of sympathy from the Filipinos, whose friendship they were avidly courting for themselves.

Earl Carroll induced them, however, to allow a committee of internees stationed at the gate to receive and send out parcels, subject, of course, to Japanese inspection. As long as the open-gate policy remained in effect, everyone in camp benefited. Some enjoyed the luxury of eating hot meals sent in each day by friends or servants outside; and even those who were strangers managed to buy extra food and other essentials.

For some weeks the Japanese adamantly refused to permit written communication between internees and outsiders, which led inevitably to smuggling notes in parcels. Whenever Japanese inspectors discovered such contraband messages, they punished the bearer, whether Spaniard, Swiss, Filipino, or German, with severe slappings or beatings, and they retaliated against the camp

23

at large by stopping all parcels for an unspecified time, usually several days.

For the administration of camp affairs, Earl set up as chief governing body an executive committee, under which were organized numerous committees and staffs. In addition to food procurement, kitchen work, parcel handling and censorship, it was immediately necessary to start a hospital, provide for sanitation, procure beds for those who could not obtain them otherwise, and find space in our overcrowded rooms for new internees arriving daily. Not always were Earl Carroll's committees models of smooth-running efficiency; yet, by and large, they overcame handicaps with a good show of ingenuity.

Possibly the most berated group was one that deserved the most sympathy: our hard-worked and harried sanitation committee. Plagued by pests that not even a magician could have charmed away, the committee fought what was often a losing battle against bedbugs, cockroaches, flies, ants, mosquitoes, centipedes, scorpions, rats, mice, lice and other vermin that abounded in Santo Tomás. They drained swamps where mosquitoes bred, trapped flies by the thousands, and issued improvised swatters to one and all, including children who participated in fly-swatting contests for prizes of candy. Bedbugs, loathsome and persistent, survived repeated attacks with disinfectants – and soon the disinfectants ran out. Complete extermination would have been next to impossible, for every blackboard, wall, desk and chair in Santo Tomás had harboured countless generations of odious creatures. Only constant vigilance kept them under control – and some rooms were less vigilant than others. To encourage competitive cleanliness, the committee chalked up outside each room a rating (Class A, B, etc.) and presented monthly awards to the best rooms in each building.

There were, in addition to the main building, three locations used as sleeping quarters: for men, the Education building and the gymnasium, situated near the southwest corner of the campus; for women and small children, the annex with its own kitchen behind the main building. Opposite the annex was the newly organized hospital, also with separate kitchen, in a small building called the dormitory.

Toilet facilities in the main building consisted of two bathrooms, one for men, one for women, on each of the three floors used by internees (on the fourth floor was a laboratory which was kept intact.) Four toilets and a single washbasin served 200 women on the first and third floors, 400 on the second floor. Only the first floor bathrooms were equipped with showers. Dishes, clothes and hair we washed outside, where we discovered here and there a few solitary taps, as it was forbidden to use building facilities for such purposes.

Earl Carroll promptly procured for the sanitation committee the necessary plumbing to install four showers in each upstairs bathroom and to construct behind the main building half a dozen galvanized iron troughs twenty to thirty feet long, spotted with faucets about three feet apart, for dish- and clotheswashing. Near the troughs they erected four hair-washing showers, which drained into a porcelain bathtub. Ultimately, we were able to draw for our shampoos limited quantities of kitchen-heated water from a faucet behind the main building — the only hot water available in Santo Tomás.

Trying to maintain cleanliness in the women's bathroom would have frustrated the most ingenious and determined of sanitary engineers. Not only were drains ancient and overworked, but they were constantly clogged by food, hair and other refuse left there by scores of rule-oblivious women. Each day squads of men gave our bathrooms a thorough scrubbing; an hour later, pigs would have turned up their noses in disgust. Within a few weeks a reasonably effective solution was worked out: the women themselves took turns by room at "bathroom duty." About once a week each of us put in an hour of toilet swabbing, drain clearing and, most difficult by far, trying to prevent rule infractions.

There was a story told of a blond young Englishwoman who

had become extremely overwrought contending with rulebreakers. The day was wet and muddy, which meant constant mopping of floors; also, frequent surreptitious attempts to rinse off dishes in sheltered bathrooms. Near the end of her hour's duty, an internee of Shanghai origin whose reputation was somewhat questionable tried to sneak a stack of dirty dishes behind her back as she bent over the mop. The maneuver had almost succeeded when the young Englishwoman turned suddenly and caught the culprit in her crime. Without a moment's pause, she let fly from her gentle lips a flood of obscenity that would have shamed a hardened seaman. Jaw agape in unfeigned astonishment, the Shanghai strumpet could only reply weakly, "My God, Mrs —— , and here I thought you was a lady!"

Chapter Four

As practical patterns of existence began to emerge from the turbulence of early days in camp, the novelty of imprisonment gave way to a wearisome monotony of routine. We were fairly well established in our rooms, each with a bed or mattress to sleep on (the Red Cross furnished camp cots or wooden beds made in Santo Tomás for those who could not obtain beds elsewhere).

Most of us had chosen regular eating places inside or on the campus, and some cooked their own meals over bonfires in the open, wooded fields behind the buildings. Gradually, charcoal stoves obtained from outside replaced the bonfires as increasing numbers of internees began preparing midday meals (provided by the camp kitchen only for children, teenagers and "heavy duty" workers).

Day began for us in room 44 when lights were switched on at six-thirty a.m. Even before that hour, early risers had been clacking down the halls in wooden scuffs called bakias, worn by many instead of shoes and by nearly all to protect feet from the concrete floor beneath the showers. Already, bathroom lines would be forming: a quick wash – perhaps a shower – then back to dress, make beds, tidy up the room.

Next, armed with meal ticket, enamel cup and plate (issued by the camp Red Cross – in the beginning most of us used tin cans), we would stand in one of four lines that led to two serving counters from our central kitchen in the rear of the main build-

27

ing. For a brief period, breakfast included not only coffee and mush (cracked wheat or cornmeal), but prunes and rolls as well, until supplies ran out.

I always ate breakfast in the west patio, one of two small garden areas enclosed by the main building's inner walls. When we first came to Santo Tomás, these patios, east and west, had been delightful havens of beauty; but very soon their lovely palm-bordered lawns were laid waste by the constant trample of internee feet: not a single blade of grass now graced the barren ground. Three circular flowerbeds, a large central garden with smaller ones at either end, had fared a little better; for a time, crushed flowers and broken shrubbery bore mute testimony to long and loving care, then they, too, succumbed to our relentless invasion.

Scores of internees breakfasted in each patio, some squatting on concrete walks next to the building, others setting up canvas chairs (sent in by friends) on what once was lawn. A few went through the smoky ritual of lighting charcoal stoves to toast their rolls. Breakfast over, internees headed by rote for the troughs, where we stood in mud to wash our dishes in cold water, with soap issued by the Red Cross; then back to our rooms to start morning chores. We took turns at essential community work: mopping the room, bathroom duty and "room guard," considered necessary to prevent thieving.

There were also innumerable personal tasks to be attended to. At nine a.m., carry outgoing parcels to the gate; at eleven, another trip to claim incoming ones. Spare moments, if any, we used for shampooing hair, mending worn garments, or, most tedious of all, laundering clothes, which were then hung to dry on public lines: an invitation to thieves unless we stood guard. Those who had volunteered to peel dinner vegetables for the central kitchen were exempted from many regular room chores. Each morning after breakfast we reported for duty behind the main building, where we scraped and cleaned the produce at long wooden tables. How long we sat there depended on the

28

nature of the day's vegetables: sometimes our benches grew hard and the sun very hot before we had finished.

Our usual fresh vegetables — camotes, squash, pechay, string beans, green onions, peppers, tiny local onions — required no more on the average than two hours, although often they were not what one would call well-prepared in that time. Tough native string beans remained tougher and stringier than need be because we could do no more than snap off ends and break them up; had we tried to string them, we should have been all day at the job. Pechay and green onions frequently arrived in such a slimy state of semi-decomposition that we could scarcely separate wholesome parts from putrid.

Deepest groans, however, were reserved for days when we had to clean dried mongo beans — a four-to-six-hour job, as the beans crawled with tiny brown bugs that closely matched them in color. Rice cleaning, too, was an eye-straining, back-breaking chore and one which we particularly disliked not so much because of weevils, abundant but easy to detect against the white grains, as because of disgusting white worms of varying sizes and temperaments, ranging from snail-like sluggishness to centipedian speed. Some months later, we gratefully relinquished the distasteful delousing of rice to women volunteer squads that specialized in cleaning cereal of all types.

At lunch time, internees went their separate ways, some to cook or to eat meals that had been sent in, others to nibble at morning leftovers. Van and I shared expenses with the Cogans for food that their cook brought to the gate three times a week: hardboiled eggs (somewhat ancient more often than not), fruit, tomatoes, bread, cold fried chicken twice a week, cold beef once. The five of us had lunched together in the grassy back fields until varying duties prevented us from meeting regularly. Van and I chose a spot in the hallway outside my room, where we set up a card table. After lunch, after having swept the hall, I would stack dirty dishes in a pail and haul them to the wash troughs, now crowded and sweltering under the midday sun. Even at this hour, and throughout the afternoon, there were internees bent over small buckets, scrubbing and wringing out soiled clothing.

During "quiet hours" between two and four p.m., I would usually undress and read awhile. We were fortunate enough to have a wide selection of books from two free libraries, one owned by the University, the other organized by our camp librarian, an internee named Glen Wishard, Secretary of the YMCA, who had procured books from the Y's library outside.

Around three-thirty p.m. I would try to take a shower: I say "try" advisedly, because water pressure on the second and third floors was whimsically erratic. During laundry and dishwashing hours, the flow often stopped entirely, except for an intermittent trickle from a single floor tap. Not infrequently we would be standing three to a shower, soaping ourselves into a lather when, with a sudden sputter, the spray would abruptly cease spraying. If we were lucky enough to find a bathroom bucket (faster than they could be replaced, buckets were "borrowed" never to reappear), we would coax a dribble from the floor tap to slosh each other off. Toilets also had to be bucket flushed, which slowed the long waiting lines.

Dinner at Santo Tomás was served from four-thirty to six p.m., an early hour for the convenience of kitchen workers as well as those whose lunch was sketchy or nonexistent. Packing dishes, soap and other essentials downstairs, I would meet Van in the west patio at about four-forty-five. Although latecomers often got smaller and less desirable portions, we generally would wait until the rush was over to avoid standing in slow-moving lines. Only once or twice did we make an exception, when the kitchen varied its usual menu of stew or beans by offering chicken or pork chops. On those rare occasions many joined the line who normally dined on food received from outside, and we feared that no meat would be left if we waited — a surmise which proved correct, to the sorrow of tardy ones whose evening meal consisted solely of vegetables.

After dinner, dishwashing and once again lumbering up and down the stairs (the equivalent of four flights because of high ceilings), I would meet Van on the front campus where, if we felt so inclined, we could watch baseball games and other sports organized early in our internment. From six to seven p.m. records were broadcast over a camp loudspeaker that had been set up to facilitate announcements: "Station STIC" (Santo Tomás Internment Camp), as it was called by our camp announcers, who at intervals told us the hour of the day at "STIC Standard Time."

At seven-thirty we reported to our rooms for roll call, after which no one was allowed outside. Residents of the main building, however, were permitted to sit in the patios, where we could chat quietly with friends, perhaps exchanging news and rumor after the day's work was done. Often we would gaze up at the tiny patch of stars caught between our patio walls: a bit of the free night's beauty that still was ours. Then lights out at eleven, and everyone in his room, to fall into restless sleep broken now and again by the moans of fellow internees whose dreams were also troubled.

Chapter Five

My room, a small one on the third floor front, was monitored capably and efficiently by Minna Nance, wife of a reserve officer who was fighting in Bataan. Supervising a room of twenty-eight women under the best of conditions would require a considerable measure of levelheadedness and tact; in a prison camp, the monitor's job was one that demanded the utmost in patience, diplomacy, good humor and hard work. Early months of adjustment were the most telling, and many a monitor, including Minna Nance, gave up in despair after a long period of gruelling and generally unappreciated service. However, Minna proved her worth in many ways before relinquishing a thankless task.

Her quick reaction to one rather frightening incident demonstrated a typical presence of mind, which on this occasion helped to calm and reassure a roomful of panic-stricken women. Late one night we were startled awake by a violent shaking of our beds, accompanied by a rattle of windows and an ominous rumbling which seemed to come up from the bowels of the earth. Women around me began to scream; some rushed into the hall. For an instant, no one knew what had happened; then it dawned on us: an earthquake!

Suddenly, above the weird roar and clatter and the pandemonium of hysterical shrieks, came a steady, unperturbed voice: "Don't rush outside, girls. You're perfectly safe here: this is an earthquake-proof building!"

Aroused from a sound sleep, Minna's wits were about her; she remembered what some of us had never known and the rest had forgotten, that our building had been especially constructed to withstand earthquake shocks. Her instant thought was to protect us, like a mother hen her chicks, against the fears of the night.[2]

However, even the protectiveness of a mother hen cannot always guide a group of women prisoners complacently through day-to-day irritations that build up inevitably as an unconscious protest against coexistence in cramped quarters. As resignation and frustration supplanted early bewilderment, the strain of worry, discomfort, weariness and lack of privacy began to tell on our nerves. Common misery does not always impel consideration and kindliness; on the contrary, trapped human beings, like trapped animals, often snarl and bare their teeth at the slightest provocation, or sometimes at none at all.

Chief cause of the squabbles that flared up among us was space, or lack of it. Early arrivals in Santo Tomás, firmly entrenched in their far-from-expansive floor plots, held on for dear life to what they had, and often refused to yield a single inch to make room for newcomers. Finally the harassed room assignment board, having allotted 30.8 square feet to each woman (twenty-nine square feet for men in the main building), was forced to measure each room in order to determine whether or not its quota was filled.

Life at times was made the less endurable by space hogs, who resented space sharing even by others in the room, lest the reshuffling might somehow jeopardize a precious iota of their own oversized allotments. I was once the object of caustic criticism on that score, along with Tillie Butler, who slept beside me. We had pushed together our beds to make room for a missionary who had been temporarily admitted while one of our

---

[2]It was reported later that after the first severe shock, one terrified man had rushed stark naked onto the front plaza.

roommates was hospitalized outside camp. Now that our roommate was expected back, the missionary was about to be shoved out into the hall, since no other room had a place for her. Despite protests from space hogs, she slept beside us for one more night; and, by sheer luck, that night won her a permanent place in our room, because our ex-roommate did not return after all.

The fiercest verbal battle I ever witnessed was waged between two well-educated women, one space-rich, the other space-poor. The former had one of the largest floor plots in our room; next to her, the latter slept with two other women on a small wooden platform. At night, the three bedmates hung their clothes on a chair at the foot of the platform. It was this chair which precipitated the violent explosion.

Resentment had smouldered for weeks between the two women, one accusing the other of bumping her bed every time she passed it on her way to the platform, which was countered with the retort, "Why don't you move your bed over? You have plenty of space; why crowd our passageway?"

After lights-out one night, the platform-sleeper stumbled over the chair on her way to bed. Next morning I was awakened by a raucous female voice screeching, "What's the idea of making such a racket after the lights are out? Why don't you go to bed before dark, you awkward old cow, waking everybody in the room!"

"Don't you dare talk to me!" hissed the other. "You shoved that chair into the passageway on purpose so I'd fall over it."

"You're a god-damned liar!"

I ducked out to take a shower. When I returned, they were still bandying about such choice epithets as tramp, space hog, trash and other similarly flattering appellations. It was gratifying to note that the space-poor victim was winning the battle of words hands down, having by far the larger vocabulary and imagination. As I departed for breakfast, the space hog threatened to sue for libel, while the other urged her to go right ahead, as all witnesses were dead set against space hogging; furthermore, she swore to bump the offensive bed every time she passed it.

Whatever might have been her sympathies, Minna Nance wisely stayed out of the dispute. Intervention between two furiously fighting females could have resulted only in drawing the would-be peacemaker into battle. Equally futile were attempts to impose consideration for others on those who innately lacked such consideration. Despite all pleas, there were always some who persisted in talking loudly during rest hours, in clattering with unnecessary noise down the hallways, in clogging drinking fountains with tea leaves, in tossing garbage from windows into the patios.

We encountered in one of our roommates a spirit of noncooperation which amounted to lack of consideration. The nonconformist, Mrs B, was a plump, intelligent woman from Shanghai who was, however, incredibly sloppy about her personal property. Boxes, bundles and clothing were strewn in utter disarray under and about her unmade bed, turning her space into an eyesore that diminished our chances of a Class A rating from the sanitation board. Moreover, she refused to have any part in room cleaning, room guard or bathroom duty.

Mrs B advanced logical arguments to support her stand. Among the first to start cooking meals in camp for herself, her teen-age son and several men, she was away from the room all day. Why, she reasoned, should she trek back to do a "silly job" of room guarding when many of her roommates seldom left the hall outside? She agreed to take her turn at bathroom duty providing that Minna gave her an evening hour; but as for her bed, if she did not mind how it looked, why should we?

On the point of bathroom duty, Minna displayed less than her usual patience and fairness. Irritated, as we all were by Mrs B's messiness, she refused conciliation and determined to have the offender thrown out of the room. A majority backed her decision: I was one of those who agreed unequivocally that Mrs B must go unless she altered her ways. Tillie Butler, one of the few who demurred, said to me, "I can't vote to have her thrown out. Where will she go?"

The rest of us did not care. What had happened to our kindness, our tolerance and understanding of another's viewpoint? Formidable indeed are the prison bars that can lock out not only the civilized world but our civilized feelings as well. However, the fight was not over, for Mrs B calmly threatened to go to the Japanese, thereby bringing upon herself the surreptitious but venomous accusation of being a spy. She disappointed spy-hunters by going instead to the internee room assignment board with promises to reform, which of course she did not do; but she remained in room 44, still a nonconformist, cheerful and sloppy as ever.

Although Mrs B was, I believe, the only permanent occupant of our room suspected by some of being a spy, there were many throughout camp who were mistrusted, a few undoubtedly with reason. Having been warned of the spy menace, we spoke guardedly when strangers were near. Word got around of conversations repeated to the Japanese, who, we were told, had planted a spy in every room. We eyed each other askance, fear and suspicion gripping every heart. Fear-warped minds often distort what is unknown and unusual into something that is evil. Mrs B, unknown to us before internment, proposed the unusual when she threatened to seek Japanese aid — sufficient evidence for alarmists among us to jump to the unwarranted conclusion that she was a spy.

Others were even more recklessly accused, the sole justification being that, counter to general over-optimism about the duration of the war, they faced realistically the prospect of a long internment. One of our spy-jittery roommates told us with uncompromisingly dogmatic seriousness that she had overheard the conversation of a "Japanese-paid" spy who was trying to wean away the loyalty of internees half-Spanish by blood, to start a "Fifth Column" in camp. Presumably their Spanish heritage made them more susceptible to enemy propaganda.

Asked what dastardly lies the wretch had insinuated into their wavering minds, our roommate replied, "Why, he said the Americans wouldn't be back for a couple of years! He said we have no supplies, and no ships to send them in!"

At a time when the majority confidently expected liberation in a matter of weeks — at the latest by May, when the rains usually started — reaction to such an opinion was understandably vehement: abysmal stupidity, said some; bare-faced treason, insisted others. The few who thought it only common sense were wise to say nothing.

This wishful thinking, pitiful and ridiculous though it was, enabled many to go on who at that time could not have faced the intolerable reality of a long internment. Dreaming of early freedom, one escaped momentarily from the drudgery of standing in long lines to get food, to collect parcels, to wash dishes, faces and teeth, to take a shower or go to the toilet; of packing loads wherever one went; of dragging fatigued bodies up endless stairs.

Hope alone made it possible, for a little while, to forget discomforts and afflictions: the mortifying lack of privacy, even in bathrooms; the incessant fight against filth; the sudden seizures of faintness from laboring under a burning sun — to forget the grotesque appearance of children's heads shaved to rid them of lice, of faces and bodies dotted permanganate-purple because of impetigo or infected prickly heat — to forget especially the fear of unknown horror in the future. There is no way to picture the perpetual weariness of body and soul in our twilight world: a weariness not from despair, for we never gave up to self-pitying dejection; but from waiting, yearning, longing futilely for an end to our present drab and distasteful existence; a weariness of people, noise, filth, toil, even thought. Above all, a weariness of the blank wall that shut off the dawn of our future day. Only the boost of optimistic rumor could send our spirits soaring.

We gleaned real news, albeit garnished with propaganda and

absurd exaggerations, from the *Tribune*, an English-language Japanese newspaper which was sent into camp (one copy per room). Rumor came from several sources: from Filipina Red Cross girls who were permitted in the early days to shop for us; from friends who brought parcels to the gate; from a handful of Filipino doctors and nurses who for some months were allowed to enter camp each day to assist our interned doctors. With the best will in the world, our neutral friends glorified the news until American defeats became overwhelming victories. They even told us that General MacArthur had broadcast that he would breakfast at the Manila Hotel on his birthday, January 26, 1942. Pleasant, well-intentioned stories — how much easier they were to believe than unpleasant truths!

When a flight of planes would roar over us, someone in the room always proclaimed, "Those are our planes! I can tell by the sound of the motors." Only one of our roommates had the temerity to deflate this bubble of over-optimism: Kitty Fairman, hard-working organizer of the camp hospital kitchen. For her outspokenness, she was soundly berated; but, since she was well-known, well-liked and respected, no one held a grudge against her. Instead, our spy-jittery roommate settled on three hospital doctors from China as the culprits. All three had been caught in Manila on their way to the States: obvious Japanese plants, according to our roommate, to dupe Kitty Fairman and other co-workers.

Although I did not commit myself one way or the other, I agreed with Kitty: they could not possibly be our planes. Only once were we sure that the planes we heard were ours: a pitiful few of them, one night toward the end of January. We heard Japanese anti-aircraft guns blaze away at them, saw shells streak across the dark sky, even read about them in the next morning's *Tribune*. Only once — yet could it not happen again? Like every other prisoner in Santo Tomás, I hoped that it might. Meanwhile, I kept silent, knowing the value of that flicker of hope that burns in human hearts long after all reason for hope has vanished.

Chapter Six

My reluctant disbelief in the widely anticipated miracle of early liberation was due to no superior wisdom of my own, but to Van's perspicacity. Literally caught fast asleep when war broke out, he had since re-read articles in prewar copies of magazines spotlighting our country's lamentable state of military unpreparedness. The easy Japanese conquest of Manila left no doubt in his mind that any immediate attempt to beat back the enemy would end in disaster; therefore, he concluded that no attack would, or could, be launched from Bataan to free us, as many hoped.

With strong faith in American industrial and military potential, he reasoned that it would take about two years to equip our armed forces, then another year before they could fight their way back to us. Luck, of course, played a part in the near-accuracy of his guess; nevertheless, sound judgment guided his estimate. Since I could not deliberately close my mind to the facts, I had to agree with him.

Convinced that we would be prisoners for three years, Van systematically prepared to meet as well as possible any needs that might arise during that time. He arranged first of all to have Edu Roxas purchase canned goods for us. Then, with Edwin Cogan, who also subscribed to the long internment theory, he discovered behind the restaurant building a small store whose owner was quietly selling out before the Japanese discovered his wares. There, as long as supplies lasted, Van and Edwin bought each day as much corned beef, Vienna sausage and assorted tinned vegetables as they could carry away with them. After acquiring some half-dozen cardboard food boxes, Van had shelves built next to my bed especially to hold them, along the unused wall space behind the door of room 44.

Meanwhile, he did not overlook suitable clothing. Since I had already worn out two of my four pairs of shoes, he sent out a tracing of my footprint with some sturdy golf shoes as models for two new pairs. To keep himself well shod, he purchased a pair of army-issue shoes, available at that time for about eight pesos (four dollars) a pair.

Late in January Aguinaldo's department store, reputedly pro-Japanese for many years, opened a small concession in Santo Tomás where we could buy slack suits, dishes, pans, knives and forks, tennis shoes, cosmetics and various other useful articles. Ten percent was added to retail prices for an internee relief fund to help the destitute.

Our most memorable purchases at Aguinaldo's were two pairs of rubber boots, one for each of us. Since the early rains began nearly three months later, these boots, the very first to appear in camp, caused a considerable stir. Although I doubt that anyone actually believed I was a spy, surely the majority of my gaping roommates thought me demented: first the food boxes, now rubber boots!

Impervious to the sensation he was causing among the ladies of room 44, Van calmly went about his business of stockpiling canned goods, the more easily now because he had undertaken a camp job which gave him access to the outside. As soon as Earl Carroll had gained Japanese authorization from the exchange of money and written messages between internees and their Manila friends, he appointed Van chief censor, with the right to go every day to the gate. There, Filipino vendors offered for sale not only canned food — much of it from U.S. Army stocks — but also local produce, which was in great demand: bread, eggs, fruits and vegetables, chickens, fresh meat — even ice. Like most of the other internee gatemen, Van bought what was available for everyone in camp who requested him to make purchases.

Few indeed, however, were those who asked him to buy canned food, although prices then were relatively cheap (fifteen cents U.S., for example, for a tin of corned beef). Many, of course, had been able to bring in, or to have sent in, their own reserves of canned goods; others did not yet realize the necessity for storing away non-perishable food; and some, even had they realized it, lacked the money to purchase in quantity. Only after Corregidor had fallen did the fearful truth sink in that our imprisonment would be a prolonged one; by that time, corned beef had zoomed to one peso (fifty cents U.S.) a can.

As chief censor, Van had full charge of all messages and money, incoming and outgoing, before they were passed to the Japanese — an astounding arrangement which enabled the censors to memorize or to pocket for later delivery any incoming notes which they knew the Japanese would turn down. Because of the risk, only messages of utmost importance were actually smuggled in; but vast sums of unrecorded money found their way into camp through the censors' pockets.

By the end of our second month in camp, money had become a pressing need, for the majority had brought in at most a few hundred pesos, and had made no such arrangement as ours with Edu Roxas, to leave funds in safe hands outside. Now there was plenty to buy, but little cash to buy it with. To further complicate our predicament the Japanese issued a warning that anyone lending money to enemy aliens would be "severely punished."

Numerous Chinese and other neutrals were willing nonetheless to chance it. For their protection as well as our own, the censors devised a reasonably foolproof scheme of smuggling in sums far too large to be passed in legitimately — that is, accompanied by a form on which were listed the amount and the names of sender and recipient — without arousing Japanese suspicion.

The first step in raising illegally borrowed currency was to request a loan through outside friends. Internees whose credit was considered good would soon receive word that the loan could be negotiated on terms ranging early in 1942 from 1000 pesos to 1400 pesos for a thousand dollar promissory note (instead of the customary 2000 pesos par value.)[3] All transactions up to this point were verbal, Van or one of the other gatemen acting as liaison between internees and neutral friends. On the final day, promissory notes would be covertly passed to the outsider, who then would hand the gateman, under the very noses of Japanese interpreters and guards, a wad of bills to slip into his pocket for later distribution to the internees concerned.

Money borrowed by individuals helped the entire community, for many insolvent internees were now engaging in private enterprise, selling services or goods, which enabled them in turn to buy what they needed. As inflation sent prices soaring, indigents depending on relief funds found their small monthly allotments (twenty pesos) quite inadequate, and more and more of the able-bodied began earning their own money.

Former beauty shop operators opened up business in camp. Amateur barbers, whose lack of skill in the beginning had encouraged a fad of beard-growing and head-shaving, soon developed sufficient finesse to entice the majority of men back to the more conventional bare-faced, dome-covered look. Boys and girls often earned a few pesos a week by washing dishes. Book owners opened private lending libraries. Vendors of foodstuffs, whether they imported wares from outside or made them in camp, could scarcely supply the internee demand for items like candy, roasted peanuts, peanut butter, jam and cake.

[3]The Japanese soon substituted pesos of their own issue for the Philippine peso. This currency, promptly dubbed "Mickey Mouse" after the comic strip play-money, was easier and cheaper to borrow than "good" pesos.

Thus, a flow of money into camp was important to buyer and seller alike. By Japanese order, internee censors made daily lists of all legitimate incoming and outgoing money and correspondence. We assumed that the High Command wished to keep strict account of our finances, for already they had distributed several sets of questionnaires on the subject — to our mild consternation, as few of us could remember our answers from one questionnaire to the next. In order to preclude any easy check on funds currently in camp, Van carefully destroyed at the end of each day the money and message lists.

Such willful obliteration of records, however wise a precaution to prevent discovery of smuggled funds, appeared to be a dangerous defiance of Japanese orders, and it made me nervous for Van's safety even though he insisted that the Japanese had never told him to *keep* the lists. As it turned out, they never once asked for them, nor apparently did they note any discrepancies in our various questionnaires.

The Japanese laid down strict rules about the length and subject matter of written notes: only "important" messages of twenty-five words or less were to be passed. Any such "unimportant" words as "love" or "thanks" were forbidden, as of course were all references to the war.

Incoming notes which contained prohibited words or subject matter were usually handed in with all other notes to the Japanese censors. Having stricken out offensive portions, the Japanese would then pass them back for retyping to the internee censors, who in due time would tell the recipient of such dressed-down messages exactly what had been deleted. Outgoing communications often proved far more troublesome to handle, for the simple reason that the censors could not always persuade internees to abide by Japanese rules. When notes were returned for rewording, irate senders frequently lashed out at the censors:

"Who the hell are you to tell me what I can say? Give it to the Japs the way I've written it, you son-of-a-bitch!"

Patiently, the censors explained that the Japanese refused to sanction certain terms and expressions; that, in fact, violations of their rule so enraged them that often the mere sight of such a term or expression precipitated the highly favored Japanese disciplinary measure of mass punishment. Many a time an endearing word caused them to cancel for a day or two not only notes, but passes, parcels and all contact with the outer world.

There were other disagreeable features connected with the censors' work. At the gate, they sometimes witnessed cruel beatings when Japanese guards turned ugly. Van told me of seeing a young Filipino kicked and pounded until he was half-dead, one sentry laughing heartily while another jumped on the boy's stomach and knocked out his teeth. His offense: bowing too carelessly. Another day, guards struck down two Filipina girls who had engaged in an argument while waiting to go through the line. Slappings were frequently meted out, and were dispensed with impartial disregard for nationality. When to expect them, or why, one never knew.

Van's special trial was a Japanese girl named Miss Coshita, who censored notes that he turned in. Before the war, Miss Coshita had worked at the Japanese consulate in Manila, where evidently her relations with Anglo-Saxons had been something less than cordial, for she made no attempt to conceal her dislike for the now-vanquished enemy. Pretty to look at[4], she was by nature cruel and sadistic.

One day there came a note from outside addressed to the writer's interned husband which revealed that their child was dying, and begged him to try to produce an immediate release from camp. When Van asked Miss Coshita to pass this note ahead of others so that it could be delivered without delay, she glanced at the message and snapped, "No, I will not pass it. Why should this man go out to see his child? What good can he do?

[4] A German-born American internee apparently succumbed completely to Miss Coshita's charms, for he used to hang around her desk all day—a pastime which earned him a high place on the camp's "spy list."

He is not a doctor!"

Van's fingers itched to strangle Miss Coshita. Repressing the urge, he hastily sought out the internee, who managed to secure a pass in time to reach his child before the end came. Later, when the Japanese inquired how he had known of the child's illness, since he had not received the note, they learned of Miss Coshita's action and expressed profound shock at her heartlessness.

When such incidents occurred, Van fervently wished to quit his job on the spot. Only a desire to help others as much as he could enabled him to control his rage and stay on the job, for he realized fully that a prisoner's impotent wrath against his gaoler's injustice could accomplish nothing: one succeeds only by outwitting the enemy.

Chapter Seven

Thus far, we had found our Japanese captors, Miss Coshita and the gate guards excepted, humane to a degree that surprised many of us. After the first few days of constant inspection, internees seldom encountered them except at the gate or near the Commandant's office on the first floor of the main building. Women who had dreaded molestation now relaxed and dispelled from their minds all lurid expectations of assault, or even of interest in their feminine charms. I, for one, emptied my pockets of razor blades which I had been secretly carrying — whether to protect or to kill myself in case of an attack, I was never very sure. Not even Van knew until afterwards that I had gone about so "armed."

However, our gaolers' self-restraint (if it was that) could be classed only as a negative virtue. On the positive side, it was to their credit that they often allowed internees to be cared for in outside hospitals and in some cases to live outside for extended periods. Many older people and women with children under two were released on periodically renewed passes, as were relatives of ill or recuperating internees, always providing that they could pay their way outside. Some stayed with neutral friends or relatives; some even returned to their own homes. Among the first to be released, for reason of health as well as age, were our host and hostess of Pearl Harbor Eve, the Stevensons, who shared the house of released internee friends, as their own home had been commandeered by the Japanese.

In various ways the Commandant and most of his assistants tried to be as kind to us as their positions allowed. His chief aide, Colonel Yamaguchi, personally helped many internees, including Van and me. At his own suggestion to Van, whom he knew as chief censor, he brought in my typewriter, dictionary and various books, magazines and articles of clothing which we had left stored in a suitcase at the Bay View Hotel. The books and magazines included several which had been banned in our camp libraries; but apparently the Japanese never noticed them, or did not care.

On one occasion, what the Japanese intended as kindness led to an extraordinary proposal: the Commandant offered to set up a "love tent" where married couples would be permitted to embrace by appointment — an inspiration which was all the more confounding because the Japanese had already forbidden physical contact between the sexes! No law of God or man could stop nightly necking parties in the patios or clandestine rendezvous in niches behind the front stairs, rented out by internees who occupied them as sleeping quarters. But a legitimate "love tent" was something to challenge even Earl Carroll's talent as a skillful manipulator. Careful to allow no echo of the derision that greeted his proposal to reach the Commandant's ears, Earl tactfully led his mind to other subjects.

Kind intentions to the contrary, we were nonetheless very much aware of the iron hand that now held our destinies. Occasional inspection parties of Japanese officers who shuffled through the halls aroused our resentment not so much because their stares affronted us as because we feared that they might be plotting some sinister change for us.

There is no such thing as security in a concentration camp, where every inmate is at the mercy of an enemy's whims; yet we had, or thought we had, a semblance of security as long as we were allowed to remain together at Santo Tomás, with friends outside to help us. Our fitful peace of mind was shattered again and again during our period of internment by the

Japanese threat to move us.

Once, in the early months, they made plans to transport us en masse to a half-finished U.S. Army camp at Tagaytay, an isolated spot some thirty or forty miles east of Manila. It was rumored that the inspection parties had recommended Santo Tomás as ideal for use as a Japanese Army hospital. Only Earl Carroll's fast thinking and energetic talking saved us from that move. Protesting that the abandoned camp had no water or proper sanitary facilities, and furthermore that all outside contacts would be cut off, Earl finally prevailed upon the Commandant to take him to Tagaytay on an inspection trip. During the long drive out, he advanced the cogent arguments that the Japanese would have to assume responsibility for our food, which was then being paid for by Red Cross money; and that trucks needed by the Army would have to be diverted to haul daily supplies to faraway Tagaytay. Moreover, Earl predicted, women and children would sicken and die of hardships in the new camp. Outpointed on every score, the Commandant capitulated.

For the moment, we were safe in our twilight dwelling: shadows of a darker world had dispersed. Yet always the fear haunted us that one day we might be immersed in the murky unknown — of Formosa, perhaps, or Manchuria, or Japan. Who could have believed, a few weeks earlier, that we would cling with gratitude to the now-familiar walls of Santo Tomás?

Sometimes our reminders of Japanese authority were less disturbing; on occasion, they were even amusing. For example, among the innumerable forms they sent us to fill in was the following:

> *Investigation of Public Opinion*
> Express your frank opinion on the following items.
> Ques. Which is more responsible for the outbreak of
>   the present war among Japan, America and
>   Britain, America or Britain?

51

Answer:

Ques.   What about your forecast of the War situation?
1. Will this war be a protracted one?
2. Will this war end in a short time?
3. Will this war end in a decisive victory for one party?
4. Do you think this war will end in an armistice instead of ending in a decisive victory for one party?
5. What is the big problem common to the countries concerned after the war?

Answer:
1.
2.
3.
4.
5.

Ques.   Which treatment is more humane, the treatment the local Japanese have received from the American Army or the one we give to the American and Britishers?

Answer:
Nationality:
Sex:

Our answers must have puzzled the Japanese, for most of us replied to each question, "No opinion."

Another incident that gave us something to laugh about was the "capture" by six armed Japanese soldiers of a harmless American half-wit who had been found rambling aimlessly through the streets. The soldiers made a ridiculous picture as they marched their captive, half scared to death, hands bound behind him, into camp at the point of fixed bayonets.

Rather than divertissement, it seems in retrospect that our reaction should have been relief that the poor man was brought in unharmed. Soon enough we witnessed a sample of the Japanese army's well-publicized brutality, which we had begun to hope we would be spared.

On February 11, 1942, three men escaped from Santo Tomás, two of them Australian, one British, all seamen who had been put ashore when war broke out. The Japanese recaptured them almost immediately[5] and, claiming that they were headed for Bataan to join American forces, the camp Commandant ordered them to be severely beaten.

A sidelight to this unhappy incident concerned Van's anathema, Miss Coshita, who begged permission to witness their tortures. Turned down by the Japanese, she seated herself just outside the room where the unfortunate men were being mauled and pommelled. As she listened through the walls for their screams of agony, Miss Coshita giggled convulsively; whether for this reason or not, she was soon afterwards dismissed from Santo Tomás.

Many hours later, when their flesh had been reduced to bloody quivering pulp, the Commandant asked that an internee doctor examine the escaped prisoners for mortal injuries. Immediately after the examination during which the doctor was permitted to render no treatment of any kind, the men were dragged away to an unknown place. Then came the shocker that withered to the roots our remote and shaky delusions of security: an announcement that the three men were to be shot. The entire camp was stunned. Why, if execution was foreordained, had the Japanese beforehand beaten them half to death? Having informed us that we were "civilians in protective custody," how could our gaolers justify this monstrous cat-and-mouse game?

The Commandant purported to be as shaken as we were. With tears streaming down his face, a Japanese interpreter told Earl Carroll that the Commandant believed he had sufficiently

[5]Another internee who escaped the following day was never recaptured. A prewar prospector for gold mining companies, he joined guerrillas in the hills and survived, we learned later, until 1944, when he was killed by a fellow guerrilla.

punished his prisoners, but that his military superiors had demanded the death penalty. Furthermore, the High Command had threatened to shoot Earl and the two monitors from whose rooms the internees had escaped. Quick-witted Earl saved himself and the monitors by pointing out that the men had escaped after evening roll call, when the Japanese and not the Americans were responsible for keeping us inside our prison walls.

Earl Carroll, in conjunction with other internees and the university priests, gained intercession of outside priests and influential neutrals, all to no avail. Finally, Earl pleaded with the Commandant himself to save the condemned men. Declaring that he had already failed in an official attempt to stop the execution order, the Commandant promised to garb himself in civilian dress (an act of humiliation to a Japanese officer) and to beg mercy as an ordinary Japanese citizen. He left camp wearing his native kimono and sandals. Whether or not he humbled himself before the High Command, we have no way of knowing; but if so, he accomplished nothing.

On the appointed day, the Japanese took Earl Carroll, the two room monitors and an internee missionary from Japan named Stanley, who served in camp as an interpreter, to witness the executions at the Chinese Cemetery, north of Manila. There, seated over a freshly dug grave, the condemned men were pumped full of tiny bullets fired at a range of about fifteen feet. When they fell, groaning, into the grave, the executioners moved close and drilled them with more shots. Then, before their moans had ceased, Japanese soldiers began shoving dirt over their faces.

At Santo Tomás a memorial service for the three murdered men was held in the peaceful garden beside the Seminary, the Fathers' Garden. Our hearts were heavy for our comrades who, seeking escape, had found their freedom only in death.

Chapter Eight

From the time of the executions, internees began to voice criticism of Earl Carroll's administration. Some, unconsciously turning their wrath at the Japanese against Earl, blamed him for not saving the condemned men — although none could suggest how this might have been accomplished. Others who held him in no way responsible for the tragedy rebelled because they had become restive under what was termed a "puppet" regime.

Earl's position was a difficult one: a Japanese appointee, he had accomplished much that was good; but he had been unable to avert antagonisms in certain branches of his administration. It is doubtful that even an elected official could have pleased several thousand prisoners of such variegated backgrounds; and the fact that Earl Carroll was *not* an elected official aggravated our grievances.

A member of Earl's executive committee, discussing with Van the prevalent agitation for free elections, put forth an oddly undemocratic defence of Earl's regime: "Why should Earl and the committee stand for election? We're doing a good job. Most internees haven't brains enough to vote for good men. I enjoy my job because I can help people."

"I enjoy mine for the same reason," Van retorted, "but I wouldn't want to hang onto it if the majority voted against me."

The committee member was "Doug" Duggleby, who had been

prewar manager of a large gold mining company. His failure to comprehend the Anglo-Saxon antipathy toward undemocratic government was all the stranger because he himself was noted in camp for a peculiarly democratic form of self-martyrdom: although he had the money to buy any number of beds, he slept by choice on a wood-topped desk because, as he explained, if others had to sleep on desks, why not he?

Possibly the most controversial division of our camp bureaucracy was the release committee, which had earned an early reputation for unfairness. We often heard the complaint that those who were lucky, or who had a friend on the committee, succeeded in getting passes, while others pleaded themselves blue in the face to no avail. Certainly it was true that ill internees were sometimes turned down, and that others who were not ill obtained releases for comparatively trivial reasons. In some cases, disgruntled internees went directly to the Japanese, claiming that the committee had allowed their requests for passes to be shelved and forgotten. The fact that the Japanese usually granted their releases strengthened a growing conviction that committee members operated in a manner which was either arbitrary or grossly inefficient.

My roommate Tillie Butler received the brush-off treatment when she tried to obtain a day pass, customarily granted in such cases, to visit her husband who was recovering in an outside hospital from a hernia operation. Carroll Grinnell, release representative for main building occupants, acknowledged her application with a curt: "I'm busy now. Come back tomorrow."

The following day, Grinnell told her indifferently that he would see what he could do. A week went by. Meanwhile, Dr Fletcher, an internee who was allowed during restricted hours to treat Santo Tomás patients at outside hospitals, brought Tillie messages that her husband, lonely and depressed, could not understand why she did not come to see him, as other patients' wives were visiting them every day. Again she went to see Grinnell, and again Grinnell shrugged her off. In tears, Tillie told me that she was going to the Japanese unless Grinnell had a pass for her on the following day. However, the following day her husband returned to camp, a week early: in the camp hospital he could at least see his wife.

Such incidents, by no means uncommon, did not increase the popularity of Earl Carroll, who, as organizer and director of the camp government, was held responsible for the shortcomings of his subordinates. Few committees, if any, escaped censure — from within by underlings who thought they could do the job better than their superiors; from without by those who rebelled against discrimination, real or fancied.

Nowhere was professional jealousy more errantly exhibited than in our camp hospital, organized by two Rockefeller Foundation doctors from Peking, Dr Leach and Dr Whitacre, whom Earl Carroll had appointed. These men had done a creditable job in creating a functioning hospital; however, they alienated many internees by spurning the help of local interned doctors. Barred from treating their own patients in the camp hospital, the local doctors were not even consulted on case histories of internees whom they had attended over a period of years.

I discovered for myself the curious resentment of the Rockefeller doctors toward their Manila colleagues when, on February 21st, I entered the hospital. The 21st of February was a memorable date for two reasons: number one, it was Van's forty-third birthday; and number two, I awakened feeling too ill to taste even the tiniest morsel of a luscious-looking chocolate and walnut layer cake that Edu Roxas had sent in to him.

Van summoned Dr Fletcher, our Manila physician in prewar days, who now practiced in a small office in the annex, assisted part-time by two Filipino doctors and several Filipina nurses. Diagnosing my case as enteritis, a common intestinal complaint in Santo Tomás, Dr Fletcher gave me some medicine and advised me to go to the hospital, where, he explained apologetically, he was persona non grata. Upon my arrival at the hospital, Dr Whitacre, in charge of the women's ward, came to see me. Under the apparently mistaken impression that doctors always wanted to know about a patient's prior treatment as well as about symptoms of malady, I showed him the medicine Dr Fletcher had given me; whereupon Dr Whitacre, refusing even to glance at my pills, snorted scornfully, "I'm sure we have the medicines here that will help you, Mrs Van Sickle."

I stayed one night at the hospital, in a tiny room with about twenty other women, most of whom had enteritis. A single toilet served both men and women throughout the hospital. Nurses (Navy and missionary) tried and sometimes failed to keep us supplied with bedpans. In the morning, too overworked to bathe even the extremely weak, they brought us each a bowl of warm water and a washcloth. I washed, dressed myself, and told a nurse that I was going to leave. "But you can't go until Dr Whitacre releases you," she said.

Feeling trapped, I was relieved to find Van at the front door waiting to see me. When he explained to Dr Whitacre that I wanted to return to my own room, the latter replied acidly, "I'm sorry you have no confidence in us, Mrs Van Sickle."

I was taken aback by this unexpected interpretation of my desire to leave, and assured him that I was motivated solely by reasons of personal comfort and convenience. I promised to take his medicine faithfully. Dr Whitacre eyed me dubiously, but gave me a release. As I passed the kitchen on my way out, my roommate Kitty Fairman called to me. "Tell Van to come here at mealtimes — I'll send you the soft diet you're supposed to have. It's against doctors' orders, but the hospital is too small to take all this enteritis, so I send out the food and keep the patients away. The diet's more important than medicine for enteritis, anyway."

I was only one of many internees who blessed Kitty Fairman for her kindly common sense. If our Rockefeller doctors had benefitted by her example of wise and sympathetic cooperation, one cause for friction could have been eliminated from the ever-growing list of vexations in our daily lives.

More and more disgruntled each day by discriminatory practices amongst our "dictator-appointed" officials, internees demonstrated their contempt for Earl Carroll and his executive committee by overt disregard for their rules. Violations became so flagrant that when regulations concerned the general welfare, Earl and the committee occasionally perpetrated the dangerous hoax that their orders derived from the Japanese. For example, when he deemed it necessary to protect women against possible Japanese concupiscence, Earl issued an "order from the Commandant" forbidding them to wear shorts or insufficient clothing. Whether this restriction, repealed after two years because clothing had become scarce, was ever needed urgently enough to justify deceit is questionable. In any case, internees who suspected the ruse became more than ever distrustful of Earl Carroll.

Under pressure of protest against his autocratic regime, Earl finally granted a measure of democracy to the camp by allowing us to elect floor and room monitors — a small concession, but enough to mollify insurgent spirits. He promised also to allow camp-wide elections for all officials as soon as conditions had become sufficiently stable to warrant full self-determination. Stability — or stalemate, one might better term it — came all too soon with the denouement of external events. The tragic manner of its coming, however, shoved into the background for the time being our dissatisfaction with Earl Carroll and his cohorts as we grieved together over a great defeat.

Chapter Nine

Our waning hope of early liberation was shattered irrevocably, heartbreakingly, by the fall of Bataan in April, 1942. Many of us could not believe the news when we read it in the *Tribune*, for we thought that by now our government must surely have been able to open supply lines. Only when Filipino and neutral friends from outside dolefully admitted that the report was true did we accept it. We all knew now that the subjugation of Corregidor was imminent, and that our stay in prison would be a long one.

Grisly tales came to our ears of the Death March, although until our liberation we never learned the name given it by the civilized world. Jack Littig was seen marching through Manila; that he survived the march we found out later from neutrals who discovered him, ill with dysentery, at one of the military prison camps in Cabanatuan. We wondered how much longer he — and all the others — could endure that nightmare of horror where prisoners were dying by the thousands, without medicine, without clothing, with very little food and few doctors, themselves military prisoners.

In our camp, the rude awakening from dreams of early freedom jolted Earl Carroll's administration into the realization that we were in no way prepared to contend with inconveniences about to be inflicted on us by the approaching rains. Behind the main building, construction committeemen hastily built two dining sheds, which were no more than galvanized iron roofs covering wooden benches and tables lined up in rows on the bare ground. When stormy weather began, rain blew in through the open sides to drench hapless internees who sat there wallowing in mud underfoot.

Camp authorities proposed also to roof over the package line at the gate, and for this project they solicited internee donations, since the Japanese declined to provide building materials except for the dining sheds. Some who could well have afforded to contribute refused to do so because they never used the package line: the thought of other men and women standing in the rain to receive water-soaked parcels troubled them not at all. However, many others donated liberally enough to make the shelter possible.

After the fall of Corregidor, our Japanese administration, now a civilian regime, became generally more lenient towards us. Probably their most extraordinary gesture was allowing the Red Cross and individual internees with prewar bank accounts to withdraw small, stipulated sums from their banks each month. This "magnanimity" backfired when the Japanese sheepishly discovered that all money in the safes of American and British banks had been removed before the Occupation. Enraged, they threatened to punish the interned bank managers, until Earl Carroll pointed out that not the bank manager, but the U.S. Navy, had taken away the money. For some obscure reason, the explanation allayed their wrath.

Soon afterwards, the Japanese permitted internees to claim possessions stored in warehouses throughout the city. Most of our own things had been burned in a storage building along the river during pre-Occupation fires; however, we recovered a suitcase which we had left at the Bay View Hotel — the same that Colonel Yamaguchi had opened to bring in our books, magazines, clothing and a typewriter. Everything else was intact. A few internees recovered such luxuries as jewelry and fur coats.

On Sundays, the Seminary gates were opened to permit Catholics to attend mass (Protestant services were held in the

Fathers' Garden), and now that Manila was no longer under blackout, we were granted the later roll call hour of eight p.m., subsequently retarded until nine p.m. We were required to return at seven to the building areas, but could stroll or sit on the front lawn and walks until roll call: a cherished privilege, because it gave us an opportunity for recreation we had neither time nor energy for during the heat of the day.

Music broadcasts, pleasantly relaxing after the day's work was done, were lengthened to an hour and a half. Programs selected from internee record collections on loan to the music department varied widely enough to appeal to every taste: symphony, opera, Gilbert and Sullivan, musical comedy, swing, sentimental love songs, old-time numbers, peppy pops and humorous novelties.

Other evening activities included lectures and play readings in the Father's Garden, over a loudspeaker which was adequate for the purpose but not loud enough to clash with the music out front. The garden, a restful place of beauty with its trees, its well-kept lawn, its tall rows of red and yellow cannas, was especially lovely in the evening, when the sky's rose, orchid and amber colors glowed through a dark filigree of leaves in the foreground. I doubt that any who have not experienced the drabness of prison life can fully realize what solace and strength one draws from the beauty of a garden, or a sky at sunrise and sunset, or a song or symphony. That we had such moments of beauty gave us much to be thankful for.

After roll call, many internees played bridge and other card games in the hallways until lights out. And so gradually we became adjusted, albeit none too happily, to the prospect of a long sojourn in prison.

Yet no sooner had we accepted our fate than we had occasion to rejoice at the imminent prospect of liberty for a few of our number: the Japanese had authorized a diplomatic exchange ship to take home non-American enemy consular groups. Before the ship sailed, we were allowed to write letters home, a

63

single sheet per person, censored by the Japanese. This was the first message we had been permitted to send, except one form cable ("Safe and Well") which the Japanese had promised to transmit through the International Red Cross. Although we had little faith that our letters would reach their destinations, we did hope to convey verbal messages through friends who were leaving.

One whom I remember as being especially kind about bearing tidings for us was a young and beautiful woman named Jesse Prismall, secretary for the British Consulate in Manila. In camp she had been a true angel of mercy, having taken upon herself the duty of carrying food trays upstairs to the ill, the aged and crippled — who, incidentally, were often cantankerous and complaining, and gave little thanks for the gracious service she rendered them. As soon as she learned that she was to be re- patriated, she began recording internees' home addresses and descriptions of their camp occupations, rooms and other perti- nent facts, personal as well as general, of our lives in Santo Tomás. All this she later wrote home to our families, her letters bringing them such consolation as it was possible to derive from an accurate picture of our prison world.

But not only were we glad for Jesse and for others who had the opportunity of leaving, but we began to nurture hope that the diplomatic exchange ship would be but the first of many ships which eventually would repatriate all of us. Americans, we feared, would remain longer imprisoned than others, since the Japanese refused to discuss the exchange of nationals as long as our government claimed the Philippines as American territory. However, even such faint hope stirred dreams of freedom as we settled down again to the long wait.

Chapter Ten

My siege of enteritis had left me weak, and soon my daily chores became so exhausting that I was compelled to give up vegetable work. The resumption of regular room duties gave me spare time which for some weeks I devoted to typing work for the censor's office, until Van refused to let me carry on with it any longer.

My fatigue was due not entirely to the aftereffects of enteritis, but partly to a minor malady which afflicted perhaps five percent of the women in Santo Tomás: complete cessation of menstruation. Although far less debilitating than the opposite state of almost constant menstruation suffered by another five percent, it nevertheless affected me with a palling lethargy, both physical and mental. The doctors surmised that these abnormalities had resulted from an unbalancing of delicate glandular adjustments, brought on by the shock of internment. Having heard that several women had been cured by a few weeks of rest outside, Van urged me to try and obtain a pass — a relatively easy procedure since the fall of Bataan. Although I dreaded the separation, I finally agreed to speak to Dr Whitacre, under whose jurisdiction came the recommendation of hospital releases for women.

Dr Whitacre rescued me from a dilemma by suggesting a series of injections and hot sitz baths at the camp hospital. The treatment, ineffectual though it was, spared me the ordeal of leaving Van, who at that time was not in good health himself.

Like many other men in camp, he had lost weight rapidly, dropping in four months from 190 to 150 pounds. Although we now supplemented our meals with cake, candy, peanut butter and other foods that we could buy in camp, Van, having no appetite, ate little of anything. He was tired all the time, and by the beginning of May he had developed such severe leg pains that he could rise from a chair only with the greatest difficulty.

After much persuasion on my part, he went to see Dr Fletcher, who referred him to Dr Hugh Robinson at the camp hospital. Dr Fletcher and other local doctors could not obtain vitamins and medicines furnished to the hospital, which forced them to turn over many patients to hospital doctors. After a thorough examination, Dr Robinson told Van that he had preliminary symptoms of beri-beri, for which he prescribed vitamin B tablets, liver, eggs, and red meat. When Van told him that he had had severe attacks of asthma in Manila, although not since internment, the good doctor stated bluntly, "If your asthma comes back now, you'd better get to an outside hospital in a hurry, unless you want to die." Then he added, "Men here worry too much and don't eat enough. That's why they're getting beri-beri. Stop worrying and start eating."

Van tried to do just that. We got ourselves a charcoal stove, an old-fashioned ice box and some kitchenware, and I started cooking immediately. Each morning at the gate Van bought fresh food and ice, which he wheeled in a small, three-wheel pushcart to our cooking site in the west patio. We both welcomed the change in diet, and for a while Van's health seemed to improve.

Because the west patio was by now familiar territory, we had followed the course of least resistance in setting up housekeeping there. Many internees had staked out claims in open ground behind the buildings, where they built shelters to protect themselves from sun and the prying eyes of passersby. In the beginning, these shacks were crude affairs made from boxes, gunny sacks, gasoline tins and whatever other materials could be found. Then, as the idea spread, internees began to import bamboo, sawali, and palm-leaf shingles called nipa, which Filipinos use for roofing and often for walls, as it gives more protection than sawali from driving rains of the typhoon season. With these native materials, picturesque Filipino-type houses were constructed, of varied sizes and degrees of elegance. Most of them stood well above the ground on bamboo stilts; many were attractively landscaped with vines and flowers.

As shanties multiplied, a camp committee was established to license and regulate them. Each shanty owner — and this classification included patio dwellers — paid a monthly "ground rent" of one peso. Among early shanty builders were the Cogans, who delighted in the comparative privacy and comfort of their little house in the fields. Although there was much to be said in favor of shanties, Van and I agreed that the patio's conveniently accessible location outweighed other considerations.

Few spaces were left by the time we filed our claim. Beds lined the eave-sheltered inner walk, which was used as men's sleeping quarters, and the three open sidewalks were filled with all manner of tables, chairs and cabinets. Internees who cooked there had set up charcoal stoves on platforms just off the walk. Space allotment, marked by windows from the first floor hallway, entitled two to four persons to occupy a one-window cubicle. Soon after we had moved in, the majority of sidewalk space-stalkers agreed on a community project to roof over our walks with wood and tarpaper as protection against the inevitable rains. Half-a-dozen "residents" volunteered to build a continuous media agua, or company, each of us paying nineteen pesos for our share.

I blessed the day that we got our wooden superstructure for the welcome shade it cast over us. May is a sultry month, and, walled in as we were, there was not even a faint whisper of a breeze to cool the rays of a sweltering noonday sun or to disperse the heat waves radiating from our stoves.

Before the builders could tack on a covering of tarpaper, the rains began. Grateful for any surcease of sun, we donned boots and raincoats, and ducked as well as we could the waterfalls that cascaded through cracks of our sieve-like roof.

Among the few who did not share in the media agua were our neighbors to the right. One of them, an ex-circus man, had strung up an old circus showboard over their space, which, however colorful, proved to be something less than an effective shield against the rain. Since the gap left our space unprotected, too, Van offered to buy them a roof, a proposal which was proudly rejected. Later on, to our comfort as much as their own, they invested in the media agua themselves.

The rains brought many afflictions, chief among them an incessant plague of ants. When their nests became flooded, ants trekked up our walls by the thousands, pouncing on any food that they encountered along the way. We placed water-filled cans around the legs of our table, cabinets and ice box — then discovered incredulously that some of the ants could swim! It was no hallucination: we actually saw them walking across three inches of water. Only by pouring kerosene into our water cans could we stop them.

If allowed to nest in wall cracks, the ants became perpetual nuisances, stealing food and biting persons, ferocious little monsters that they were! Consequently, whenever they began their safaris up the wall, I would drop everything and start boiling water over our charcoal fire. Floods of boiling water discouraged them temporarily, but there was no relaxation until the last stubborn ant had succumbed, which often meant that the battle would rage for hours.

Once the rains had started, it did not take long for our patios to become oozes of sodden mud which clung tenaciously to boots and barracks, eventually to be trodden into the hallways and room floors. While it was actually raining, we walked through one another's spaces for the protection of the roof, an arrangement which was ruled in order by the mayor and board of officials whom we had elected to run our patio community. However, between rains we tried to respect the privacy of others by wallowing through the mud that lay between our cubicles and doors to the building at either end of the patio.

One minor phase of camp life which had given most of us pleasure in the beginning became a source of irritation to patio dwellers during the rainy season. An interned professional entertainer named Dave Harvey, assisted by his two teammates, the Dyer sisters, had organized internee talent to stage free variety shows each week in the west patio. An entertaining novelty and morale-booster at first, their showmanship soon lost its sparkle; and as time went on, patio residents came to dread show nights, partly because the thieves took advantage of crowds to steal food and kitchenware, but principally because in the rainy season the mess and confusion lasted for days at a time.

Each afternoon before an evening performance was scheduled, children, and a good many adults, too, would spread out blankets and petates (woven grass mats) over the mire to reserve spaces for the show. Internees crossing the patio had no choice but to trample on them with mucky shoes, as they covered every inch of the grounds. Usually a downpour would force a postponement, which meant that owners would gather up their filthy, soaking mats, only to repeat the entire procedure the following day, and each day thereafter until the show could finally go on.

The rains interrupted all outdoor evening activities, forcing us to huddle together in crowded hallways or to retire early to rooms that were stuffy because windows had to be closed in order to protect the beds near them. It had been suggested that window media aguas be constructed, but when it came to raising funds, too many whose beds were not near windows failed to perceive the personal advantage of such a project. Now we all suffered alike from lack of air.

During the day, necessary activities were slowed a hundredfold by seasonal inconveniences. Damp charcoal made fires hard to light; clothes would not dry; mud-splashed floors required constant mopping. By far the most serious consequence of the rains for us personally, however, was the return of Van's asthma. His general health, too, had worsened; he still suffered with severe leg pains, and by mid-June, although his appetite was better, he had lost another seven pounds. Yet, despite his illness, exhaustion and anxious pleading from a worried wife, he continued to work eight hours a day at his censor's job. Asthma finally forced him to give up and seek Dr Robinson's help again.

Because brandy had often relieved his attacks in the past, Van asked Dr Robinson whether he could possibly procure any in Santo Tomás; to which that worthy physician, with a twinkle in his eye, instantly retorted, "If you were about to die, I'd send for brandy. But by the time it got here, you'd be dead, and I'd drink it."

Then, mincing no words, he told Van that his condition was serious and that he must go immediately to an outside hospital. When Van explained his reluctance to leave me, Dr Robinson assured him that I could undoubtedly get a pass to join him, as the Japanese had now established a policy of releasing wives to care for husbands who were hospitalized or recuperating outside.

In order to obtain his release, it was necessary for Van to interview Dr Cho, a disagreeable little Korean appointed by the Japanese to pass on chronic ailment cases for outside hospitalization. Everyone disliked Dr Cho because, whether through lack of medical knowledge or lack of humanity, he often turned down internees who badly needed care and rest outside. When Van arrived at his office, so choked with asthma that he could scarcely breathe, Cho listened for a moment to his chest, then grunted, "You go out."

Van interpreted Dr Cho's ambiguous instructions as a dismissal from the office, but fortunately he meant "go out" to a hospital. Dr Robinson wrote his release, specifying at Van's request the Hospital Español de Santiago, one of a number of hospitals approved by the Japanese for internees. Van chose Santiago Hospital, located at Makati, a barrio (or town) near Manila, for two reasons: first, because there he could occupy an air-conditioned room, of inestimable therapeutic value to asthma sufferers; second, because two Spanish friends, Edu Roxas and Juan Elizalde, were directors of the hospital.

As we walked together to the gates of Santo Tomás on the afternoon of June 21st, 1942, my heart ached for Van, who looked very ill. He would not let me help him, yet he was so weak that he could scarcely wheel his bags down the path in our little pushcart. Before he climbed into the hospital ambulance, he kissed me and told me he was going to return to camp unless I could join him within ten days. A sudden unreasoning fear seized me that he would never come back — that never again would I see him. Forcing myself to smile, I admonished him gaily not to dare think of such a thing, that if he returned, I would have no excuse to leave — that it might take a little time, but I'd surely join him there.

When the ambulance had pulled away, I felt the hot tears in my eyes. In vain did I tell myself that he would be well cared for, that soon he would be in good health again: I could not shake off those horrible fantasies that gripped my mind. Together we had walked through the shadows of our prison world; now we were separated — who could say for how long? Although he was returning to a world we both had known before, it seemed to me at that moment that he was about to step across the threshold of life itself, into the vast unknown of eternity.

Then from nowhere Edwin Cogan appeared and began to talk of friends outside, whom Van would soon be seeing, and of the good, stiff drinks they were sure to bring him — and gradually the concrete realities presented by a kind friend drove away my dire imaginings. The tears dried up unshed as I walked with Edwin across the campus, thanking God in my heart that thus far the Japanese had been merciful to the sick in our camp.

71

Chapter Eleven

Dr Aboitiz, a Spaniard who was Van's doctor at Santiago Hospital, came into Santo Tomás on June 25th to arrange for my release — a routine matter, although Dr Leach, administrator of the camp hospital, tried to make it difficult by refusing to sign my application on the grounds that the Japanese might object.

"Object to what?" queried Dr Aboitiz. "Every day they are releasing women to take care of their husbands."

Dr Robinson, who had drafted the letter for Dr Leach's signature, signed it himself, with a quizzical shrug for his colleague. The Japanese readily granted me a renewable one-week pass, effective beginning July 3rd.

The intervening days passed slowly, yet finally time ushered in the eve of my departure. It was late afternoon; I had just finished packing and my thoughts were far from Santo Tomás when one of my roommates called me over to the window. Looking down on the plaza below us, I saw several truckloads of army nurses from Corregidor arriving at the front entrance. The nurses looked desperately tired. Many were standing; some were slumped over duffel bags and suitcases. Japanese guards summarily halted a score or more internees who had rushed out to greet the nurses and to ask news of husbands and sons who had fought at Corregidor. One or two momentarily eluded the soldiers, but they were quickly intercepted and turned back. After an hour's wait under steaming sun (the rains having let up for a few days), the nurses were ushered into Santa

73

Catalina, a Catholic girls' school across the street from the east wall of Santo Tomás. Since they had with them only what they had been able to carry from Corregidor, we donated whatever we could spare in the way of bedding, towels, soap, and food.

Long after the nurses had gone, I lingered at the window, watching evening shadows lengthen across the campus that was dotted with gay pastel figures which formed colorful, changing groups as casual strollers drifted by or paused to join others who were seated in canvas chairs on the lawn. The scene, reminiscent at that distance of a summer resort, drew my attention to the many changes that had occurred since our early days of internment.

Then we had been too busy or too tired to care what we wore; now, although the daytime clothing was drab, we blossomed forth on clear evenings in our freshest slack suits and dresses, most of them newly purchased at Aguinaldo's or from outside stores which had extended credit to internees with prewar charge accounts. When it rained, we attired ourselves in raincoats and boots if we had them. Many donned instead the more picturesque, if less convenient, native costumes of bakias, palm leaf capes and Chinese-style wide-brimmed straw hats that looked like huge, inverted trays.

The face of the campus itself had altered as shanties mushroomed over fields and lawn; a few had sprung up even around the Fathers' Garden. So numerous were these private dwellings that plumbing facilities had been installed in shanty areas, and public paths had been laid out and named for convenience. The compounds, too, had names: there was Glamorville with its Park and Fifth Avenue, Pechay Street and Talinum Drive after local vegetables; Garden City, Jungletown, Jerkville, Foggy Bottom and others. Internee regulations forbade shanty building on the central portion of the front lawn or in the camp garden behind the Education building. Formerly the garden had served as a garbage dump, but after the fall

74

of Corregidor the Japanese permitted a city garbage wagon to enter Santo Tomás each evening; and now the enriched soil nourished our camp-grown vegetables.

Except for rainy season inconveniences, our daily life in many ways was easier and better organized than in the beginning. Now we could send out soiled clothing to "camp laundry," operated by an internee whose Filipina wife, living outside, employed launderers to wash and iron for us at reasonable rates. In camp, women volunteers who operated sewing machines repaired mosquito nets and mended men's clothing. Children now attended regular school classes, presided over by interned teachers. For the edification and instruction of adults, there were two internee bulletins, one for camp news, the other a sanitation and health publication.

On Saturday evenings, dances for teenagers were held on the plaza or, when it rained, in the lobby of the main building. The resulting bedlam that reigned for a few hours not unnaturally caused complaints. My sympathies, however, were with the teenagers, lovely girls and fine lads who often did an adult's work with never a word of complaint. Those boys and girls were missing most of the carefree fun that is the adolescent's usual expectation; instead of wonder and romance, their portion was monotony and toil.

The children, too young to realize what privations and what dangers beset us in a concentration camp, enjoyed themselves with all the bubbling, heartwarming enthusiasm that is God's gift to childhood. We who were adults had already lived our precious and glorious moments on the threshold of maturity; but lost forever to those teenagers was the radiance of awakening to a world of mystery and beauty, a world whose magic was theirs alone, to hold until the rose-lit morning of youth yielded its delicate glow to the harsher noon of maturity. Surely, had they remembered their own youth, none could have begrudged those teenagers their one bit of fun on Saturday nights.

Yet fun in a concentration camp is such a rare thing that

possibly it caused resentment among some of those who felt deeply, as most of us did, the precariousness of our future in the hands of the enemy. One thing had not changed: we lived in fear, for although there had been no more executions, the Japanese Kempei-tai from time to time seized from our midst internees whom they held incommunicado at Fort Santiago, the dread stronghold in the old Walled City where political prisoners were starved and tortured.

Recently incarcerated was an internee named Joe Yetti, who had formerly served as a petty officer in the U.S. Navy. His arrest had greatly upset Van, for Joe had worked ably as one of his assistants in the censor's office. There were few in camp who did not know Joe Yetti, not only through the censor's office, but as star player and especially, in the early days, as the most dashing of our volunteer servers on the mush and corned beef line. Short, swarthy, with a pleasant smile, black mustache and sparkling eyes, he somehow cut an adventurous figure even when shouting to the kitchen for "More mush!" or "More stew!"

We later learned that Joe had been left behind in Manila by the Navy to carry out a secret mission of paying government money to ex-government workers, both within and outside the camp. His job with the censor's office had enabled him to make necessary contacts at the gate, which in the end, however, had aroused Japanese suspicions. At Fort Santiago, he was beaten and strung up by the thumbs from the ceiling; his arms and legs were bound for hours on end. When his torturers unbound him, he suffered agonies as the blood trickled back into benumbed limbs. Still he refused to talk, and his silence saved many others from torture.

I knew none of these things at the time. Shortly before my departure, he returned to Santo Tomás, too shaken, I was told, to speak of what had happened during that fortnight he must have thought would never end. I knew only that he was back, and was grateful that I could convey that news to Van.

And now, on the eve of leaving, as I turned from the window view that had started this long train of reflection, I wondered what changes I might see when I returned — and I realized suddenly that my vision ended with the morrow. To see Van again: that was enough for the time. Whatever might come later, God willing we would see it through together.

PART II: THE INTERLUDE

Chapter One

A handsome, exuberant young Spaniard leapt from an ambulance that entered Santo Tomás on the morning of July 3rd. Introducing himself as Dr Campa, one of Santiago Hospital's Residents, he proceeded to help me aboard, and enlivened the twenty-kilometer drive to Makati with a sprightly stream of patter about street scenes, the Occupation, war news, and life in general under the Japanese. I was immediately struck by his quaint manner of prefacing various and sundry remarks with one of two American slang expressions: "Oh boy!" or "Hot dog!" The words fairly bubbled over each other as he elaborated on sights which I could barely glimpse through the clear edges of our frosted windows. "Look at the sandbags! Oh boy, the Japs say the Americans won't be back, but if they really thought so they wouldn't barricade those buildings, would they?"

For miles, we paced our speed to the slow-moving traffic of horsedrawn carromatas, bicycles and hand pushcarts. The rare sight of a car made Doc's black eyes flash. "Hot dog! You don't see many cars now. The Army shipped most of them to Japan. Even the lucky ones who still have cars can't run them more than once a month — alcohol rations are too short. No gasoline now, except for planes. Oh boy, just wait till the Americans get back!" He seemed to expect them in a week or two.

As we entered the hospital, a buxom, white-haired lady wearing the starched white uniform of a sister of charity greeted me with a warm smile and a spontaneous, heartfelt embrace. Dr Campa introduced her as the Mother Superior. Beside her stood several Filipina sisters, waiting their turn to welcome me.

Mother Superior was a Frenchwoman, Santiago's only non-Filipina sister. Despite age and a painful malady that caused her legs to swell, she ran the hospital with a firm hand; no detail escaped her vigilance, yet so tactful was her guidance that an atmosphere of harmony always prevailed. Radiating kindliness and efficiency, she inspired instant confidence, an impression which only deepened on further acquaintance. She pressed my hand gently as she led me to Van's room. "I will leave you with your husband. Now, he will be happy here."

Van looked terribly emaciated: somehow, I had expected him to gain pounds during those two weeks we had been apart. It had seemed so much longer. . . . Then I realized that he thought I did not look well, either, because he said, "Thank God I've gotten you out of camp! Here, you'll have nothing to do but rest." I admitted that I was tired; at thirty-one, I felt as though I were an old woman of eighty who had worked hard all her life. A glance in the mirror confirmed the suspicion that my looks matched my feelings. For a moment I stared at the scarecrow apparition with pale brown hair skinned back in two long braids, the top screwed up in a string spiral; eyes that were lusterless and deeply shadowed; face drawn and haggard: the "Santo Tomás look" that nearly all of us wore at one time or another.

Then, turning away from my unattractive reflection, I accepted gratefully, albeit somewhat fearfully after six months of unwilling abstinence, the drink that Van poured for me. Soon, nurses brought our luncheon trays — what heaven to have someone bring in a tray once again, to relax over a cocktail in an air-conditioned bedroom — above all, to be alone together!

That first night, I slept in a separate bedroom. Van had arranged it because he thought that after six months of sharing a room with twenty-seven other women, I might enjoy one

night just by myself. Just to myself— how very lovely! Too lovely, in fact. Has anyone ever heard of such a thing as "the shock
of absolute privacy"? That there must be such a thing is the
only explanation I can offer for what happened to me.

I slept fitfully, arose early, and was combing my straggly hair
at seven a.m. when one of the sisters entered my room with a
breakfast tray. Quite unwittingly, she startled me. We chatted
a few moments, then after she had gone I most unexpectedly
burst into tears. Heartily ashamed of myself, for I had never
had visible nerves and seldom cried, I dashed across to Van's
bedroom, which we then shared happily ever afterwards, until
we returned to Santo Tomás.

Life at the hospital was like a dream. It was a place of peace
in the midst of turmoil, a quiet haven, secure, for the moment
at least, from most of the tribulations that beset the worried
world around us. The grounds, which included meadowland
and a lovely garden and lawn, covered about two square
blocks. A road to Fort McKinley ran past the hospital's northern
boundary, and beyond it flowed the leisurely Pasig River,
winding its way toward Manila from green hills to the east.
Native houses, clustered along the riverbank, marked the barrio
of Makati, whose residents tilled and planted fertile rice paddy-
land west of us. The barrio church spire stood out against a
background of beautiful ruins: the lacy stonework of Guada-
lupe, an ancient Spanish cathedral which loomed gracefully
against distant hills. Southward near our fence lay the tracks of
the Manila-McKinley streetcar, and farther on we could see
Nielson Airport, one of our few reminders of war.

When it was not raining, we used to stroll through the
grounds or sit on the roof, which could be reached by an elevator.
At dusk, the overcast horizon would suddenly catch fire; with
magic swiftness, its molten colors blazed across the entire sky,
transforming our world into a technicolored wonderland as
watery rice fields below reflected their brilliance. Our nightly
music was the song of a million frogs, mingled now and again

with the lazy hum of passing streetcars. I kept remembering Swinburne's lines: "Here, where the world is quiet. . . . I watch the green field growing. . . ." Only during the day did roaring planes shatter the quiet of growing fields and peaceful barrio.

Various neutral friends came to see us, although such visits were forbidden by the Japanese. Edu Roxas and Juan Elizalde made regular trips, Edu by bicycle, Juan by horse carriage. They planned, if questioned, to explain their frequent calls as Board of Directors' business. In prewar days, the Elizalde family had owned gold mines, rope and paint factories, sugar plantations, shipping interests and just about everything else under the Philippine sun. Juan, with three of his brothers, had built a handsome polo club where they had played together in a nineteen-goal brother team until Mike, the elder, had gone to Washington, first as Resident Commissioner, later as Philippine Ambassador. The brothers, Spanish-born, had become naturalized Philippine citizens for business reasons.

Now, instead of playing polo and motoring in chauffeur-driven Cadillacs, Juan harnessed his best polo ponies to the small carriage that he used for transportation. A distillery which before the war had been a mere sideline now was the family's sole source of income: a shaky source at that, for the Japanese threatened repeatedly to commandeer it for their own use, as they had commandeered already all other interests in the vast commercial empire that the Elizaldes had owned. From the output of the distillery, Juan kept us supplied with rum as long as we were in the hospital.

Edu, too, had been a polo player. His wealth had come from sugar plantations which now, by Japanese order, had been converted to cotton. Edu and other sugar planters had fought the change, explaining in detail why cotton would not grow on their land; but the Japanese had replied in effect, "So sorry to disagree with you" — and that was that. The experiment failed as predicted, and as a result, Edu derived no income from his properties during the Occupation.

Another constant visitor was Fred Guettinger, a Swiss auditor employed by International Harvester of the Philippines. It was Fred who had borrowed money for interned local Harvester employees, at considerable risk to himself, since he had not only delivered large packets of currency to the Santo Tomás gatesman, but also signed papers and held receipts to protect both borrowers and lenders at the war's end.

Short and plumpish, Fred rather reminded one of a penguin because of his long nose, round glasses and short arms and legs — if only he had worn a dress suit! Like a penguin, too, he was courteous, friendly and unafraid — and much more besides. There was a certain quiet heroism inherent in his nature, and a great-hearted sympathy and generosity which motivated innumerable deeds of kindness, regardless of the potential danger involved. Fred used to ride the streetcar out to the hospital, usually waiting for the last car (ten-forty p.m.) back to Manila. How he got home before the eleven o'clock curfew, we never learned. Often he would bring us food from the Swiss Club: great kettles of spareribs and sauerkraut, or spaghetti, or chicken soup with whole chickens floating in it. Once or twice he procured loaves of bread, which, after soaring to twenty pesos for a small loaf, had altogether disappeared from the market about mid-June. Fred bought his loaves — at what price, we dared not guess — from a bakery that still possessed a few sealed tins of wheat flour.

To protect him in case of a Japanese inspection, Mother Superior devised the story that Fred was a patient at the hospital, which was in fact true during one month of our stay, while he was undergoing treatment for a spot on the lungs. She kept a room in constant readiness for him.

From Fred, Juan and Edu we learned much about the hazards of life outside. Neutrals — and even Germans — were in constant danger of arrest for questioning at Fort Santiago. Some were held incommunicado for days at a time. Filipinos hated the Japanese because, friendly overtures to the contrary, the army pauperized the people by confiscating chickens, pigs, rice or whatever other property they wanted. Juan told us a story typical of Philippine Occupation humor: "The Japs did something in two weeks that the Americans couldn't do in forty years: they made the Filipinos love the Americans!"

Internees living in homes outside fared precariously, also, because at any moment the army or navy might decide to commandeer their houses. Often they were forced out on a few hours' notice; some moved half-a-dozen times. Occasionally our friends brought news of Jack Littig and others who were prisoners at Cabanatuan. That any still lived seemed a miracle. Juan had sent money and medicine into the military camps, and had tried to send clothes, which many had requested, only to have them turned back by the Japanese.

The one bit of good news that came to us concerned our families at home. Fred Guettinger, through a reluctant and fearful Swiss consul, managed to achieve the next-to-impossible for us: he transmitted via Tokyo and Geneva a cable to International Harvester in Chicago. Replies came back within a month, telling us that our families were well.

War news from the outside world was consistently bad; yet Mother Superior, whose faith in the American army was unshakable, kept regaling us with tales of glorious American victories. Sometimes we would slip over to the sisters' quarters, where we listened ourselves to broadcasts over a concealed radio; but never did we hear such glowing accounts as she reported with all the ardor of true belief, about triumphs on land and sea. Since Mother Superior was as alert mentally and spiritually as she was handicapped physically by her lameness, I have often wondered whether her optimism was not entirely for our benefit. Or could she have believed that her "news" had any foundation in fact? Throughout our stay at the hospital, she firmly and invariably maintained that the Americans would be back "within three months." Thank God she lived to see them return, at long last.

Chapter Two

The hospital's first newcomer after our arrival was a Japanese patient, a civilian from Meralco Power Plant. When the Japanese took over Meralco they interned its American owners on the premises for several months to explain the plant's operation, and they also retained permanently the company's Dr Moreta, a highly reputed Spanish physician and surgeon. For years, Dr Moreta had been sending Meralco patients to Santiago Hospital. At the start of his assignment with the company's new staff, he had a heart-to-heart talk with Mother Superior on the subject of caring for his Japanese patients.

Always dependent to some extent on donations from wealthy Spaniards, the hospital now was hard-pressed for money, as few patients could even pay full fees, much less offer gratuities to help with the upkeep. Since the Occupation, Juan's mother, Doña Carmen Elizalde, had almost single-handedly kept the institution going. In addition to financing direct hospital needs — equipment, nurses, medicines, food — her contributions supported some two dozen aged and indigent Spaniards who lived in a separate house on the grounds and depended for their existence solely on the hospital's charity. Although Doña Carmen gave generously, the money was spread very thin to carry a sizeable overhead. Consequently, Mother Superior readily agreed that Japanese patients, at twenty pesos a day in the hospital's best rooms, would be a godsend.

Unused to Manila's climate, these civilian Japanese often contracted tropical fevers and intestinal diseases, which generally kept them hospitalized not more than four or five days. While they were sick enough to stay in bed, Van and I would discreetly venture out from time to time; but, always nervous, we remained in our room as soon as they began to wander through the halls. Our reticence disturbed Mother Superior, who assured us that they would not bother us at all.

"It isn't that we think they'll bother us," Van explained. "But if the tables were turned, how many Americans would tolerate Japanese internees strolling along garden paths of their best hospital? These Japanese must feel the same about us. If they were really annoyed, they might even complain to the military authorities — then we'd be sent to some other hospital."

Although patently convinced that we were unduly timid and over-cautious, Mother Superior soon devised an ingenious scheme for keeping Japanese patients in their rooms. On arrival, each was given a large stool-chair, with the admonition not to walk to the bathroom. "You must stay very quietly in bed," Mother would say. "It is important to rest *all* the time until you are able to leave the hospital." Trained in obedience, the Japanese thereafter seldom stuck their noses outside the door.

Dr Campa, no lover of the Japanese —"mosquitoes," as they were contemptuously termed in Manila — used to drop in to report on the progress of Dr Moreta's patients.

"I hope the bastard dies," Doc would exclaim. Then hastily he would add, "But not here! If a mosquito ever died here, the whole stinking army would investigate us."

Fearless and irrepressible, Doc told many an amusing tale of official and unofficial encounters with members of that "stinking" army. Once, two drunken soldiers tried late at night to enter his house, mistaking it for a brothel. "Oh boy, when the first one climbed up the stairs," Doc related, "he tried to get rough, so I socked him on the jaw and he fell flat. Then I yelled so loud at the second that the s.o.b. got scared and ran away. Hot dog!"

"Doc, you are going to end up in Fort Santiago," I predicted, laughing at the picture he had evoked of terrified Japanese soldiers stumbling away from this dynamo of muscle and energy that had lashed out at them in the dark.

"Oh boy, I've been there already," he announced triumphantly. "I didn't stop for a sentry. Why should I stop? I had a doctor's permit on my car." He was detained only a few hours; I imagine his ebullient spirits won over even the Japanese. But it was just as well that he usually rode a bicycle, and that he took off for the hills to join the guerrillas some months before we were liberated; otherwise, I doubt that he would be alive today.

Dr Campa was not the only one to defy the Japanese; Mother Superior herself did so on many occasions, not with violence, but with courage equal to Doc's. Angel of wisdom, mercy and goodness that she was, she bore no hatred for the Japanese, but only for the evil which they perpetrated against God and humanity. Never was there a more ardent defender of the Faith than Mother — not in words, but in action: her whole life was a prayer dedicated to the service of God and His children. When it became necessary to risk her life in that service, she did so with unwavering devotion to duty and faith in Divine Providence.

Mother's most dangerous undertaking while we were at the hospital was to shelter three American soldiers who appeared at the hospital, haggard and ill, having escaped to the hills, they said, to join the guerrillas after Bataan fell. She opened her arms and her hospital to them and cared for them until they were well. One stayed only a short time. The two others lingered five or six weeks, on the very threshold of Nielson Airport, at which they often peered with interest from our roof. They were risky patients, for Japanese soldiers sometimes came to Santiago for treatment, and parties of officers had more than once mistaken the hospital for the airport. Although none had ever entered the wards, who could predict when some Japanese — even a patient — might suddenly decide to make an inspection tour?

Proud and happy to be able to help American soldiers, Mother sensibly invented alibis for their protection: in case of a Japanese inspection, the convalescents were to remain silent while Mother Superior explained that the swarthy, dark-haired lad was a Spaniard while the other, a blond, was a German. I am confident that she could have convinced any possible inspectors; however, none appeared at the time. That no word of the soldiers' presence ever leaked out was proof of the adoration and esteem which Mother's Filipino staff felt for her.

When the two were well enough to leave, Mother gave them food and money to return to the hills, as they had said they wished to do. Unfortunately, they proved themselves unworthy of her kind assistance and care — and unwise in the ways of war — by hotfooting it to Manila, where Japanese soldiers caught them brawling in a tavern and proceeded to shoot them.

Mother was grieved at the fate of her American soldiers, but there were other problems to occupy her time and energies. For about a week, she was kept on the *qui vive* caring for an insane patient from Tomás who, in sudden fits of violence, would struggle free of his nurses, rush for the window and try to dash out his brains on the pavement below. Only Dr Campa could restrain him, and only Mother Superior could calm him. In quieter moments, he wanted to kiss Mother, and he talked incessantly of his wife and his beautiful car. Then another spasm would seize him, and the cycle began again. His room being next to ours, we heard all the scuffling through our wall. On alternate nights when Dr Campa was not on duty, the commotion really frightened us, because the other Resident, a slender, gentle young doctor, was palpably no match for his husky patient.

It was a relief to everyone when he was removed to a hospital better equipped to care for mental cases. After an operation for hemorrhoids, he recovered his sanity and returned to Santo Tomás.

As time went on, Santiago came to be crowded with internees, some staying only a few days or weeks for operations or treatment, others living there, as we did, for months. Most of the latter were women, often with babies and small children. Several internee babies were born at the hospital.

Juan Elizalde paid expenses for many internees at Santiago, for although Santo Tomás allowed a nominal monthly stipend for each patient, actual expenses ran considerably higher, and few were in a position to pay the difference. Van and I were fortunate in this respect, having left our money in safe hands.

The access of relatively healthy resident patients might have created a food crisis had Mother Superior not carefully rationed us. Despite her indomitable optimism, she sagely realized that hospital stores of rice and other food might have to last a long time. Consequently, the hospital's normally scanty portions became skimpier than ever. Internees who felt the pinch began bringing in extra food which they cooked in three tiny "diet kitchens," formerly used for preparing special diets and baby formulas. It was not long before Van and I followed their lead. After Dr Aboitiz had administered a series of vitamin B injections in "shock doses," Van's appetite began to improve noticeably. Except for severe and frequent asthma attacks, his health was better, and from the time we arranged extra food, he slowly regained some of the pounds he had lost so rapidly.

The internee onslaught must have driven the poor nurses frantic, for we overran their miniature kitchens like a chefs' convention; but they were wonderfully patient with us, and if they longed for the peaceful days of yore, they never showed it. It was the nurses who brought in our supplies — fresh fruit, liverwurst, bologna and sometimes a bit of fresh meat — whenever they went to market. Infallibly kind, faithful and courteous, they delighted wholeheartedly in any service they could render us.

Eggs we could buy at the hospital, fresh from Mother Superior's flock of about a hundred chickens. She also kept a few pigs, survivors of a once-sizeable drove, the majority having been stolen from a sturdy concrete pen near the fence. After the theft, Mother moved the remainder to a less elaborate structure closer to hospital buildings. Later, she converted the concrete pen into a doghouse to accommodate two pets belonging to one of our fellow patients, an internee named Delilah Endicott. Blond, pretty Delilah, a sister-in-law of Juan Elizalde's brother's wife, had been teaching English at the University of the Philippines when Manila fell. In the early days of the Occupation she had experienced internment at its worst in Villamor Hall, a building of her own university. There, for lack of space, internees had been forced to sleep — if sleep they could — sitting up, while Japanese guards had brutally kicked and abused many of them. After two days in that unsavory prison, Santo Tomás had seemed like a luxury hotel.

Another terrifying experience had precipitated Delilah's entry into the hospital. While she was in Manila on a week's pass to take care of a sick friend, a drunken Japanese soldier had forced his way into the house and had attempted to attack her. As soon as Juan learned of it, he rushed her to Santiago Hospital, where, hysterical from shock, she soon responded to the gentle ministrations of Mother Superior and the sisters and nurses.

After Mother had provided a home for her dogs, she became as idyllically happy as one could be in a land conquered by the enemy. The pigpen made an admirable doghouse despite the unmistakable redolence that repeated scrubbings failed to quell; which, however, neither Delilah nor her dogs found objectionable. Having been friends before the war, we saw her frequently during her stay at the hospital. She usually spent her evenings playing cribbage in our room, with Fred Guettinger making a fourth whenever he came out.

Only one thing ever upset Delilah during those days of reprieve: the periodic application for release extensions. None of us ever knew, when our passes went in for renewal, whether we would be called back to camp or allowed to stay outside longer. We all worried a little, but Delilah's dread of the inevitable reincarceration became a morbid obsession. On days when her pass was due, she became violently ill with blinding headaches and spasms of vomiting that brought a greenish pallor to her face. After the renewal came through, she quickly recovered.

Mother Superior, who suffered and prayed for each one of us on pass-extension days, was particularly concerned about Delilah, knowing her inordinate fear of returning to camp. We used to wonder whether Mother, in her kind, human way, did not sometimes threaten St Joseph, the hospital's patron saint; we could so easily imagine her shaking a warning finger at the good saint, exhorting him please to help Miss Endicott, "Or else, St Joseph, I'll pick none of my pretty white flowers for you next Sunday!"

In September, a new civilian Japanese group took over our camp administration. Before retiring, the old administration extended passes for liberal periods, up to six months in some cases. Delilah, Van and I were given a month. Now, no longer so frequently on edge about the "when" of returning to camp, we could all relax and enjoy our transient security.

Chapter Three

Early in the autumn of 1942, there was talk of a repatriation ship to exchange American and Japanese civilian prisoners. Mother Superior told us that one of her new internee patients was scheduled to sail on the boat; and that is what led to our meeting Daré Frances Kaeding.

A more unusual personality I have never encountered. We invited her to our room for a drink, knowing nothing about her except that she was some sort of writer. She asked us to call her Daré, her pen name; and this is the only specific bit of conversation that I recall from our first meeting, for try as we might, we could elicit no understandable response to any remark or question we ventured.

She made a first — and lasting — impression on us of extraordinary vagueness; so vague was she, in fact, that when she left our room, we doubted that she even remembered our names. She seemed to dwell in a realm apart, worlds away from practical realities of this life. In discourse, she lacked coordination of thought, and I marvelled that she had written two books and was about to embark on a third. She talked incessantly and irrelevantly, asking questions without a moment's pause for an answer, then later asking the same questions again. When I knew her better, I would sometimes say to her, "Now just be quiet a minute, Daré, and listen while I tell you what you want to know." Eventually, she would.

After our first meeting, Van remarked that she was an un-likely prospect for bearing news home to our families. However, since she was our only prospect, we agreed to see as much of her as possible in an effort to impress ourselves firmly on her consciousness.

As I came to know Daré, I grew fond of her and I felt rather sor-ry for her. Although at times her egocentricities irritated me, I found her a fascinating enigma. When we met her, she was fat and fortyish, with little trace of the beauty that pictures proved she had possessed in youth. For ten years or more, she had lived in Paris as a fashion writer, syndicating her columns in Ameri-can newspapers. That she had artistic talent I did not doubt when I read one of her self-illustrated books about feminine beauty, style, and fashion. Her philosophical reflection, delight-ful style and manifest clarity of expression amazed me, although of course I did not tell her so. She lent me the book reluctantly.

"It seems so trivial now," she explained, "so unworthy of what we should truly seek in life. Beauty that is skin-deep is not really beauty at all. Spiritual beauty is the only thing worthwhile. I have devoted years of my life to the study of esoterics, and now I want to teach the world what I have learned. But it is so intricate. How can I hope to encompass in a book what it has taken me years to learn myself? I can't expect the ordinary person to have my intelligence, but I am sure that everyone has spiritual yearnings. I feel that my life's work should be to explain how to attain spirituality."

That is the gist of what she said, although she conveyed her thoughts less concisely than I have recorded them.

"Daré, I think your previous book is a splendid foundation for spirituality," I told her. "You haven't concentrated on skin-deep beauty. You have emphasized the qualities of character and spir-it that create loveliness in humanity. I think the ordinary human being needs a more earthly means than esoterics to achieve spirituality."

"Yes, perhaps you are right. But you *do* think there is spiritual longing among people, don't you?"

"Of course."

"Have you ever studied esoterics?"

Thinking, Here is my chance! I replied, "No, but I'd like to know something about it."

That was the beginning of a close association which lasted for several months. Each morning Daré would take me to the roof to practice esoteric vocals, gestures and exercises, each with its own meditation. While teaching, she was a different person, coordinated and exact. I am not sure that her teachings were accurate: she sometimes told tales of seeing demons that made me wonder. I shall never find out, because I am too much of the Western world ever to study under Oriental priests of esoterics; but I did sense the potential spiritual power of a true student, and I learned much about Daré.

Before devoting her soul to the pursuit of esoterics, she had lived a full life, which included several marriages. Then she had gone to Japan, where she studied for several years at a Zen Buddhist temple. Just before the war she had come to Manila en route to California as a guest, in some capacity, of the Japanese Tourist Bureau. We guessed that she might have written or illustrated pamphlets for them in exchange for passage home, as her studies had used up all her money.

Instead of sailing immediately to the States, Daré fell in love with a naval officer and stayed in Manila. After the debacle, she was interned for a week at Santo Tomás, then was released at the request of the Japanese Tourist Bureau, she told us, to live at a convent. A Catholic herself, she related that she had been discreet about mentioning her esoteric studies, of which the priests and sisters would surely not approve. Six months later, the Catholic Fathers sent her, because of ill health, to Santiago Hospital, where they paid her expenses. She was a victim of many ailments, varying in seriousness from infected ant bites to heart and glandular troubles, and severe headaches which had resulted, she said, from eight mastoid operations. Because of the operations, she wore her hair straight and unbecomingly short, being unable, she explained, to endure the heat of permanent waves, or even of a hair dryer. Her usual attire—three or four dressing gowns or kimonos, one on top of the other—gave her the bizarre and shapeless look of a multi-colored sack full of feathers. However, on the rare occasions when she "dressed up," concealing her shorn locks beneath the folds of a turban, she looked very attractive. Her large brown eyes, whose luster was undimmed by the passing years, were beautifully expressive.

She could have been an asset to our internee gatherings if only she had not chattered so eccentrically; for example, it was disconcerting to the raconteur of some not-so-old story to be told suddenly by Daré, "I cannot understand your stories. But I will give you a meditation. If this is the sound of two hands"—she clapped her hands sharply together—"what is the sound of one hand? You must meditate deeply. Even I could not understand it for many years."

Although she never adjusted herself to people, Daré in many ways adapted herself better than anyone I know to the circumstances of internment. It was one of the enigmas about her that, although she often appeared to be a square peg in a round hole, she never had the least difficulty accepting—or ignoring—any situation that confronted her. She had no regrets about her stay in Manila, and lamented only the loss of her trunks, which had been stored near the piers. They contained all her notes and publicity: spiritual consideration to the contrary, Daré delighted in publicity.

Soon after her arrival, a kindred spirit in the person of Edgar Kneedler moved with his family to the hospital. Before the war, Edgar had managed the Bay View Hotel, one of his father's many valuable properties. The Japanese had retained him for some months to run the hotel, and he had succeeded in securing from them a release for his elderly parents and a promise that they could continue indefinitely to live in one of the buildings that had belonged to Dr Kneedler. Shifted from apartment to apartment, the Kneedlers were finally ordered out by the Japanese and, having no other place to go, they gratefully accepted Mother Superior's invitation to live at the hospital until they could find a house. They came in force: Dr and Mrs Kneedler, Dr Kneedler's secretary and her little girl, Edgar and his wife and small daughter. Mother Superior turned over to them the isolation ward in back of the hospital, a four-room house with kitchen and bath, where they stayed until Spanish patients with communicable diseases needed it some months later.

Edgar often invited Daré and me to hear his splendid collection of classical records, which included such interesting modern compositions as Mil'haud's "L'Oreste d'Eschille" and Stravinsky's "Symphonie de Saumes." Tall, blond and artistic, he was a talented young musician himself, having studied piano, voice and ballet. Even more important to Daré, his was a soul that responded readily to esoteric studies; after joining her morning classes, he quickly became her star pupil and told me that he benefitted greatly from her teachings. As he approached the threshold of her spiritual realm, Daré proudly rejoiced in the improvements she detected in his character. I noted no marked change in Edgar, but no doubt I lacked esoteric perception.

Soon Daré acquired still another pupil: Father Sastre, a Spanish priest who had been sent to Santiago to recuperate from several days of torture by the Japanese. During convalescence, he carried on his priestly duties at the hospital chapel. Father Sastre's voice when he said mass was rather harsh and indistinct, a fault which he recognized. Having observed Daré's classes with Edgar and me, he asked her permission to join our "voice lessons." It tickled her sense of humor — she did have one, even though commonplace jokes eluded her comprehension — to teach Father Sastre esoteric vocals whose meaning he would heartily have disapproved had he understood it. Whether from the unconscious absorption of esoterics or from beneficial exercise of the vocal cords, Father Sastre's voice developed a new and richer resonance, to his delight as well as Daré's.

Chapter Four

Released internees fared particularly well for a period toward the end of 1942. There was little doubt that Allied reverses explained the oft referred to "magnanimity" of the Imperial Japanese Army, for never was the panorama bleaker for our side. Americans were struggling to protect the Australian coast, while Russians grimly battled Germans at the very gates of Stalingrad, Leningrad and Moscow. Relaxed and happy over this pleasing state of affairs, the new Japanese administration at Santo Tomás emulated the previous regime in issuing renewals of a month or longer. Furthermore, they often granted interned husbands permission to join wives and families outside. Many a reunion took place at Santiago Hospital as husbands arrived to spend several weeks or months.

By Christmas, a season as happy and festive as Mother Superior and her devoted staff could make it, we were a community of some two dozen internees, men, women, and children. Most of the adults attended midnight mass on Christmas Eve in the little hospital chapel. Then on Christmas Day, Mother arranged a visit from Santa Claus, bearing gifts fashioned by the sisters' skillful fingers for grownups and children alike. At dinner we enjoyed extra dainties heaped on our plates.

That night, with no Japanese patients around, Van and I gave a party in our room for the internees and everyone else we knew at the hospital. There were rum eggnogs to drink, and more food than we could possibly eat, thanks to the generosity of Juan, Edu and other friends who had sent us turkey, cake and all manner of holiday delicacies.

I remember that Daré, vivacious and attractive in a bright turban and becoming dress, remarked, "Next Christmas I will be home, but I shall be thinking of all of you, and the fun we are having tonight."

By now, few of us believed that there would ever be another repatriation ship, but we said nothing to chill her wishful thinking. And who knew? She might be right.

January — the most perfect of months in Manila, when days are cool and sunny and fields still green from recent rains — opened auspiciously for us in 1943 with the receipt of Red Cross kits from the diplomatic repatriation ship. Each internee, in camp and outside, received a kit from Canada, New Zealand or South Africa, and half a kit from Great Britain. Each kit contained several tins of meat and fish, a small can of tomatoes, a chocolate bar, a can of condensed or powdered milk, tea, jam, a can of cheese crackers, a tin of butter or margarine, sugar, salt and pepper, soap, and a box of prunes or raisins. Delilah, Van and I gave our powdered milk to mothers with young babies.

There arrived at the hospital about the same time as our kits a more abundant source of milk: several cows which Doña Carmen Elizalde had sent to Mother Superior from her farm in Baguio, a hill resort north of Manila. The newcomers occupied a part of the pigpen that housed Delilah's dogs, who accepted the intrusion philosophically. Tapping this copious source of supply, however, presented unforeseen difficulties: not one of the hospital's Filipino employees had ever been near a cow, and the mere thought of milking one terrified them. Delilah and Daré came quickly to the rescue, each claiming to have had experience with cows. Mother Superior gladly granted them permission to try their techniques. Delilah's cow cooperated beautifully, but Daré's was a disgruntled beast which promptly kicked her. Never again did she boast of her prowess, much less attempt to show it off. I suspect that her previous bovine associations had been confined to those mystic realms of the spirit wherein cows, I presume, yield milk on esoteric impulse. Delilah's knowledge was of the more practical sort that could be passed on, which she proceeded to do, to one of the gardeners who soon became a credible milker.

A newly purchased carrometa pony now unexpectedly gave birth to a colt; then several goats joined Mother Superior's fast-growing herd of domestic animals. No scene more peaceful and bucolic could have been imagined than the hospital's lush meadowlands, which now served as pasture for grazing cows, nibbling goats and an ever-wary mare whose frolicsome colt kicked up his heels delightedly in this playground of shaggy grass.

Just beyond Santiago's boundaries, however, a discordant sight marred our idyl with a reminder of war, for the Japanese were utilizing the fair weather to enlarge Nielson Airport, leveling the field all the way to the streetcar track. As we observed their progress we noticed with sudden interest that some of the workmen, tall and gaunt in the distance, looked like Americans. Our suspicions were soon verified by a Filipino employed on the job, who told the sisters that a number of his co-workers were American civilian government employees and military prisoners who had been captured at Cavite. They lived at Fort McKinley, walking the several miles to and from the airport. Every evening we watched them trudge down the road, weary and droop-shouldered after eight or nine hours of heavy work in the sun.

There were sounds, too, that reminded us of war: the zoom of planes, the chants of Japanese troops swinging along the McKinley Road, the haranguing of officials in the Kalibapi — a Japanese-Philippine political party whose barrio headquarters, equipped with loudspeakers, were next door to the hospital. Many a night their raucous propaganda entertainments and political ratings shattered the beauty of a dreaming countryside, driving us down from the roof to our closed room, where still their clamor pursued us: a relentless symbol of Japanese aggres-

101

sion and tyranny.

And now, disconcerting news came to us from Santo Tomás: because of imprudent internee behavior, Japanese "magnanimity" was wearing thin. It was no wonder that they had lost patience with us, because both in the camp and outside, certain internees had violated the Commandant's explicit orders. In camp, the Japanese had discovered a number of pregnant women, some married, some not. Remembering the "love tent" proposal of a former Commandant, one might wonder why this revelation should create such a furore. But consistency was no attribute of the Japanese, and subsequent commandants had clearly manifested their ideas of propriety by prohibiting all demonstrations of affection, and by further decreeing that all shanties have two open sides to expose the interiors to passersby. Internees had perforce obeyed until the rainy season, when fast-growing vines covered the openings to give a semblance of privacy. At intervals, the Japanese would order vegetation torn down, but between times nature took its course, with predictable results.

Outraged at this arrant insubordination, the Japanese rounded up the fathers-to-be and put them in the camp jail for about a fortnight. One of the unauthorized fathers was a missionary who, when questioned about his indiscretion, reputedly replied, "My wife and I thought this was a good time to have a baby. There's nothing else to do and it won't cost us a cent." As was to be expected, individual punishment alone did not satisfy the Japanese. They denied shanty privileges to everyone for some days, and promptly inaugurated a policy of separating husbands and wives on the outside.

The Japanese were further vexed by the all-too-free wanderings of certain released internees. Those living in houses were allowed to market, but some took advantage of their restricted freedom to frequent restaurants and bars, where they were often picked up by infuriated guards and promptly sent back to Santo Tomás. To facilitate quick identification, the Commandant ordered every released internee to wear in public places a red armband label; yet some internees flagrantly continued to visit spots that were strictly off-limits — a futile defiance of orders that brought only trouble to themselves and to others who were innocent of offense.

At the hospital, patients from Santo Tomás were clearly interned on the premises and had no right to wander. However, there were some, like the Kneedler family, who were not patients and who had formerly lived in the city with permission to shop. Since nothing to the contrary had been indicated, they assumed that they retained the same privilege at the hospital. Various others who had never been given such authorization went out anyway from time to time, until finally the Japanese put a stop to all roaming. Undeterred, a few still defied the warning when it suited them.

One of these, an internee who was visiting his wife and two children, got himself into trouble — through thoughtlessness rather than willful disobedience, but the result was the same. Having volunteered to help the hospital gardeners, he stepped outside the gate one day to borrow a special garden tool from a neighbor. As he entered the nearby cottage, he was nabbed by the barrio constable, a Kalibapi leader, who thought he was an escaped military prisoner. Taken to Fort McKinley, he convinced military authorities that an error had been made, and he was escorted to Santo Tomás. Although the Japanese then allowed him to return to the hospital, they did not renew his pass when it expired a few days later. Possibly he may have scored a second black mark in their books by leaving behind him a newly pregnant wife.

Because of Japanese determination to separate husbands and wives, I felt that my days in the hospital were numbered. When my pass was due on January 25th, Dr Aboitiz, busy with an operation, asked the gentle young Resident to request a renewal for me. He brought back news that I had expected, although not quite so imminently: I was to return in four days to Santo Tomás.

Dr Aboitiz's amicable relations with the camp administration had led him to ignore that ever-present element of doubt in pass renewals and to take for granted an automatism which in fact never existed. Now, startled at the realization that the Japanese were dead serious about enforcing their birth control program, he still was not prepared to give up easily. When my four days were up, he presented my pass in person and secured a month's renewal on the basis of my own health (instead of "to take care of my husband") so that he could continue treatments started when I first arrived at the hospital.

Soon afterwards, the ax fell on Delilah Endicott. Since she was unmarried, it appeared that there must be another explanation for her recall: the recent incident with the Kalibapi official had probably focused unfavorable Japanese attention on internees at Santiago Hospital. We were all sorry that it had to be Delilah, the one who most dreaded returning to Santo Tomás, and one of the very few who had never left Santiago Hospital premises.

Chapter Five

At the end of my month's extension, Dr Aboitiz took me into Santo Tomás to request a renewal. Only once before had I, at his suggestion, gone in myself; I had waited, with others seeking pass renewals, on a bench outside the Commandant's office while a member of the release committee presented my case to the Japanese. This time, I had come in for an examination by Dr Fletcher, and Dr Aboitiz took me directly to his office in the new camp hospital.

No greater improvement had taken place during our absence from Santo Tomás than the organization of this new hospital under the direction of Dr Fletcher, whom the Japanese had appointed some months before, when former administrator Dr Leach had failed to control a dysentery epidemic. Larger and better equipped than the old dormitory, the new hospital was located in Santa Catalina, the school building where army nurses had been housed after their arrival at Santo Tomás. An entrance had been cut through the camp's east wall, and the street between blocked off by wooden fences which enclosed Santa Catalina within the university grounds.

Personnel had altered almost as much as the hospital's physical appointments. Dr Leach had retired; Dr Whitacre was released to carry on research work at Philippine General Hospital; the Filipino doctors and nurses were now barred from camp. Only Dr Robinson and several other missionary doctors remained to assist Dr Fletcher; yet the hospital functioned with greater efficiency than ever before. Army nurses, reluctant at first to take care of civilians, had agreed to staff the new hospital after the Japanese refused their request to be sent to military camps. Navy and missionary nurses were ousted at the insistence of the army group, who had consented to work only as a solitary unit. Although some internees complained of indifference and roughness, the majority found them a cheerful, efficient, hardworking outfit.

During our interview with Dr Fletcher, Dr Aboitiz explained the treatment he had been administering to bring on menstruation and to relieve other related complications. After the examination, Dr Fletcher recommended a month's extension for a minor operation. I have always doubted that my ailment was serious enough to justify prolonged hospitalization, and I believe that Dr Fletcher advised my release because he knew that Van, who desperately needed the outside care and rest, was determined to come in when I did.

My operation, which should have been completed in five minutes, became something of an ordeal when the electrical implements failed to function properly. I was not a brave patient, but Mother Superior's sympathetic words and reassuring presence helped me to endure the hour that seemed like half a day on the operating table. After it was over, she followed the stretcher to my room and poured me a drink of straight rum, the best medicine in the world at that moment.

About three weeks later, when I was quite well again, we had a sudden inspection by two Japanese release officers from Santo Tomás, our first in all the months we had been there. Van and I were just sitting down to lunch when a sister, dispatched by Mother Superior to warn us, burst into our room. Always cool-headed and alert, Mother Superior outdid herself that day. While she escorted the two Japanese through the first and second floor wings, sisters and nurses rushed to our room to carry out fine instructions covering everything from hiding the demijohn of rum (sent by Juan to be divided among all internee patients) to whisking me off to another room. After they had us chastely separated, the sisters and nurses hastened away to help other internees.

Van lighted asthma powder and burned it until the air was thick with smoke. When the inspectors poked their heads in, they hastily withdrew them and gasped for breath. Still coughing and choking, one of them demanded, "What's that smell?"

"Asthma powder. The poor one suffers constantly," truthfully responded Mother Superior.

Brief as their inspection was, the Japanese had observed the two beds in Van's room, and asked who slept in the other bed. Never at a loss, Mother instantly replied, "That is for the special nurse who is with him at night when the attacks are bad." She felt no need to explain that the "special nurse" was Mrs Van Sickle.

When they entered my newly acquired room, one of the inspectors asked me how I felt. Slow as usual on the uptake, and knowing furthermore that my healthy color would belie any pretence of appearing gravely ill, I faltered in what I hoped was a weak voice, "Pretty well, thank you."

Mother Superior rallied the conversation. "She is getting a little better now." Smoothing my hair and patting my cheek, she spoke of how ill I had been, until the inspectors departed.

They covered the hospital thoroughly. Mother tried to divert them from the roof, but they nosed their way up — and voiced disapproval. There, with Nielsen Airport at our feet, we had a perfect grandstand for spying, although what harm they thought our "spying" could do, we never learned. They ordered the roof closed immediately. We later heard that the inspectors had reported Santiago Hospital much too good for Americans. One of them, Ohashi, particularly mentioned Van's air-conditioned room and complained with irrefutable logic, "Even I do not have an air-conditioned room." However, he continued to extend Van's pass.

It seemed no time at all before my pass was due again. I went to camp alone to interview Dr Cho, the Korean, who told me to return in two days with my doctor. On the second visit, he agreed to recommend another month's extension, then evidently changed his mind, because he put no such recommendation on the card he sent to the release office. Dr Aboitiz, enraged, protested to Ohashi, who finally told us to come back in two days for another interview. On our return, Dr Cho hissed, "What is your chief complaint?" I kept quiet and let Dr Aboitiz do the talking. Cho's supercilious indifference so angered him that finally he demanded to know why the Korean had broken his word to recommend my extension. This approach brought swift and untoward results: the insulted Korean brusquely ordered us out of his office. I was glad to leave before the two men came to blows. While Dr Aboitiz, livid with rage, nursed his injured pride and wounded feelings outside in his car, I presented myself at the release office, where I was given four days to come into camp.

Although Dr Aboitiz reported him to the Japanese medical authorities in Manila, Cho stayed on in camp—probably because the Army wanted a doctor there who could be tough. The Japanese administration in Santo Tomás evidently thought little of his medical skill, for they often ignored his recommendations and released sick internees whom he had turned down. In my case, the only complaint against Cho was that he had changed his mind without notifying Dr Aboitiz. Medically, there was no longer any reason for me to stay outside, as the operation and treatments had at last accomplished the desired result.

Dr Aboitiz wanted me to try again for Van's sake, and I promised to apply for a new release after I had stayed in camp a week or two. We persuaded Van to wait that long, in case I might be allowed to return. But I felt there was little hope, and only prayed that Dr Aboitiz might be able to induce Van, who so badly needed hospital care, to remain there as long as the Japanese would renew his pass.

PART III: TWILIGHT AGAIN

Chapter One

The turmoil of Santo Tomás struck me anew as I stepped down from the ambulance on the afternoon of April 12th. Internees, many of them weary and worn-looking, walked ceaselessly hither and yon, this way and that, each bent on his own private errand. Yet most immediately I perceived that the direction of all this activity had changed vastly during my nine months of absence from camp. When I had left the previous July, Santo Tomás was, commercially speaking, a village emerging from the wilderness; now the village had grown to be a full-sized town of many stores, services and businesses, both private and camp-sponsored.

Upon arrival, I availed myself of a private baggage service arranged for by Delilah, who was waiting at the main building entrance for the ambulance. After an exchange of greetings and farewells, Dr Campa and attendants who had accompanied me from the hospital drove away, leaving us a bit wistful. But this was no time to indulge in happy memories or futile wishes; my first concern was to find a place to park my possessions. I had wanted to go back to room 44, but there was no space; in fact, space was still at a premium everywhere. The room assignment board, desperately trying to allocate half a dozen other new arrivals, had not the least idea where to suggest putting me.

Feeling forlorn and orphanish, I had begun to envision myself setting up squatter's rights in the hallway, when Delilah told me of a temporary space in her room, number 50 on the third floor. She introduced me to her monitor, who, wonder of wonders, did not deflect me with the customary declaration that "we have too many in this room already"— although at a glance I could see that here, if anywhere, it was more than true: beds were lined up like soldiers in a tight parade formation, with nowhere a wasted inch. As though unaware of her room's cramped condition, the monitor graciously informed me that I could stay for a few days in the space occupied by someone visiting relatives outside. My gratitude was all the more heartfelt for her cordiality.

After my bags had been brought up, Delilah volunteered to take me on a tour of the camp — and many were the marvels to behold! First of all, she showed me the camp-run cold store which sold meat, eggs, lard and various internee-made products such as rice bread sandwiches and "potato" salad concocted from white camotes. Open only in the morning, the cold store was situated in a small room which fronted on the west patio. During the seven or eight months of 1943, there was an abundance of chicken, ham, carabao pot roast, frankfurters, bologna, liver-wurst, pork roast and chops. Tenderloin carabao steaks were not uncommon, and on a few occasions the cold store offered for sale Birdseye frozen vegetables obtained from Manila cold stores when it was feared that they would spoil.

Scarcely less fabulous were other camp-run stores: canteen for canned goods, staple foods and seasonings; a bakery that sold rice and bread and cookies brought in from outside; a personal service shop where internees could order medicine, drugs, cosmetics, shoes and many other articles. No longer was it necessary to arrange for purchases through gatemen: nearly everything could be bought directly in camp, or ordered through the personal service department. Like buyers of our line chow, internee buyers for the canteen, cold store and other camp projects went outside daily to order and purchase in the city.

Private industry had kept pace with camp-sponsored developments. I was astonished to see that the western end of the roadway behind the main building had become a sort of Main Street where shoppers could buy anything from clothing to a meal of steak and French fried camotes. An internee named Rosie Rosenbaum, who had owned an exclusive Manila dress shop, now displayed her stylish apparel, sent in by former employees, in an open-fronted shanty, one of many such stores that lined the road. Other stall owners sold toys, cosmetics, soft drinks, cakes and cookies, candy and peanuts, canned goods, native cigarettes (American ones had long since vanished) and almost everything else one would find at a corner grocery or drugstore. Several restaurants, well patronized despite their slum-like atmosphere, served tempting meals which could be eaten on the spot or carried away, as one preferred.

Delilah told me that in the evening, when these shops closed, there were refreshment booths which came suddenly to life in the patios and main building. There, internees revived their flagging spirits with hot coffee, cocoa, soft drinks, rice bread sandwiches, cakes and other light snacks.

If Main Street lay behind the main building, the road in back of the "restaurant" building (which now housed Japanese and internee government offices) was Market Street, for here each morning one could buy fruits and vegetables from any one of four Filipino-owned stalls. Prices were higher than outside, because Japanese gate guards, we were told, demanded a share of whatever was brought into camp.

Across the road, two Japanese concessions sold canned goods and staples. A third handled fresh meat and excellent Japanese fish cakes. Further along were located other internee businesses, both public and private: a camp lumberyard, the office of the camp laundry, a repair shop for shoes and umbrellas, a canned goods broker's stall, a building material contractor's office. Various other projects were scattered sporadically across the campus.

111

I noticed that Aguinaldo's no longer maintained a concession in camp, and I remembered reading in the paper several months before that their main store in Manila had been closed and its owners arrested because they had dealt in "forbidden" (i.e., American) currency, and had sold American newspapers and periodicals. Whether or not they had sold them, they had indeed to my knowledge distributed old American papers, as wrappers for goods purchased. I had discovered in a New York paper encasing my rubber boots a scathing cartoon about the toppling "House that Jap Built," and also the following clever parody of Father William which, however, was scarcely calculated to amuse the Japanese:

"You are young, Hirohito," the old man said,
"And your thinking is reasonably clear;
But what is this Co- that you have in your head,
Along with Prosperity Sphere?"
"By Prosperity Sphere," Hirohito replied,
"We mean but our share of the biz,
While Co- is the share of the chap we have pried
As loose as we dare to from his."

Probably the closing of Aguinaldo's concession had helped our internee government secure permission to open camp-run stores. If so, it had worked to our advantage.

After our sightseeing tour, Delilah and I had dinner together. To my amazement, the line served meat loaf, squash and rice with a tasty tomato sauce. Delilah assured me that this was now normal fare in Santo Tomás: after several shakeups, the kitchen was finally staffed with men who took pride in preparing palatably such *piéces de résistance* as chile con carne, hamburgers, beef stew, pork and beans (with plenty of pork), and a variety of healthful, if not elegant, vegetables. She told me also that a noon meal was provided for all who were willing to work two hours a day, six days a week — not an undue hard-

112

ship for the healthy because, volunteer labor having failed to supply enough workers, every internee was now required to do some camp job. The lunches, usually rice and beans, were no gastronomic delicacy, although undoubtedly they provided nourishment enough for those whose digestive organs did not rebel against daily beans.

I wondered how our internee buyers could possibly pay for all this expensive food: with local produce selling at three to four times its normal cost, and corned beef at five dollars a can, the minute Japanese allowance of fifty centavos (twenty-five cents) a day per adult would not even begin to cover our needs. I soon learned that Earl Carroll and other internees had borrowed for the camp considerable sums of money, underwritten by the Red Cross, to make up the shortage.

We had reason to believe that the Japanese administration knew about these borrowed funds, for Kuroda, the new camp commandant, once jokingly told Earl that he knew money was flowing freely into Santo Tomás. Why should the Japanese ignore such flagrant violation of their own law? We could only suppose that Kuroda and his civilian regime were humane and decent enough to conceal the facts from the army. Had it been otherwise, many who are alive today might never have lived to be free again.

Chapter Two

The morning after my return I set out on another tour of the camp, this time alone and with a specific destination in mind: a shanty which a friend had secretly purchased for us several weeks before my return. Secrecy had been essential because camp regulations forbade internees living outside to own shanties: an unjust law that often caused trouble to released internees who had lent shanties to obliging friends, only to discover upon returning to camp that the friends were most reluctant to relinquish their property. In at least one case, the caretaker refused to budge, which left the rightful owner holding a bag, a victim of legalized theft. Our newly acquired shanty was not yet legally ours, because no transfer of registration could be made until Van returned. However, since all parties involved in the transaction were honest, it was, for all practical purposes, my very own.

Strolling out to investigate our property, I passed the Cogan's shanty and stopped a moment to chat with them. Helen, thin and looking far from well, had only recently returned to camp after an operation. When I left, Edwin accompanied me up the path to see our new purchase. At first glance, the shanty was no mansion, and subsequent scrutiny confirmed my original impression that here was a tumbledown shack, six feet by eight, with nipa roof, bamboo strip floor and sides of open bamboo slatwork situated at the camp's northwest corner between a drainage ditch and a dumpsite for burning trash. For this aristocratic dwelling, furnished with a small, screened cabinet and a large, cushioned bejuko chair, we had paid 150 pesos. Nevertheless, I liked it immediately, and considered the price by no means exorbitant for these times. Edwin, not so favorably impressed, exclaimed, "Good God, you certainly picked an elegant neighborhood!"

"Smelly, but private," I retorted, sniffing the delicate aroma of smoking rubbish mingled with ditch sewer gas which gently wafted its way to our nostrils. On two sides, the camp wall bounded our property, a tall acacia tree shaded us on a third, and already I pictured screens of bougainvilla hiding ditch, trash heap and all neighbors beyond. "The smells should discourage long noses," I added.

We planned, when Van returned to camp, to tear down the old shack and to construct in its place a wooden shanty with a sheet iron roofing, substantial and rainproof so that Van could comfortably sleep out at night, as men were now allowed to do. Because there were no more vacant sites, we had bought this shanty for its ground space; meanwhile, it served me well as a place to relax during free hours.

Edwin offered helpful advice about building the new shanty, and engaged one of the camp's best carpenters to make a survey and estimate of materials needed, which Van hoped to buy outside. Shanty building had grown into a vast industry run by internee contractors and sub-contractors who hired internee gangs of carpenters, laborers, nipa tiers, etc., to construct shanties from diverse materials that they brought into camp to sell. Certain contractors imported prefabricated, native-type shanties which had only to be assembled, but Edwin warned against these: although they looked pretty, they were too flimsily built to withstand typhoons.

Only two other shanties stood near ours, one across the ditch, the other facing it on the opposite side of the path. The first was occupied by a quiet couple with whom I never exchanged more than a passing greeting. The second, a makeshift affair with toppling walls, sagging roof and the ground for a floor, was used by a half dozen young men and one girl, who gathered there not only for sociability but to work. During the day they roasted peanuts and boiled fudge and peanut brittle in huge cauldrons over bonfires and charcoal stoves, to sell in front of the main building at night.

Delilah introduced one of them to me, a young man whom she had known in pre-internment days when they had rolled bandages at the same Red Cross unit. Through him, I met the rest of the gang, most picturesque among them a chap I shall call Duke, who, I gathered, was half-owner of the shanty and business. Tall, dark, and thin-featured, with a devil-may-care twinkle in his eye, he wore a wide-brimmed straw hat tilted at a rakish angle—and the girl, whose fictitious name was Georgie, belonged to him.

There was not the slightest doubt that Georgie, a plump, not very attractive girl of about sixteen, adored her Duke — despite the fact that she knew he was married to a Filipina woman who lived outside, and that he had several Mestizo children. Her mother and father, I was told, had protested and threatened in vain: the child followed her heart's desire, and her parents disowned her. So now Georgie worked her fingers to the bone for Duke, cooking through the heat of the day and selling during evening hours when most of us were strolling or reclining, watching ball games or listening to lectures and play readings. Such is the power of love, even in a prison camp.

For me at that time, life was certainly easy enough; yet suddenly I discovered what a soul-searching experience internment can be, not innately of itself, but in one's personal reaction under stress: my own reaction. If it is not pleasant to discover one's own worst nature, it is still less pleasant to reveal it brashly and unwittingly to others, which is precisely what I did.

The incident was trivial enough: one afternoon I met an

acquaintance whom I shall call Arlene, wife of a military prisoner at Cabanatuan. Arlene asked me if I was going to buy my sugar ration — sugar, that is, which had been brought in by the Japanese to be sold, half a kilo per internee, for twenty centavos, a price much lower than the standard market rate. I replied that I was not, as we used so little sugar that what I saved from my breakfast ration was more then we needed at the present. She suggested I let her have my ration, to which I acquiesced reluctantly — not because I begrudged her the sugar, but because it meant that I would have to stand in line to present my meal ticket for identification. It happened that I was not feeling well, and wanted only to go to the shanty where I could rest quietly by myself.

When I got my ration, the internee behind the counter said, "twenty centavos." I looked blank and started to walk away.

"Hey, you haven't paid yet," he called after me. Realizing then what he was talking about, I looked at Arlene.

"Well, pay him," she said. "Haven't you got twenty centavos?"

A sudden tide of anger swept away all reason, and I snapped, "Can't you even pay for your own sugar?"

As soon as the words were spoken, I could have sunk through the earth to bury my shameful resentment of doing a favor. Her answer, spoken with detached amusement, only emphasized the manifest meanness within myself: "I'll pay you back. I don't have the money with me."

I paid, mumbled an apology and, figuratively speaking, slunk away to the shanty to lick my spiritual wounds. No doubt Arlene though no more about it, but all day long I carried her mocking smile in my soul.

Probably it is a good thing occasionally to be humbled by one's own evil nature, if only because it teaches understanding and sympathy for others who fail themselves and their fellow men. I though then of a man who was abhorred by all because he had betrayed and caused to be condemned to death by slow starvation, illness or torture, some two dozen of his associates. His was a tale of tragedy brought about by his own undisciplined character.

It had happened months before, while I was still at the hospital. I remembered the man, because he had been assigned to a room next to my old room 44, and he used to sleep in the hallway outside our door. When we protested, he claimed that he slept there because it was cool. However, his roving eye and swaggering, impertinent manner convinced us that something less chaste than atmospheric temperature motivated his choice of sleeping space. Determined at last to get rid of him, the women of the third floor monitors' council demanded that he move to the gymnasium, threatening if he refused to inform the Commandant of an incriminating fact which they had discovered: he was a deserter from the army.

"Go ahead and tell them," he retorted, "but if you do, I'll name every man in the army and navy who was left behind in civilian clothes."

Soon afterwards he observed two of the women enter the Commandant's office: not, they later averred, to report him as a deserter, but to complain that he was a nuisance and menace to women. Whatever their purpose, he carried out his threat, although, whether intentionally or through ignorance, he failed to mention Joe Yetti and several others.

The betrayer was imprisoned and tortured along with the betrayed; not one of them survived.

Chapter Three

A week from the day I came back from camp, Delilah rushed up to me and announced breathlessly: "Daré is here!"

"Not to stay?" I inquired incredulously.

"Absolutely, bag and baggage. You should see the baggage!"

"Where is she?"

"Room 30-A."

I gasped, for 30-A was a room of notorious ill-repute, a melting pot of nationalities, including many "undesirables," that was ever on the verge of boiling over. Meztiza fought Meztiza, Russian fought class-conscious Russian, and each fought each other. Possibly the scrappiest of all was the Filipina wife of a black American who battled snubs and insults on all sides.

Among the more questionable characters inhabiting 30-A was a middle-aged Shanghai Russian kleptomaniac who, rumor had it, at one time thought she was pregnant but was not sure just which internee had fathered the supposed child-to-be. Another inmate, an unattractive blond prostitute who slaved at laundry work to support some man she loved, caused considerable dissention at siesta time when she would stretch out bare-bodied on her bed to be caressed by the afternoon breeze. Not far from the nude were the beds of a seven-year-old boy, offspring of a mixed marriage, and his Indian mother. Horrified at the lascivious sights to which her son was daily exposed, the poor Indian woman complained bitterly. Other decent occupants, including navy nurses, offered wholehearted sympathy and support; but the nude appeared blissfully unaware of

121

scandalized remarks directed towards her.

Holding down the lid of this bubbling pot was an American monitor, a hairdresser by trade, who was by no means abashed by the tough characters in her charge. Frequently and with maximum effectiveness, she tongue-lashed her difficult wards into orderly behavior.

This, then, was the motley group that Daré had joined. I suggested to Delilah that we take a look to see how things were working out, and off we went to 30-A.

It was a huge corner room, airy and cool, but a veritable rat's nest of untidiness: clothes strewn everywhere, beds unmade, rolls of dust blowing hither and yon. Squatting atop the untidiest mess of all, on a bed with rolledback mattress, was Daré, looking for all the world like the goddess of disorder in person. On, under and around her bed we beheld a bewildering conglomeration of open boxes and tampipis, bulging with all manner of jars, bottles, tin cans, clothing, knives, forks, bedding, pots and pans, toilet articles and heaven knows what.else. Several jars were filled with melted candy; others were empty, but unwashed from previous batches of unidentifiable substances, edible or otherwise. The general impression was that an angry junkman had grabbed whatever was at hand and stuffed it into Daré's boxes and empty tampipis.

"Daré, what on earth are you doing here?" I asked in unfeigned astonishment.

"I am so glad to see you, dear," she replied, "and I'll tell you all about it. But I am a wreck — simply a wreck! Look at this bed! It belongs to someone outside in a hospital, and I am to sleep in it. Of course, it's a very nice bed, springs and everything. But the mattress! Just look at the mattress! Filthy! I wouldn't think of sleeping on it. But they tell me I cannot remove it because there is no place to put it. I'll have to put it under my bed, I suppose. I have a straw mat to cover the springs."

"That won't be comfortable, Daré. Haven't you a bed of

your own?"

"I have a camp cot, dear, but there is no place to put it. I can't even move this bed out."

I had bought a hospital bed from Mother Superior, and consequently had no use for the cane-bottomed one I had used before. I offered the old bed and mattress to Daré, and arranged to have the mattress brought to her immediately. Practical matters having been attended to, I could no longer contain my curiosity, and I burst out again, "Please tell me what you are doing here! I know your pass is good for another month, and as long as anyone is allowed to work outside, you'd have no trouble getting a renewal — so, why?"

Daré rolled her large brown eyes upward and chortled loudly. "The Japanese guard at the gate asked me the same question. He was utterly astonished. At first he refused to let me in. 'No, no," he insisted, 'pass is good.' 'But I want to go back to Santo Tomás,' I told him. His jaw dropped a mile, but he finally let me in."

"You still haven't told me why you came back," I reminded her.

"I'm coming to that. Just give me time, dear. I am so exhausted that I can't think. Oh, that reminds me, Van said to tell you he is definitely coming back. Poor Mother Superior almost wept. Her little family is all leaving her. Do have a bite of candy —" Daré grabbed at one of the jars beneath her bed — "I made it yesterday in the midst of packing. Oh, such a rush! I'm surprised I am still all in one piece."

After many more digressions, Daré told us that she had returned to camp because the Catholic father could no longer afford to keep her at the hospital. Later on, Van recounted the full story, which Daré herself did not know.

For months, her relations with several of the sisters and nurses had been something less than cordial. I think that Daré had a mild persecution complex, because she often told me that the sisters did not like her and had shown it by slighting her in various ways: omitting from her plate some little delicacy that other patients received, or serving her smaller portions of dessert, or speaking sharply to her about leaving the diet kitchen in a mess. Her special *bête noire* was a male nurse whom she had accused of stealing coffee from a tin in her room. The male nurse, backed by the sisters, reported his grievances to Mother Superior, who in turn told Doña Carmen Elizalde what had occurred. Incensed, Doña Carmen announced that Daré must leave forthwith.

"We turn away patients who could use her room, and all she does is make trouble for us!"

"But where will she go?" queried Mother Superior.

"Back to Santo Tomás, I suppose," retorted Doña Carmen. "I will arrange everything."

Soon afterwards, Doña Carmen prevailed upon the fathers to explain to Daré with diplomatic sadness that their funds were so depleted that they could no longer afford to keep her at the hospital.

I felt sorry to see Daré in camp, for, although she accepted the situation with philosophical cheerfulness, I knew that she lacked the two essentials for getting along reasonably well: good health and money, or some means of earning money. Moreover, I feared that her supersensitive disposition and her obtuseness concerning the reactions of others would precipitate many a clash in this place of confinement where personalities grated against each other daily and hourly.

Just two days after Daré's return, I joined her, from necessity rather than my choice, in room 30-A. Because I was not as strong as I had supposed, I was forced to reduce stair-climbing to a minimum, which meant moving to the first or second floor. Reluctantly, I accepted the only available space, hoping to move elsewhere later.

When I entered 30-A with my transfer slip, the monitor greeted me with, "My God, who is this friend of yours? Is she nuts or something?"

"You mean Daré? What happened?"

"Happened! She's upset the entire room. First she can't sleep on Mrs Blank's mattress — says it's dirty. Now I know Mrs Blank and I know she isn't dirty. If you ask me, this Daré is the dirty one. Just look at that junk pile under her bed! So she sticks the mattress out in the hall where anyone can steal it. Along comes Mr Blank and finds it, raises hell with me. I give her the devil for it and tell her if she doesn't want to sleep on it she has to keep it under her bed — and what do you think? She gives me the barmiest look, as if she doesn't understand a word I'm saying, and turns on her heel and walks out! Can you beat it? I think the woman's crazy."

"She is a little odd, but she's all right. Sometimes she just doesn't think before she does things."

"Doesn't think — you mean she can't think! She had junk of hers spread all over everyone else's beds and floor space, then acts like I'd slapped her in the face when I tell her to move it pronto. Believe me, I felt like slapping her, too. Then she takes somebody else's bath towel and starts wiping off her filthy bottles with it. But the payoff came today when she deliberately took a bamboo pole that supports the mosquito net wires — and what do you think she does with it? Just try and guess!" The monitor's voice hoarsened with rage at the very memory.

"I can't imagine. Surely she didn't ride it hobbyhorse?"

"Maybe you think it's funny," she retorted, "but I don't think it's one bit funny. Where are we going to get another pole?"

"What happened to that one?"

"Your nitwit friend deliberately threw it out the window! One of the girls saw her do it. By the time we got downstairs the pole was gone. This Daré has to buy us a new one, that's all there is to it. God, that woman gets in my hair!"

I told the monitor that I could not imagine Daré throwing a pole out the window, but I volunteered to replace it and to talk to Daré who, I assured her, meant well regardless of appearances.

"Maybe so, but she could have killed someone with that pole." The monitor stalked out of the room, and Daré walked in a few minutes later. When I told her she had a new roommate, she was delighted, and went on to say that 30-A was a nice room even though some of the people were a bit peculiar. "I get along with most of them," she said, "except that awful monitor. Really, I have never encountered such a low, vulgar creature in my life." Daré slumped down on my bed and rolled her large eyes meaningfully.

"What's the trouble?"

Daré gave me her version of the several tales I had just heard, which proved to be a serial-comedy of errors. The bath towel, for instance, she had found on her bed and, after having asked her nearest neighbors if it belonged to any of them, she had decided that the owner was not to be found and began to dust off her bottles; whereupon the owner, who lived across the room, spotted the towel and complained to the monitor.

"You should have turned in the towel to the monitor," I told her.

"Turn in anything to that impossible person?" Daré replied indignantly. "Undoubtedly she would have kept it for herself. You should have heard the outrageous things she said to me. She actually accused me of throwing a bamboo pole out of the window, one of these poles that hold up the wires. How could anyone suppose that I would throw a pole out the window? She does not like me, and tries in every way to upset me. Her language was most revolting, but I simply ignored her. I looked at her calmly and did not say a word. I shall never allow my composure to be disturbed by such contemptible trivialities." When I asked her why the monitor accused her of such a thing, she replied that, while airing her pillow on the balcony, she had accidentally knocked over a pole balanced against the rail. As she tried to catch it, someone in the room had seen her and had reported to the monitor that she had thrown it over the rail.

I breathed an inward sigh of relief. Until Daré told me, I had not been quite certain myself whether or not she had heaved the pole overboard.

Chapter Four

Aware of Daré's vagueness about matters non-esoteric, I did not accept as final her assertion that Van positively was going to return to camp, and I prayed fervently that he would stay out as long as possible. On April 24th, Dr Aboitiz brought him in to apply for another renewal. My heart sank when he announced that he was still determined to come back unless I was released again. The release officer, Ohashi, said, "Mr Van Sickle is the one with the air-conditioned room, isn't he?" — then extended Van's pass for another month.

Dr Aboitiz explained to him that I was not well and that Van refused to stay outside without me. Ohashi considered a moment. Obviously I was not sick enough to be released again.

"Mr Van Sickle can stay outside or he can come in, I don't care," he said. "His wife cannot go out again."

"Suppose I come back to camp, can my wife go out?" Van asked. "If you want to separate married couples, I'd rather have her outside."

"Very sorry, no." It was just as well, because I would not have gone without Van.

Neither Dr Aboitiz's urging nor my own pleading could shake Van's resolve to return. He replied only, "I'll come in day after tomorrow. I'm packed already."

I turned back from the gate with a heavy heart, remembering how ill Van had been only a year before — and this was the beginning of his bad asthma season. At the hospital he had suffered attacks so severe that Dr Campa had been forced to administer artificial respiration. I dreaded what might happen in camp, where each one had to look out after himself; where rugged living conditions sapped the strength even of the healthy; where the hospital, albeit better than before, still was overcrowded, understaffed and ill-equipped.

As I walked toward the main building, someone hailed me, and I looked up to see a well-known Manila newspaperwoman, Winifred Bissinger.

"Wasn't that Dr Aboitiz I saw you with?" she asked.

I replied in the affirmative, and she continued, "I understand he has pull with the Japs — what is his fee for getting people out of camp?"

All of a sudden my dejection turned to rage. "He has no fee, and that's a rotten thing to say," I lashed out at her. "He doesn't even charge for treatment unless patients can afford to pay. The Japanese respect him because he has the courage to tell them what he thinks — and as for pull, he tried just now to get me out again and was turned down!"

"All right, don't be so huffy about it," retorted the irreprovable Winnie. "I'd like to get out awhile myself, and thought I might work it through Aboitiz."

Still fuming when I returned to 30-A for my afternoon shower, I found Daré sitting crosslegged on her bed, the center of an inconceivable chaos of assorted bric-a-brac. "Come here a minute, dear," she called to me. As I approached, she went on removing bottles, pots, cups, knives, forks, jars, glasses, can-openers, et cetera ad infinitum, from a large wooden box beside her.

"What on earth are you doing, Daré?"

"Just rearranging my things." She turned her eyes slowly up to me. "Emily, you look glum. That is not like you. You must not allow yourself to think thoughts that put such an expression on your face. Are you remembering to meditate, as I taught you?"

"I've had no time for meditating since I came back to camp, Daré."

"You must meditate. Project yourself away from these tawdry surroundings. Only by meditation can we achieve what is really important."

"All right. But I have to take my shower now." I started to walk away.

"Wait!" Her voice was resonant and imperious. "I have a gift for you."

I turned around a little impatiently, expecting another pearl of wisdom to fall from her lips. But instead she handed me a cologne bottle filled with dark brown liquid. "It is for you," she said. "I have another for Van, and one for Delilah."

"What is it?" I inquired.

She pulled me down and whispered loudly and mysteriously into my ear, "Rum."

"Good Lord, Daré, suppose they had searched your things at the gate?"

"That is why I used small bottles. They would never suspect that it was rum." I marvelled at the strange mixture of cleverness and naïveté that was Daré.

"But you shouldn't give away your small supply. You may need it yourself."

"I have some for myself, too. I want you to have this."

"Well, I don't know how to thank you. It's a better balm than meditation right at the moment."

"It is nothing. Nothing at all." Daré raised her arm shoulder-high in a regal gesture with a gracefully posed hand. "You have always been kind to me. This is a very small thing that I can do in return."

I do not know why Daré thought that I had been so kind to her. While we had occasionally shared food and rum with her, she on her part had invariably reciprocated with candy, delicious coffee and other "extras" which she had concocted from time to time at the hospital. Whatever her shortcomings, there was no lack of generosity or appreciation in Daré's soul. Later, when the three of us were dining together, Daré presented Delilah's bottle to her, omitting the dramatic effects she had used on me, but revealing the contents in an equally mysterious stage whisper. After appropriate thanks, Delilah suggested that it might be well for Daré to lock up her precious liquid where thieving hands could not reach it — which led to a general discussion of the heterogeneous cluster of humanity with whom we were so intimately associated with in room 30-A. Suddenly Daré uttered one of those classic observations which set her apart from the others.

"It isn't that I object to being in the same room with prostitutes," she said. "I have found them very kind and goodhearted. But wouldn't you think," she continued, "that the room assignment board would size people up as they come in, and try to put them together in congenial groups? They could easily tell by the luggage. Now mine, for instance — it may be a little makeshift, but they could tell at a glance —"

Delilah and I looked keenly at Daré: she was absolutely serious. We did not dare look at each other.

The evening held a special treat in store for the camp: we were to have a movie, the second film to be shown thus far in Santo Tomás. The previous one, exhibited at Christmastime, we of course had missed. A screen was erected above the new stage at the west end of the plaza, where Dave Harvey had been holding his shows ever since a nine o'clock roll call had allowed internees to stay out front. We knew nothing of the picture to be presented except the title: *Sullivan's Travels*. Of all subjects on earth, it was about a chain gang prison camp in the swamps of Georgia!

Daré, Delilah and I suffered alike through the picture, which seemed to have been selected by Japanese sadists for our special edification. "Here you are, prisoners of the Japanese," our unknown torturers seemed to say. "Now observe how your own people treat their prisoners. We are much kinder to you

130

than this. You are so lucky to be prisoners of the Japanese."

Other friends I talked to thought the film a poor one, but not cruel or horrible to show in a prison camp as did the three of us. Could it be that our prolonged stay outside had made us super-sensitive? Quite possibly; and it is equally possible that the Japanese intended to inflict no such excruciating mental anguish on their prisoners.

When the movie was over, Daré went to bed exhausted. Delilah and I returned after roll call to the plaza, where we were now permitted to stay until ten forty-five. As we paced around our restricted area, gazing at the remote stars far above us, the free night air washed over us and helped to heal the raw hurt of *Sullivan's Travels*.

The next morning was Easter Sunday. I went with Delilah and Daré to the Seminary chapel, where a fine choral mass, composed in camp by an internee, was offered to God. I remembered that in 1942 the only Easter mass in camp had been a simple outdoor one on the lawn near the plaza, offered by Father Kelly, an Irish priest who had come into Santo Tomás expressly for that purpose. How different was this year's chanted mass to the Resurrection, conceived by an unfettered spirit behind the stone walls of our prison: a prayer, a hope, a vision of dawn breaking through the twilight, of suffering left behind: a casting away of prison shackles for the glorious rebirth!

Chapter Five

After Van's return, we quickly got back into the swing of camp life: performing camp chores, shopping at the market and cold stores, cooking in our patio space. Legally, the patio space was no longer ours, since no one in camp was allowed to own more than one piece of property at a time. However, we were able to use it while our new shanty was being constructed because it was still listed under the names of three men from Van's room who had kept it for us while we were outside.

Under the camp's new work system, vegetable duty (my assignment) was no longer the ordeal it had been in early days. Different groups of workers were called daily, so that each individual (except "regulars" who worked for a noon meal) averaged no more than three or four hours a week.

Throughout the morning, the camp bustled with activity. First, the breakfast lines: coffee, cornmeal mush, brown sugar (ration: four tablespoons, soon cut to two), coconut milk, sometimes a banana. Then dishwashing. There was now a semi-automatic three-tub dishwasher, but I, like many others, preferred the old cold water taps, as the "clean hot water" tubs were usually lukewarm and greasy.

Dishwashing over, laundry work started. Nearby, under the welcome shade of the dining sheds behind the main building, vegetable workers busily scraped and peeled. Men with long canvas aprons hauled away heavy baskets of prepared vegetables, then trotted back with more to be processed. Beyond the tables clattered rice-, bean-, and cornmeal-cleaning machines, the invention of an ingenious internee who thereby earned the everlasting gratitude of all who had ever hand-picked cereal, rice, or beans. Trucks bumped noisily over the road, laden with ice, meat and tomorrow's vegetables. A staccato chop-chop-chop from the screened meat house off the kitchen signi- fied stew for dinner, or pork and beans. Internees passed busily up and down the road, some well-shod, others in bakias. Most of them carried market baskets or bayong (shopping bags wo- ven of flat straw strips), en route to market, canteen or cold store.

When vegetable preparation was finished — generally before eleven a.m. — a cleanup squad of men swept away the refuse and wiped off the tables, which, their efforts not withstanding, never looked really clean. One wondered why, when money and materials were still plentiful, the camp did not build a clean, dry, decent dining room for those who had no other place to eat.

During the afternoon, activities lessened; the vegetable mar- ket, Japanese meat and fish booth, cold store, bakery and other camp stores closed at noon. Only the canteen and a few barter booths reopened at two p.m., and from time to time some booth where special products, such as camp-made pea- nut butter, were rationed and sold on presentation of meal tick- et, at a lower price than the current market rate.

There was no surcease of toil for kitchen workers, of course, or for men of the coconut squad. The latter went to work after lunch just beyond the dining tables, cracking shells and scrap- ing out meat for our morning coconut milk, which was made by squeezing water through the grated pulp.

All workers drew their allotted camp activities from a work assignment board. Internees could indicate preferences, but whether or not they would be given assignments of their choice and capabilities was problematical, for inevitably, now as always, "pull" was often the determining factor. Those who were ill — Van among them — were exempted from camp duties.

By internee law, able-bodied internees who refused to work could be put in the camp jail: a small, barred room on the first floor front of the main building, where an internee jailer kept prisoners locked up and saw to it that they received no food except line chow. Several men were jailed for job-shirking, but no women, since there was no suitable place to lock them up. Women who broke internee laws were punished in other ways: one was confined to her room for a week because of drunk and disorderly conduct, and several who refused to help with room cleaning were evicted from their rooms.

Jail offenses for men included stealing, drunkenness, bootlegging, disorderly conduct and gambling. The maximum sentence allowable was thirty days, in accordance with Geneva Convention rules, a copy of which had been smuggled into camp by an interned lawyer named Clyde DeWitt. A three-man board, appointed by our internee governing committee, tried the accused, who were allowed no legal counsel and no appeal except to the same board. Sentences and offenses of those found guilty were broadcast over the camp loudspeaker along with the evening news and announcements.

Van and I were shocked when we first heard such a public broadcast, which we considered a cruel and unnecessary additional penalty to impose on a man just about to be jailed; but what really appalled us was the resounding internee applause as each sentence was read. What happens to human beings, imprisoned themselves, that causes them to delight in another's greater hardship? Admittedly, there were some who deserved all too well to be jailed; for example, a crook hired small boys to steal whatever they could lay hands on: food, dishes, clothing, pots and pans — loot which he then sent outside to sell. No one could be sorry that he was caught and sentenced to thirty days. Certain penalties, however, smacked of personal grudges. An internee who bootlegged alcohol went unmolested for months until, so the story goes, he angered a customer, one of the camp authorities, by cutting his alcohol with water. Internee policemen who had previously winked at his activities were then posted to pick him up on his daily trip across the camp with a bayong full of alcohol. He was tried and sentenced. Another convicted bootlegger received an apology from one of the legal board members, a regular customer. "Sorry I had to be a party to this," he said in effect. "Camp law, you know."

Such hypocrisy was by no means uncommon; nor was the inequity reserved exclusively for lawbreakers. On the contrary, it was actually written into the law itself as it applied to those who earned money in camp. Everyone engaged in private enterprise was required to take out a work permit fee, one peso per month, whether earnings were twenty pesos for dishwashing or 1000 pesos for selling food, clothing, or building materials. Internees who employed others to work for them were not taxed, although presumably they could far better afford it than their helpers, especially those hired at small salaries to perform menial tasks.

The one peso fee went into the camp relief fund for needy internees, whose monthly allotments was twenty pesos per person — a sum which would buy the barest modicum of extra food. Yet no one on relief was permitted to supplement his meagre portion by working for money, even the smallest stipend.

All applicants for work permits, whether to tie nipa or to wash dishes, were required to undergo time-consuming monthly medical examinations, which included Wassermans and typhoid-dysentary tests. Because of the nuisance, many self-supporters simply refused to apply for work permits and, if questioned, maintained that they were working gratis to help friends. Internees convicted of violating work permit regulations were sentenced to jail. Soon after our return to camp, we hired a dishwasher, a nice lad, who, however, did not bother to get a work permit. It made no difference to us: like most internees, we had little respect for laws that we had had no part in making.

Any discussion of camp law and our reaction towards it must inevitably lead to an analysis of the internee government which formulated and enforced the law, and which had changed as much during our absence as had camp activities. Some months before our return, Earl Carroll, having established an orderly system of operations in camp, kept his promise to hold a general election. In lieu of the old executive committee, internees elected a central committee, of ten members. It is interesting to note, in passing, that "Doug" Duggleby, who had condemned elecions because he thought internees too stupid to choose good officials, was himself elected to the committee.

A man named Calhoun, manager of the National City Bank's Philippine branch, received the largest number of popular votes; nevertheless, the committee elected as chairman another member, Carroll Grinnell, Far Eastern manager of General Electric Company, and a former member of the camp release committee. Grinnell grasped the reins of power firmly in his hands. When he became chairman, he was widely popular among internees, although by no means universally so. Some, like my ex-roommate, Tillie Butler, who had experienced his indifference about obtaining releases, wasted no enthusiasm on their new leader. By April, 1943, many others had come to share their lack of cordiality. Only a superman, I believe, could have retained substantial popularity after a few months of camp leadership, for, in trying circumstances, one is prone to blame on the head man all that goes amiss. Grinnell was not superman; moreover, his arrogance and impatience towards internees did nothing to endear him or to revive his public's waning trust.

He was performing what he considered a fine job for us, although many thought that someone else could have done it better. A major grievance against him, as against Earl Carroll, was that he refused to tell us what went on in his conferences with the Japanese. Internees believed that they had a right to know, since everything discussed concerned the welfare of all. Grinnell, however, was far more secretive than Earl.

When the first election took place, it was understood that camp elections would be held every six months. At the second election, on schedule, Grinnell was voted out. Ironically, it was Earl Carroll, ousted in the first election, who captured the largest popular vote in camp. But — Grinnell refused to step aside, claiming that the Japanese would not allow him to leave. Possibly this was true; certainly the Japanese had evidenced their willingness to deal with him. Yet, as time went on and the Japanese regime changed again and again, one could only conclude that it was Grinnell's indomitable egoism which caused him to cling to the power that the majority wanted to wrest from him. Rightly or wrongly, we came to believe that it was Grinnell himself who persuaded the Japanese to retain him — pleading that his leadership was essential for maintaining stability and continuity of policy. Convinced that he was our natural leader, he believed (and said many times) that no one else understood Japanese psychology as well as he — hence, implicitly, no one was fitted to replace him. Thus, in our first attempt at democracy, we found ourselves saddled with the very monstrosity that our soldiers were battling to free others from the world over: a dictatorship.

Government by dictatorship can arise wherever citizens become apathetic about their leaders; against the people's will, it can occur when a would-be dictator is supported by sufficient armed force — in our case, the Japanese. The seeds of dictatorship, fertilized by fear and fostered by a gaoler's protection, flourish well in the fetid soil of a concentration camp. Loudly though we denounced a system of government that we abhorred, it availed us nothing; for as prisoners we were weaponless and powerless.

Under a democratic government, free people choose their representatives by free election; thus, they may control to a large measure the purposes, plans and principles of that government. The citizens of a democracy may openly follow the course of their government's legislation; may guide and direct that course by criticism and suggestion; may even reverse it, in time, at the polls. Their country's destiny is theirs, in theory, to plan and execute.

Could we, the inmates of a concentration camp, believe it possible to enjoy the benefits of a system whose very essence is freedom? Could we hope to share in the planning of our communal destiny when our very lives were dependent on the mercy of an enemy?

No such sweeping hopes or beliefs deluded us. Yet, because we lacked means to defy our enemy, we cherished more than ever the right of free men to choose their leaders. Although we accepted our primary loss of freedom to the Japanese, we did not acquiesce in a secondary loss to fellow internees. Freedom to run our own internal affairs was all the more urgent as a safety valve to ease tensions of frustration built up behind prison walls. Since Grinnell, ignoring criticism, rejected our expressed will, it was against him that we turned the full force of our pent-up anger, defiance and fear, which might otherwise have been reserved exclusively for the Japanese.

Meanwhile, the Japanese had appointed Earl Carroll to take charge of the camp's finances, a job which was not under Grinnell. Many suspected that Grinnell was jealous of Earl's steadily rising popularity, a possibility that was borne out in a revealing statement which Earl once made to Van: the Japanese, he said, had told him that Grinnell had asked them not to repeat to him what went on during their conferences.

Like Earl, Grinnell borrowed money under his company's signature for camp food purchases and private loans to internees. Unlike Earl and others who borrowed for the camp, however, he did not ask the Red Cross to underwrite his notes. We wondered, perhaps unjustly, whether his motive might not have been to prove himself a more generous benefactor than Earl.

139

Chapter Six

Our growing dislike of Grinnell was not mitigated by a passing remark made soon after our return to a Japanese inspection party, one of whose members had commented on congested living conditions for internees at Santo Tomás. "They are used to it," responded Grinnell. "They don't mind it."

Small wonder that we were restless and dissatisfied. We sensed, too, something in the air that our unrest did not wholly explain, something that crystallized in alarm when passes were suddenly stopped on May 3rd. What did it mean? Possibly nothing: it had happened before. Perhaps some released American had misbehaved again; perhaps it was a mere whim of the Japanese.

Not until Sunday evening, May 9th, did we have an inkling of the reason. Then came an announcement over the loudspeaker, each word falling like a physical blow: the Japanese proposed to open a new internment camp at Los Baños, about sixty-five miles from Manila. Eight hundred men were to be selected to leave Santo Tomás on Friday, May 14th. The new camp would be situated on part of the grounds of Los Baños Agricultural College, where a few buildings were available for living quarters on a site described as "beautiful and healthful." Men not holding essential camp jobs could volunteer for transfer and the complement of the 800 would be drawn from single men and married men with no small children. Barracks were to be built at Los Baños by Filipino labor so that additional internees could be transferred there later. The original 800 would organize a kitchen and other facilities to accommodate themselves as well as later arrivals.

Tidal waves of surmise crashed over Santo Tomás that night. Now, the thing that we had feared from the first was about to happen to us: separation. Some whispered that the Japanese planned to do away with all the able-bodied men from our camp, that Santo Tomás was to be a place of internment solely for women, children, the aged and ill. Conjectures as to why the Japanese had planned to move and who would be among the unlucky 800 replaced the usual lengthy dissertations on how we should win the war and what should be done about running Santo Tomás. Anxiety and fear gripped many a heart that Sunday night.

Criticism of Grinnell now swelled to a tempestuous roar of condemnation. Why had he done nothing to stop the Japanese plan? Many of us remembered that Earl Carroll had dissuaded them more than a year before from taking us to Tagaytay. Possibly Grinnell's belittling of our cramped quarters was a clumsy attempt to quash the Japanese motive for moving us, for they had announced their intention of re-interning many more from the outside, and had declared Santo Tomás already overcrowded. Why had Grinnell not thought of building barracks? There was no lack of open space, nor of building materials.

Furthermore, although Grinnell admitted knowledge of the Japanese proposal weeks before its announcement, never once had he hinted that anything unusual was underway. In our own case, he allowed Van, who had spoken to him just eleven days before, to buy sheet iron roofing and lumber for the shanty we planned to build: no intimation that it might be well to wait awhile. Now the roof was on our shanty, and the floor was laid. We halted further construction until we decided what to do: not that we thought Van would be among the first 800, but if more, possibly all, were to be shifted later to Los Baños, what would be the use of a shanty in Santo Tomás?

On Monday it was announced that the gate would remain closed until after the 800 had departed: no notes or packages, no one permitted in or out of camp. Monday evening three internees who had accompanied the Japanese to the new location broadcast their conclusions about Los Baños. The three were Doug Duggleby, Calhoun the banker, and a professional engineer. Their impression: the proposed site was indeed beautiful, but so wild that only rugged pioneering could transform it into a habitable internment camp for several thousand men, women and children. The engineer sounded a warning that the water supply, completely inadequate, could probably not be substantially increased.

Approximately 200 adventurous men volunteered to transfer, among them Calhoun, who was selected to head the group. The remaining 600 names were drawn and posted. Then came the howls: nearly every selectee protested, some with reason, some with merely an overpowering desire not to go. Errors, such as the drawing of a man with four children, were corrected. Those who applied for exemption on medical grounds awaited examination in lines, four-deep, that extended from the doctors' office the full length of one corridor and halfway down another. After a second drawing, the list finally stood completed on Wednesday.

Among those selected to go was the "boyfriend" of one of my 30-A roommates, an attractive, hot-tempered Meztiza whom we called the Duchess. The man had a wife in camp, a well-known Manila girl whom he now refused to support, although he drew an allotment for that purpose from the company that employed him. This, and public exhibitions of his ardor for the Duchess, had won him no admirers in camp: in fact, many suspected that his name had been deliberately drawn.

His paramour, the Duchess, was quite a gal. Once she had tangled in a fight with her boyfriend's wife, whose rather caustic remarks about home-wrecking she resented. After assailing her rejected rival with a mile-long string of two-fisted invectives, the Duchess rounded off her attack with a resounding slap across the face.

Yet in other ways she resembled those proverbial "good-hearted bad women" we hear about so often. I had benefited personally from her kindness. One morning when I was lifting up Daré's paraphernalia from under her bed to sweep, the Duchess came over and said, "Here, let me do that. Daré told me you had an operation. You gotta take care of yourself in this place, you know." Despite my protestations of feeling all right, she insisted on hoisting, with no apparent effort, not only Daré's various boxes, but my own suitcases as well. As she was quite slender and tall, her strength amazed me no less than the generous gesture which was so unlike what one had learned to expect from others in Santo Tomás. Many times thereafter she helped me, always lightly brushing off my deprecations and thanks.

Although I liked the Duchess, I had no sympathy for her boyfriend, who as soon as his name was posted for Los Baños, tried his best to avoid going. On Wednesday night he had a violent attack of vomiting. Tears streaming down her face, the Duchess rushed for Dr Fletcher, and told us the poor chap was so ill that he could not possibly go to Los Baños. After a thorough examination, Dr Fletcher discovered that the nausea had been induced by a glass of warm soapsuds. His strategy having backfired, the boyfriend then received an ultimatum: "Get your bed and heavy luggage ready by morning. Ready or not, you'll leave Friday morning with the rest."

The navy nurses, who had been forced out of our hospital when army nurses took over, volunteered in a group to go to Los Baños to take care of the 800 pioneers. At first the Japanese turned down their request on grounds that there was no suitable place as yet for women to live. Their refusal had a dire ring: were they, then, going to make no provision, in the event of illness, for the care of our 800 men?

On Wednesday evening, the Japanese reversed their decision. We felt a bit easier now about the men who were leaving us. For the nurses, however, the sudden notification meant a scramble to get ready. Each departing internee was allowed to carry two bags containing immediate essentials: drinking cup, plate, knife and fork, clothing, mosquito net and toilet articles. Beds were to be sent Thursday morning to Los Baños, and additional baggage was to be ready also, to follow "as soon as transportation was available."

In addition to personal effects, the nurses owned jointly a circulating library, which they crated for shipment. With mingled admiration and regret, we watched our splendid navy girls of room 30-A pitch into their packing: much as we hated to lose them, we honored the spirit that motivated their departure.

Early Friday morning, May 14th, 1943, awakened by a blast of bugles over the loudspeaker, most of the camp got up to see off the pioneers. Breakfast was served at four-thirty a.m.; then the 800 reported to the plaza where, divided into alphabetical groups, they stood or sat on their bags in allotted spaces. We who were not leaving wandered from group to group, saying goodbye to friends. All of Duke's gang was going, except Duke himself, and of course Georgie. The men who had kept our patio space were also leaving. Japanese army trucks, each staffed with armed guards, began rolling into camp around six a.m. Carrying their luggage aboard, internees piled on, group by group, while hearty band music blared from the camp loudspeaker to cheer them. Japanese fashion, the women were last to go. As our nurses waved their parting goodbye, a resounding cheer from the lips and hearts of those they were leaving behind swelled above the music into the morning air and followed after them: our final blessing on their courageously unselfish deed.

When the last echo of rumbling trucks had faded away, we

turned sadly to the routine of daily tasks. Tears filled many an eye that morning, not only of those whose husbands and sweethearts were among the 800. What would be the fate of the men and women who had left? What obstacles and hazards would they encounter in their new, untried abode? Would we ever have news of them — ever see them again? We could only pray — and work, for the day's jobs must be done, and brooding does not help. We gritted our teeth and went ahead with the tasks necessary for maintaining existence.

Chapter Seven

A ray of light pierced the gloom when the gate reopened on Saturday, the day following the Los Baños exodus. Soon the norm of prison life returned, and after a time, as communications were established, the outlook concerning the new camp brightened considerably. Reports indicated that in the beginning living conditions there left much to be desired. However, new barracks were under construction, some to accommodate families. Each would house one hundred persons: two rooms for families of four, with a private portion of veranda; one room for each family of two, who should share their veranda with another couple for cooking and eating. Room dimensions were adequate by Santo Tomás standards. Not long after the great migration, a Los Baños bus began making biweekly trips to Santo Tomás, carrying back food and other parcels which wives and friends of the 800 were permitted to send. Fruit was plentiful at the new camp, but there was a scarcity of meat; hence, on bus days the cold store meat line was twice as long as usual. Commiserations among lonely wives made up the bulk of conversation; to the amusement of many, the Duchess always took a prominent place among commiserators.

The loss of 800-odd internees made no lasting dent in our Santo Tomás population, for fresh hauls by the Japanese brought released internees trailing back to camp by the hundreds, until practically none but the seriously or chronically ill were left outside. Entering Santo Tomás, the newcomers encountered grave inconveniences. Japanese guards now opened all baggage at the gate for inspection. There was no longer a baggage service, the men who had operated it having departed to Los Baños. Volunteer "emergency squads," subject to call at all times as a camp work assignment, did fine work, but often the luggage piled up faster than they could carry it away. When the High Commissioner group was herded in, part of their possessions had to be left outside overnight. Before morning, a hard rain had fallen which thoroughly drenched the clothes and bedding packed in their trunks. Instead of manifesting sympathy, a good many internees said, "Humph! Serves them right! After all, they've had a year and four months of soft living while we've been taking it the hard way here. I'm glad their stuff got ruined."

Judging from what I heard, members of the High Commissioner's staff had suffered their share of discomforts outside. Although they escaped the rugged start-from-scratch in Santo Tomás, they were confined almost as much as we were, some two dozen men and women living under one roof, cooking, cleaning and marketing for themselves. To offset the advantage of a private house with a bathroom, the Japanese watched them so closely that they dreaded going outside even to buy food. Taut-nerved from close association and fear, they were nevertheless persecuted in camp because of the "soft" time they had enjoyed outside.

A month before coming to camp, one of the staff secretaries, a woman of about forty, had undergone a serious operation, the aftereffects of which were severe, both physically and emotionally. Although it was obvious that she was far from strong, she insisted on doing a full share of the room work; yet, instead of helping her to get established, her roommates treated her with malignant cruelty, insinuating that she was a slacker for having lived outside. Finally, no longer able to endure their taunts, she moved to another room.

It was not only the High Commissioner group who were singled out for reprehension by the self-righteous. A charming and gracious Austrian named Ada Aplin suffered what probably was the most brutal of all reproaches and calumnies: the accusation of being a spy. Released because of tuberculosis in the spring of 1942, she was joined soon afterwards by her British husband, ill with stomach ulcers. They lived outside camp until the general roundup in May, 1943. During this period, they had associated with an old friend, Max Kummer, anti-Nazi leader of the German community — which caused internee busybodies to whisper that Ada and her husband had received their passes through German influence, an innuendo which was as untrue as it was unkind. On her return, they heckled her in every conceivable way, even stooping to the device of threats by anonymous note. In despair, Ada yearned to escape. At length, she succeeded in getting a pass to San Juan de Dios Hospital in the Walled City — grossly inadequate as a TB sanatorium, but at least a refuge from slanderous attacks.

Some of the newly interned fared better. Several groups occupied rooms to themselves, where they arranged camp life in the easiest way possible by employing other internees to do their room cleaning, bathroom duty and vegetable work. Holier-than-thou internees censured that method of getting camp work done. "We are no sissies," they scoffed in effect. "We'll do our own share of the camp work, and everyone else should do the same."

Well and good, for those who were able. Those who were unable helped not only themselves but their needy employees as well.

One of those who earned money by doing bathroom duty was a roommate from 30-A, the little Indian woman, whose British husband had gone as a willing volunteer to Los Baños, leaving her to fend for herself, her seven-year-old boy and an older son. She came to me one day to ask if I knew of any place where she could set up a charcoal stove. "A friend gave me building materials for a small shelter," she said, "but I can find no place to build. What good is the money I earn to buy my children food if I can't cook?"

There was in our patio a vacant space large enough for the type of shelter she wanted. However, when Van asked about it, the mayor informed us that no more shacks were permitted on the grounds. Soon afterwards, someone else — apparently more socially acceptable — was allowed to build on the very site we had asked for. We were gratified, though by no means appeased, when the Indian woman later managed to find another place.

As more and more internees poured into camp, room space dwindled to the vanishing point. The congestion became so critical that the room assignment committee decided to vacate for women and children a number of men's rooms in the main building, among them Van's.

Like most of his roommates, Van was in a quandary over the prospective change. Soon after the Los Baños move, we had dismantled our half-finished shanty, had sold the materials (at "used" prices) and had let the site go in order to hold our patio space. Now, belatedly, we wished that we had gone on with it. Unless he could find another shanty, Van had to choose between moving to the Education building or to the gym, both overcrowded and undesirable. A shanty was far preferable, despite the manifest disadvantages of sacrificing our convenient patio space and of risking substantial loss if we were moved to Los Baños.

It happened that Van's room monitor, Ralph Baskerville, was also looking for a shanty, which he wished to share with two other men. He found a desirable one for sale at 450 pesos, which, however, was small for three. Van offered to pay two-thirds of the price in order to live comfortably. As the grounds were not large enough for an extension to be added for cooking, the two men agreed to use their shanty only for sleeping. And since Ralph had it registered in his name, we were able to retain our patio space. Van and Ralph further agreed, in case both decided later to keep house, that they would draw straws for the shanty, the winner to buy out the loser at cost. If only one wanted to set up housekeeping, the other would buy him out and let him find his own shanty.

Just before moving, Van had the incredible good luck to acquire enough wire screening to build a sort of cage around his bed, which protected him against the plaguing hordes of mosquitoes when he had to sit up for hours at night burning asthma powder. The screening had been purchased for twenty-eight pesos by the men who lived in his room. Although screening was now difficult to obtain at any price, they sold it at cost, and no one but Van wanted it.

Ralph and Van moved to their shanty on Sunday, June 11th, a day of steady rain. The deluge continued on Monday, turning the ground to a slimy marsh. While Van was putting together the parts of his screened room, he slipped on a mud-splattered board — and suddenly his face contorted with pain. A nail sticking up through the board had perforated his rubber boot and had penetrated deeply into his foot. When he went to the hospital for treatment, Dr Fletcher advised against antitetanus serum because of his asthma, an opinion in which other doctors concurred. Replying to my anxious query, Dr Fletcher said that the danger would be over in about two weeks.

I did not have an easy night's sleep during those two weeks; but they came to an end at last, and all was well. Van and Ralph found their new shanty comfortable and convenient, far more so than the crowded room that they had had to leave. Meanwhile, I also had found more comfortable living quarters. A vacancy had given me the opportunity to move to room 25, a large corner room at the opposite end of the corridor from 30-A. There I was assigned to a space next to my old acquaintance Arlene, whom I had seen only in passing since the humiliating episode of the twenty centavos. (After promptly repaying me, she had never again referred to

151

the incident.)

Arlene, well-rounded where a woman should be round, used to lie mermaid-fashion on her bed at siesta time, bosoms bare, chin poised appealingly on her palms, buttocks clad in the shortest of tight-fitting shorts. Sometimes while so reclining, she would call over to her side a six-year-old boy who lived in the room, and would carry on lengthy discourses while his mother took an afternoon shower.

One day the mother walked in on their tête-a-tête. The picture of bare-breasted Arlene enticing her innocent boy into conversation outraged every protective instinct of motherhood. Indignantly snatching the boy away, she instructed him firmly never to go near that woman again — "that woman" acquiring an aura of unflattering adjectives as the injured mother repeated her lurid tale. Arlene found her reaction exceedingly entertaining.

Having lived outside camp for a number of months, Arlene had been re-interned about the time I was. Now, her sole objective was somehow to get another release. Before her first departure, and again after her return, she had exasperated friends by a constant pose of languid ill health; she wore no make-up, and claimed to feel weary all day. In the evening, her parting words, emphasized by a malingering yawn, were invariably, "Good night, girls, I must take myself gently by the hand and put myself to bed." It was rather unsympathetically suggested that she save her act for the doctor; but Arlene always remained in character. Perhaps the rehearsal amused her; perhaps she wanted to live the part so that she would never forget her cue. In any case, she knew what she wanted, and day after day she parked in the Japanese release office to talk to Ohashi about getting it.

"Why waste your time?" I asked her one day. "They're dragging in more from outside each day. Do you still think you'll be released?"

Arlene shrugged. "It doesn't cost anything to try — and Ohashi thinks it's terribly amusing that I come to see him every day. He told one of our release committee so. Who knows?"

"What do you say to him every day?"

"'Oh, Mr Ohashi, I'm so ill —'" Arlene cast an imploring look in my direction, in lieu of Ohashi. "'I want to go to the Doctor's Hospital for an operation.'"

"If you get out, you'll have to have the operation."

Arlene smiled faintly. "It's not too serious."

Where there's a will, there's a way. On June 15th, Arlene got her pass. Even those who resented her act had to admit reluctant admiration for the actress's persistence.

Chapter Eight

Soon after I had moved, Daré also departed from Room 30-A, not because of the company (except the monitor), but because the stairs were too much for her. She found space in a first floor room where she was happier, albeit she found her new room-mates exceedingly drab and mediocre — and most of them thought her more than a little "touched," which seemed to amuse her. It was not surprising that they thought so. By now, she had started several esoteric groups in camp, the most spectacular a pseudo-Yoga class which Daré explained was not exactly Yoga, in fact not Yoga at all, but an application of Judo, the Japanese science of muscular manipulation. It made little difference what she called her class: by any name it would have attracted considerable attention and comment.

Daré's star pupil and devoted disciple, Edgar Kneedler, a recent arrival in Santo Tomás, displayed an even more ardent interest than before in things esoteric. Half-a-dozen other adherents, most of them merely curious, I suspect, rounded out the group, which met in the Fathers' Garden. Members as a rule wore cutoff slacks, allowing the greatest possible freedom for mystic movement. It was a startling scene to come upon suddenly in a prison camp: a group of young men and women, oblivious to surroundings and the rude remarks of curious onlookers, esoterically elevating bodies bound to earth by mere forces of gravity — subjugating nature's law by sheer spiritual will. Even passing Japanese stopped, rigid with astonishment, when they happened upon these extraordinary performers, and Daré related with evident pleasure that a soldier, bowing and smiling, had proclaimed to her, "Judo!"

When she invited me to join her classes, I excused myself on the grounds of being too busy, which was no lie even if only a half-truth.

"Well, dear," she insisted, "in the midst of turmoil, esoteric study and meditation will do you more good than anything else."

I remained firm, and did my esoteric duty by occasionally inviting Daré, who had by doctor's prescription a noon meal ticket but could not digest the rice-and-bean diet, to lunch. Because our patio space was small, I fed Van first, or sometimes when he was late I would fix a snack to hand Daré through the window (her room faced the corridor inside).

Other friends invited her to lunch fairly often, one of them a kindhearted Englishman named Tommy Pratt, whose lovely wife Daré and I had known well at Santiago Hospital (where she still remained, very ill). There came a time, however, when Tommy rued the day that he had ever brought Daré to his shanty. Poor man, I well remember the comically woebegone expression on his face as he explained why never again would Daré be *persona grata* with him. It seems that she had asked to borrow his shanty "for about two hours" to make cocohonee during an afternoon when he would not be there. Masculine courtesy compelled acquiescence. When he returned to the shanty at five o'clock to pick up his dinner bucket, he saw what looked like a typhoon-struck glue factory: cooking apparatus strewn high and low; shelves, stove and floor be-stickumed with splotches of cocohonee; every dish, pan, jar and glass a gooey mess. Over this wreckage presided a wild-eyed, dishevelled, exhausted Daré: the very spirit of the chaos she had wrought.

Poor Daré was abject in her apologies. She had not realized that the process would take so long. Unable to decide which jars to use, she could find no tops for some that she had already filled (I did not wonder, remembering the topsy-turvy array of jars and bottles she had brought into camp). Wilting with weariness, she had poured the concoction from jar to jar; and, dismal denouement, her coconuts has produced less than half the cocohonee she had anticipated.

Tommy rose gallantly to the occasion, picked up Daré's dinner from the line along with his own, and after dinner, cleaned up her mess. "But never again," he declared firmly.

Daré gave both Tommy and me a jarful of her cocohonee. It was good, but not *that* good as far as Tommy was concerned.

When the rains started, he had an excuse for no longer entertaining Daré in his shanty, which was inaccessibly situated on a swampy piece of land at the far end of the garden. Only with boots could one reach the spot, and Daré had none. Having ascertained that she could not possibly make it, he continued to invite her to lunch from time to time, which led to the remarkable comment by Daré: "Tommy is kind to ask me to lunch, but you know very well that if he really *wanted* me to come, he could easily carry me across the garden."

I looked at her appraisingly and estimated that, even though she had been losing weight, she must still top the 150 mark on the scales. For her own self-esteem, it was just as well that she did not see herself as others saw her.

Occasionally she did things that so exasperated me that, although I could not hold a grudge because her intentions were always the best, I almost wished I would never again have to lay eyes on her. One afternoon she leaned through the window to ask me if I would keep a piece of bologna in our icebox for her until the next day. "Someone gave it to me, dear," she explained. "I want to save it for lunch tomorrow."

I was busy turning rice bread melba toast (which we preserved in tins for future use) and did not glance around as I replied, "Sure, just stick it on the ice." She reached over and dropped it in. After I had finished the melba toast, I took a shower and changed for dinner. It was fairly late in the evening before I opened the icebox to get Van some cold water — and behold, our icebox was crawling with red ants!

How they got there mystified us, for no part of the box was touching ground or wall, and we had just filled the leg cans with fresh kerosene. Swiftly I hauled out the piece of bologna, spoiled and reeking. Numbers of clinging ants viciously bit my hand. Then I discovered that the ants had carried germs of decomposition from the rotten bologna to some bacon which I had purchased that morning. I felt rather sick about the bacon, because it was hard to come by these days. It took an hour and a half to purge the ants. Just as I was finishing, Daré passed by and I told her what happened.

"I'm sorry about your bologna," I said.

"It smelled rather funny," she replied. "I thought it might be spoiled before I put it in your icebox. And I am so sorry about the ants. The meat was on my bed and a lot of red ants got on it, but I put it on the windowsill in the sun and I thought they had all gone away."

An access of anger flashed through my veins, and it was all I could do to restrain the harsh words that came to my lips. "Just be calm," I told myself. "Don't say anything. She didn't do it on purpose." I managed to subdue the devil in me, but for a few seconds it was touch and go.

Chapter Nine

About mid-rainy season, when internee spirits were approximately as sodden as the ground around us, there came an announcement that lit up the camp like a sudden burst of sunshine: a repatriation ship for Americans was on its way. A list — not necessarily final, we were told — which purported to have come from Washington announced the names of the internees who were slated to go. Names included, as well as those omitted, led us to deduce immediately that Washington had had nothing to do with its preparation. To this day, I do not know its origin, although it appeared to have some connection with Shanghai, all internees named, so far as we could determine, being transients from China, principally Shanghai. On the other hand, many transients from Shanghai and other parts of China were not on the list.

Internee reaction to repatriation ranged from jubilation to sour grapes, some whose names were not on the list maintaining firmly that nothing could induce them to leave Manila. Many hoped to God, as we did, that by some stroke of luck their names would appear on the final list.

Van and I longingly discussed the possibility. If all transients should be listed, we would be among the fortunate; or if Washington should really have something to say about it, we felt sure that either International Harvester or my father would have influence enough to get us back. I prayed that somehow the miracle might happen, because I feared that

Van, whose asthma attacks grew worse each day, would never live through another rainy season in Santo Tomás.

On August 27th we read in the *Tribune* details of the proposed exchange. A Swedish ship, the *Gripsholm*, carrying Japanese nationals, was to meet at Goa (Portuguese India) a Japanese ship bearing an equal number of Americans from Japan, Manila, Hong Kong, Shanghai and other localities. The Shanghai group included some seventy ex-Santo Tomás internees who had elected to go there in the autumn of 1942, when the Japanese had offered the opportunity to any who wished to make the change.

With a posting of the final list on September 10th, I could not help feeling a pang of disappointment: Van's name and mine were not on it. Not that we had expected them to be — but we had hoped so ardently. Most of the original names appeared again, and in addition some new names which had been added locally, Daré's and Arlene's among them. Even before the final listing, Daré had never doubted that she would leave, as the Japanese Tourist Bureau had promised to send her home if ever there was an exchange ship.

Grinnell and his committee threw a dark blanket of secrecy around the selection of the supplemental group, insisting still that the list "came from Washington." Even those who in the beginning had believed the Washington myth were now compelled to give Grinnell a lusty horselaugh, for outstanding on the new list were the names of several young women known to have been unduly friendly with Kodaki, chief commandant of Santo Tomás, and other Japanese officials.

Grinnell himself had evidently recommended some who were selected, and had entrusted to one of them, a prominent Manila lawyer who had served on his staff in camp, the official report on conditions in Santo Tomás. We were told that Grinnell's secretary, a loyal and hardworking young woman, was given, along with her sister, the option of leaving; but since she elected to remain in camp with her father, only her sister's name appeared on the supplemental list. The head of the American Red Cross in Manila was slated to leave — while Tommy Wolff, Philippine representative of the International Red Cross, whom Grinnell had bypassed when he borrowed money, was not mentioned. The new list included a few sick internees, most of them diabetics, and three doctors from China (Drs Robinson, Leach, and Whitacre) were named on both lists. Dr Robinson promised to do all he could in Washington to push further repatriations, especially of the sick. He confided to me that Van was among the first he had recommended, at the request of the Japanese, to leave. "But they aren't taking any of the sick," he added.

All bona fide Canadians were offered repatriation, and most of them jumped at the chance. An exception was a retired Canadian executive whom I shall name Mr Gross, who turned it down, we surmised, to spite his wife. Mrs Gross (the *second* Mrs Gross) was most anxious to leave, but the Japanese would not permit her to go without her husband. We gathered that the old man had found life not much to his liking with the youngish Canadian woman whom he had married just after Pearl Harbor. The first Mrs Gross, deceased for more than a year, had shared to the utmost his every pleasure and interest, which might have been summed up in a single word: food.

At the Manila Hotel, where the roly-poly old couple had lived, they had relished their meals as joyful rituals, ordering and consuming thrice daily every item on the hotel's long menu. To wind up the day after a long evening of gourmandizing, they would shuffle, Humpty Dumpty fashion, once around the dance floor; then would retire, to secure knowledge that the morrow held in store three fulsome meals.

The new Mrs Gross, trim and attractive, offered no such companionship in gluttony. Released from camp early in 1942 to take care of her husband, she had entered Santiago Hospital as a patient some seven or eight months later, then resided alone in Manila until re-interned in the spring of

1943. She told us that Mr Gross had begged her to marry him so that he could look after her — then, to her chagrin, she found the tables turned so that she had to look after him, until finally, fed up with gratifying an old man's needs and self-ish demands, she had left him for a long rest cure. In camp as outside, the Grosses continued to have nothing to do with each other.

When repatriation came up, Mrs Gross futilely vented her fury on the willful old man, and referred to their marriage as her "worst day's work," a statement not hard to believe, because had she been unmarried, her own Canadian nationality would have entitled her to go home.

Another near-repatriate was a man named Virgil Crowe, Shanghai representative of a large automobile company. A Crowe with a different initial had appeared on the first list — and there happened to be in camp a Crowe with such an initial, an old-timer whose Filipina wife lived outside. The Japanese asked him if he wished to leave; he did not. Because the first list included so many internees with Shanghai connections, Virgil Crowe petitioned the Japanese to request verification of the Crowe initial, a favor the Japanese declined to grant. What matter to them if an initial were incorrect? Each internee who spurned their invitation gave the Japanese one more place to fill with repatriates of their own choice. Thus, added to the yearning that haunted most of us, Virgil Crowe bore the cross of frustrated hope and probable injustice.

Mysteries and mistakes notwithstanding, there appeared to be one clear-cut category for repatriation: the press. To the best of my knowledge, every American newspaperman was offered a chance to go home.

An amusing incident occurred when the Far Eastern manager of a large press association spotted his name on the final list. Previously, piqued because the name of a subordinate who had gone to Shanghai in 1942 appeared on the first list while his own was conspicuously missing, he had vowed that under no circumstances would he leave, even though the opportunity were offered. "A newsman's job is right here," he had averred. "Who's going to send out the stories when our boys come back?"

When he found his name included after all, he whooped and cheered. Not another word about staying to greet the boys!

Three other newsmen, all editors of local papers, seriously believed that their job was to stay in Manila. Before the war, they had written scathingly anti-Japanese articles, for which the Japanese army had imprisoned them for many months at Fort Santiago. Tortured and starved, they were barely alive when finally released to Santo Tomás. Yet, now that they had the chance to leave, all three elected to stick to their posts: victims of the old Santo Tomás malady, over-optimism.

After the list was published, Edwin Cogan met one of the trio, Ford Wilkins, in the hallway, and congratulated him.

"Thanks," responded Ford, "but I'm not going."

"You're not — what? Are you crazy?" gasped Edwin.

"This thing is going to be over by Christmas," retorted Ford Wilkins. "I'm a newspaperman and I want to be here when things begin to happen."

"Which Christmas?" demanded Edwin. "Personally, I think you're nuts, and God help the world if it depends on the prophecies of newspapermen!"

Many another old Manila resident agreed with the three local editors. Dr Fletcher's wife, a sincere, intelligent, straightforward woman, was astonished when I told her that I wished we were on the list to go. "Why, I wouldn't leave for anything," she asserted, and I knew that sour grapes did not grow in the garden of her thoughts. "Our boys are so close now that I'd be afraid of missing them before we even reached Goa. Our eldest son will be right with them."

"I wish I could believe they were that close," I replied.

"You are worried about your husband," said Mrs Fletcher, who knew how often in the small hours of the morning Dr

163

Fletcher had been summoned to administer life-giving doses of adrenalin when Van had several asthma attacks. Exhausted though he was from overwork, the faithful doctor never failed to come promptly and willingly. "Don't worry too much," Mrs Fletcher continued kindly. "You and Van will be sailing home on an *American* ship before you know it!"

Ah, how sweet to dream! But would the dream ever, ever come true? One ray of hope flickered in our hearts: perhaps there would be other repatriation ships — perhaps next time we would be lucky.

Chapter Ten

Each internee was permitted to send his nearest relative a brief censored note, the first we had been allowed to write since the diplomatic repatriation ship in June, 1942. Several friends offered to transmit verbal messages, but our best hope of all was Daré, who guaranteed that she would smuggle in an uncensored letter for our families. Long before, we had promised that if her ship ever came in, we would buy whatever she wanted to sell at any price she named, and would arrange for her to collect the money at home, since she had no funds at all in the States. Each repatriate was permitted to take out a small number of Occupation pesos, the only currency allowed, presumably to be exchanged for American dollars at Goa. In addition, Daré possessed a few travellers checks which she planned to conceal, along with our letter, on her person. The letter, two pages of typed onionskin, contained our request that International Harvester (identified only by the initials of a company executive known to my family) immediately send Daré a sum of $340.

She had little to sell: a few canned goods, mostly from the kits we had received the previous Christmas; two or three cooking utensils, a thermos jug, a few odds and ends. After forewarning us that she was going to "sock" us, poor Daré acted guilty as a predilected profiteer when she charged current dealers' rates, but she cheered up a bit when we predicted that prices would soon double. We were very glad to help that prices would soon double. We were very glad to help her, and moreover it was worth any money to get our message back.

Included in the canned goods were seven pounds of powdered milk (fifty pesos a pound), which Daré requested us to offer, if we decided to resell them, to Edgar Kneedler, whose wife had recently had a baby. She suggested also that we give Tommy Pratt first option on three pounds of coffee (five pesos a pound) and a pound of tea (twenty pesos), because his wife, who remained ill at Santiago Hospital, would be grateful to have them.

We assured her that we would resell the goods immediately if Edgar and Tommy wanted them. Both were delighted; perhaps Daré's thoughtfulness helped to wipe away Tommy's nightmare memories of a shanty wrecked by runaway cocohonee!

When she delivered her wares, she brought along an extra pound of coffee, which she presented to me. "You gave it to me for Christmas last year," she explained.

"But it's yours," I insisted. "We ought to buy it along with the rest."

Since she threatened to become insulted if I mentioned again paying for it, I accepted her gift with due appreciation. She brought a gift for Van, also, which she asked me to keep for him until after she had left. It was a sample bottle of Scotch. Again I was touched by her liberality: of the little she had, she gave so generously.

When we wrote our letter, we phrased it with no incriminating names or addresses, in case it should be lost or discovered. We mentioned only first names, and referred to Daré as "our friend who is bringing you this message." I spoke of "Van," but my signature was a family nickname. Daré had written my family's address in a notebook, passed by the Japanese, such as each repatriate was allowed to take.

In due course, she sent the letter to my family and received $340 from International Harvester. My mother wrote to which rather troubled Mother at the time, its esoteric flavor and references to our "classes" together causing her to wonder whether the strain of internment had affected my sanity.

As the time of departure grew near, Daré blossomed like a tropical flower whose beauty, long dormant in the tangled wilds of the jungle, bursts suddenly to life at the touch of a slanting sunbeam. Stimulated by the near miracle of repatriation, her personality diffused a many-faceted radiance over friends and acquaintances. Daily I discovered new things about this strange young woman — not so young, at that, but younger looking now than ever before since I had known her. A loss of weight, slow at first, but greatly accelerated of recent weeks, which had left her some twenty-five or thirty pounds lighter than when she entered Santo Tomás five months earlier, revealed a shapeliness long hidden beneath cushions of fat. Her dark eyes, always her loveliest feature, sparkled now with new light which mirrored the faint flush of excitement aglow in her cheeks, vitalizing and transforming her appearance as though a magic wand had waved away the shielding chrysalis of flesh to reveal the spirit within, semisomnolent but awaiting its moment of wakening to spread new and glorious wings.

One day she showed me a book of poems, written by her some eight or ten years before: poems of passion that flowed with exotic imagery through heavy-scented gardens and languid, moonlit seas. Again I marvelled, as I had when I read her book on Lovely Ladies, that Daré could so coordinate her seemingly disjointed thoughts to mould them into rich, meaningful form. As I praised her poetic outpourings, I could see that something troubled her.

"Dear," she said at last, "I am wondering whether I dare show this book to Edgar. Do you suppose he would think me a horrible person? Our relationship has been purely spiritual, you know, and he has progressed to such heights that I'd hate to shake his faith in me. It might make him lose all that

167

he has attained. Of course, he still has far to go before he can acquire the truly esoteric approach to life. I want to show him this book to make him realize that what one is now has nothing to do with what one can become. Once, I was this —" Dramatically, Daré swept the sinister pages with her hand — "and now look at me!"

I knew that Daré was sincere, yet I could not help smiling within the depths of my unesoteric soul that she, who would completely deny the ego, was herself a supreme example of egoism in the world of egoistic human beings. Perhaps it was partly because of that enigma that I was fond of her; probably the egoistic demon within myself enjoyed the superiority imparted by observing such ludicrous foibles and the inconsistencies in a human being who, in some ways, was a remarkable person.

"Do you think that Edgar would understand?" Daré demanded urgently.

"I'm sure he would if you explained it. Edgar's of age. If he is shocked by a little passion, then it's high time he had a dose."

After that brief conversation, I met a mutual friend who added spice to the mental stew Daré had cooked up: Daré, she said, had revealed that she was in love with Edgar. "She says he knows nothing about her feeling, and never looks at her as if she was a woman at all. She vows that she doesn't want him to know, or to give her that kind of look, but — well, you know Dare!" ("Aha!" smirked that gleefully mischievous demon inside me, "perhaps the subconscious in her esoteric soul wants to dedicate these poems to Edgar!" What a nasty little demon!)

Whether or not she showed him the book, I do not know. She made me swear not to mention it to him. . . but then, she often enjoyed glamorizing her actions by shrouding them in secrecy.

On September 20th at about ten a.m., Daré, smartly dressed

in a red blouse, white skirt and shining white turban, poked her head through the window of our patio space. "I'm having lunch with the Commandant and some other officials outside the camp," she announced. "I wanted you to know where I was in case anything happens."

Before I could answer, she had vanished. I was dumbfounded, and as the day wore on, I became rather worried. What had she meant, "in case anything happens"? I asked Van what we should do if she failed to reappear in camp. He lightly dismissed the possibility of any danger befalling her. "She was just being theatrical," he said. "The Japanese Tourist Bureau is behind her — why would the Japs want to do anything to her?"

"I don't know." Nevertheless, I was uneasy.

Late in the afternoon, Daré returned, still immaculately groomed and looking quite attractive and happy. A group quickly gathered around her to hear the day's happenings. "We had a delicious lunch at the Jai Alai," she recounted. "Cocktails and excellent food. I was guest of honor. They pumped me quite a lot — asked me what I thought about the war and the Japanese people. I told them that I was an artist and knew nothing about the war except that it was abominable. I said that I like very much the Japanese people whom I had known in Japan. The Tourist Bureau representative told me that they were sorry war had broken out while I was their guest. 'Yes,' I replied, 'I have lost thirty pounds as your guest in Santo Tomás.' Kuroda told them that it was a shame how people have to live in camp. 'You don't have to see it,' he said, 'but I see it every day. I feel very sorry that conditions in the camp are so bad. We do all we can to help, but we are not allowed to do much.'"

Kuroda, Commandant Kodaki's deputy and the number one Japanese official living inside camp, was a decent chap, a civilian, and I believe that his remarks as quoted by Daré were sincere.

As soon as the crowd around her dispersed for the dinner line, Daré whispered cryptically to me, "I want to talk to you later in the evening when we can be alone."

I found her again at about eleven p.m. Never knowing whether her mysteries surrounded a plot or a vacuum, I was scarcely prepared for what she had to tell me.

"I was taken to Fort Santiago this morning," she confided in a hushed voice.

Stunned, I could only stammer, "You — ? Why?"

"To sign some papers absolving the Japanese from any accusations of mistreating me when I was there before."

"Before?" I asked in amazement. "Good Lord, Daré, I didn't know you were ever in Fort Santiago."

"Yes. I was there for three days and three nights. I sat on the floor the entire time, and had nothing to eat but a little rice. It was just before I came to Santiago Hospital. They picked me up while I was living with the Sisters of the Convent."

"Did they mistreat you?"

"No. They questioned me, and finally released me."

"Why did they arrest you?"

"They suspected me of being a spy. They could not understand an American woman living in Japan for so long, particularly an ex-newspaperwoman, unless she was a spy. When I explained what kind of work I had done, they seemed satisfied."

"Why didn't you mention it before?"

"It's not healthy to mention such things. I am telling you now only because I am leaving very soon and I wanted you to know. Don't breathe it to anyone else — at least, not until you know I am home."

"What did they say to you today?"

Daré's eyes held a faraway, amused look. "In retrospect, it is really funny: Kuroda told me this morning that it was necessary to go to Fort Santiago before the luncheon. He was most apologetic and terribly embarrassed about it. I was naturally startled, but I kept my poise perfectly. He went inside the Fort with me. We entered an office where we were greeted by a small Japanese army officer with an enormous sword. I was given some papers and asked to sign them. One was in English, the other in Japanese.

"I read the English paper. It was a statement that I had not been mistreated during my detention at Fort Santiago. I signed it. The Japanese paper I handed back unsigned. The officer asked me again to sign it. I refused. 'I cannot read Japanese,' I told him. 'I have no idea what this paper says.' 'It says in Japanese the same as the English paper,' he replied. 'You tell me this, but how am I to know whether it is true? I refuse to sign any paper that I cannot read. You have my statement in English. That is sufficient.' I glanced at Kuroda. He was perspiring profusely and looked extremely ill at ease. The Japanese officer glared at me. I remembered a little trick that I had learned in Japan of out-glaring an adversary. I glared back at him unperturbed. His eyes dropped. 'Very well,' he said. When we drove back through the gates of Fort Santiago, Kuroda mopped his brow and breathed a sigh of relief. 'Now we can relax,' he said. I felt just as relieved as he did, if not more so. But I gave no indication that I had been in the least ruffled."

Amazing person, Daré. So that was what she had meant....

Having told the tale, she dismissed it from her mind. "There is something else I want to talk to you about, dear. Times may become very bad before this imprisonment is ended. If you are ever faced with starvation, remember these words of wisdom.

"There was a holy and ascetic monk who lived for a long period of time on a diet of a single almond a day. He chewed the almond thoroughly, and chewed and chewed. And while he chewed, he meditated that the almond was a tiny seed from which grows the almond tree. He meditated on the growth of each branch, and each leaf and blossom, and each nut on the almond tree. And when he had finished chewing and meditating, the tiny almond gave him the strength of the entire almond tree. Remember that, dear. It may help you come through."

Chapter Eleven

The Japanese fine-combed all repatriate baggage on September 23rd, even tearing off wrappers from brand-new cakes of soap to make sure that no messages had been written inside. Yet for all their subtle searching, they amateurishly overlooked many an obvious hiding place for smuggled goods. I know specifically of one man who carried private papers safely home in the false bottom of a packing case, and I am sure there must have been others who similarly hoodwinked the inspectors.

On the 24th, the Japanese showed a good film for the express benefit of repatriates and I presume for the rest of us as well, as this was the fourth or fifth movie since my return to camp. Beforehand, Kodaki made a speech in which he gave Grinnell the lie about the supplemental repatriation list and verified our hypothesis about its preparation. After repeating the old farce about the original list coming from Washington, he went on to say that he had heard considerable criticism from the internees because so few of the sick were among those later selected to leave. However, he continued, illness was not a prime factor in this repatriation, although certain individuals were chosen for that reason.

The supplemental list had been compiled, he said, from joint recommendations of our doctors and our committee, and from recommendations of the Japanese administration. Scornful snickers greeted his statement that the Japanese had selected internees whom they personally knew and who, they hoped, would report favorably to the American people about their treatment during internment. He added that he had immensely enjoyed his relationships with interned Americans, and that he hoped some day in a diplomatic capacity to be able to renew those pleasant associations in our own country.

On the 25th, the date of departure at last was announced: repatriates would leave by train the following morning for an unannounced port some distance from Manila to board their ship, which would sail on the 27th. That evening I fixed a lunch for Daré to take with her; then, like most of the camp, I dragged myself out of bed at four a.m. on the 26th to say a last adieu to the lucky departing ones. After breakfast we gathered in the darkness on the plaza, just as we had done four months earlier to speed the 800 on their way to Los Baños; but with what a difference now, for this time our friends, and likewise some who were not our friends, were heading for certain happiness.

No one that day was happier than Edgar Kneedler, who rushed jubilantly back and forth between Daré and his own mother and father, also to be repatriated. During the time he had managed the Bay View Hotel for the Japanese, Edgar had secured a promise from high officials that if ever an exchange ship should leave the Philippines, his parents would be among the passengers. The disappointment which he must have felt when they broke their word about allowing the Kneedlers living quarters was forgotten now that they had honored this far more important pledge. I rejoiced with Edgar in his parents' good fortune, for they were elderly and his mother far from well.

The Japanese provided a bus for the aged and ill, and loaded others onto army trucks. After assisting his mother to her seat on the bus, Edgar helped Daré and his father climb aboard their truck, where Daré, making her way forward, lounged gracefully against the cab, one hand poised piquantly on the crown of a wide-brimmed hat which gave her the look of a slightly windblown belle reclining on a rustic fence at a garden party. As the truck pulled away at five-thirty a.m., she raised her right arm in a dramatic, typically Daré gesture. "Goodbye, Edgar," she called, in a voice resonant with the rich tones of a blessing.

There in the dusk of morning, we watched with mixed feelings the line of trucks roll by. We were happy for most who were leaving, contemptuous of a few. As the first misty tints of dawn began to color low-hanging clouds on the eastern horizon, we turned away. But oh, how hard it was to be left behind!

The afterglow of repatriation lingered awhile throughout the camp. A last tale about Arlene, told by an internee who had helped her aboard the bus for the aged and ill, amused us for days. Arlene, he related, had leaned out the bus window to remark, "There may be plenty of people in this camp who are sicker than I am, but there's no one who's smarter!"

In the *Tribune* we read about the exchange of nationals when the ship reached Goa, and Dave Harvey featured in his next stage show a song all about going to Goa. Then gradually the echoes of repatriation faded away into the dull, familiar sounds of camp life: the clomping of wooden shoes, the slurp of dishwater, the din of voices in the hallways, the unending splatter of rain.

Chapter Twelve

The peak of prosperity in Santo Tomás had already been surmounted and the long downward descent begun when our repatriates sailed from Manila. Inflation and dwindling supplies caused living costs to soar, so that by the end of August, Lux toilet soap was selling for 3.50 pesos a cake, Baguio potatoes for 4.50 pesos a kilo (2.2 pounds), lard for 7.10 pesos a kilo, chicken for six pesos for a kilo, and all other commodities in proportion.

The camp still issued certain staples, such as laundry soap (one cake a person per month — no bath or face soap) and toilet paper. The latter, however, was in too short supply for distribution among men — although it could still be purchased for an exorbitant price at camp stores. Women received four sheets a sitting, then three, and finally, as the vanishing point neared, twenty sheets a week to ration as they chose. Because of Van's foresight in the early days, we had sixteen rolls of our own, and twenty-four cakes of bath and face soap: enough to last, with care, for more than a year.

Meat for camp kitchens began to disappear in August, when the Japanese military banned it after discovering that camp buyers had been purchasing from the black market. By the end of the year, no fresh meat at all was available for the line, although it was still sold at the cold store and restaurants. Consequently, those who depended entirely on line food began to suffer months earlier than those who had money to buy what meat was available.

One wondered why internee officials had not provided adequately for all. Admittedly the job would have been difficult, yet many of us believed that it could have been done by men with foresight to envision hardships that lay ahead. Numbers of individuals had protected themselves from future starvation by laying in supplies of rice, beans, sugar and canned goods. Surely our leaders should have attempted to store away quantities of food while it still could be had.

That they failed to do so undoubtedly fanned the flames of internee rancor, which now blazed with new fanaticism against Grinnell. We found a champion for the cause of democracy in an interned minister named Dr Holter, member of a voluntary group called the public relations committee, to whom we carried our complaints and suggestions. Largely because of Dr Holter's agitation, Grinnell finally agreed to another election, but only for monitors and for a new representative on the central committee, whose members, one at a time, would now be replaced every few months by popular vote: all strictly democratic, except that Grinnell himself was to remain in charge of the camp.

During the election campaign, Dave Harvey produced on one of his stage shows a Charlie McCarthy-type dummy to run against our dictator, at whom he hailed and jibed, to cheering applause from the audience. Yet, in the face of this insulting attack, which indicated almost universal disapproval, even condemnation, Grinnell continued on his solitary way, ignoring ridicule, defying the wishes of the governed, adamantly refusing to stand for election. How could any American justify to himself such ruthless disregard for the opinions of those whom he governed? Grinnell disclosed the answer, I believe, in a remark which he made to Van about repatriation.

"I wouldn't have gone even if I could have," he stated. "I am too valuable to this camp."

Therein, concisely expressed, lay the key to his character and reasoning: sincerely believing in his mission as our leader, he fancied himself a Man of Destiny.   Van learned from certain of Grinnell's associates that he had actually been offered repatriation, and had turned it down.   A man of such egocentricity could scarcely be expected to waver before ridicule, or even mass hatred, so convinced was he that his was a just and righteous leadership on which depended our welfare and our safety — even, possibly, our survival.

Our champion, Dr Holter, won by a large majority the central committee membership; and thereafter, he stopped agitating on our behalf.   What is there about achieving a position of honor among the powers-that-be that so effectively silences a would-be crusader, as though victory in itself were the objective rather than the reform whose promise won him victory?   In all fairness, I must add that Dr Holter probably realized the futility of challenging Grinnell.

We often wondered why the entire central committee did not resign en masse in protest against Grinnell.   To him, the committee members were mere figureheads; why, then, did they cling to their positions?   Did they flatter themselves that they, too, shared a few crumbs of power?   Or did they nurture the illusion that they might someday alter the situation from within?   Surely by now they should have known better.

Shortly after the election, a new Commandant who was reputedly a Socialist took charge of Santo Tomás.   A diplomatic repatriate from England, he gave every indication of cordially disliking Europeans.   Frequently and pointedly, he told us that we were lucky to be prisoners of the Japanese, as we were receiving far better treatment than Japanese internees in England.

Unsympathetic though we were toward many of the new Commandant's statements, we could only agree with him when he expressed shocked surprise at the lack of provision for our underprivileged.   Why, he inquired, did they have no place to cook, no decent place to eat? Spurred by a threat to communize private property in camp, Grinnell and his committee presented plans for building cooking sheds, but the idea was soon shelved.

The Commandant did nothing to improve the quality of food for the underprivileged, who ate rice and vegetable stew four or five times a week. Those of us who had money could still buy meat, if only a piece of bologna, by standing several hours in lines which grew longer each day; and some of the underprivileged earned money to buy meat for themselves by standing in line for others.

Chapter Thirteen

Time in a prison camp resembled a sluggish stream, its never-ending procession of nights and days flowing vapidly along in a flat, unvaried monochrome broken only occasionally by some subtle coloration, some slight ripple catching a facet of light, some event which sets one day apart from others. Seldom were there events as momentous as repatriation, yet even minor incidents, good or bad, speeded the dragging hours.

During the dismal rains, punctuated by equally unpleasant periods of muggy heat, we spent our days trudging through mud, fighting ants, standing in dripping lines, sleeping in stuffy rooms damp from soggy clothing and watery foot-tracks. When the skies cleared momentarily, we rushed to air mildewing clothes, luggage and bedding. Yet the rain had its own compensations. Flowers and ferns grew tall, their lush verdure hiding some of the squalor of makeshift lean-tos which crowded our patios. In shanty areas, a jungle-like drapery of vines formed natural secluding walls over many a shack to cover the required "open" sides.

Often at sunset, towering stormy-weather clouds would burst into gold and scarlet flame with here and there a splash of pale lemon, orchid and rose overlaid by masses of crimson and glowing purple. Sometimes there were starry-fingered twilights, and lovely evenings when the moon, rising in cloudy skies behind a screen of trees, would cast a magic silver mist through the dark lace pattern of leaves. Such glimpses of beauty our prison walls could not shut out.

Often, too, we forgot our troubled existence as we listened, huddled under umbrellas, to the evening music in the plaza, or to classical concerts Thursday afternoons and Sunday mornings in the Fathers' Garden where, amid flowers and green trees, we listened — if we had time — to glorious symphonies and concertos that have inspired and will continue to inspire mankind under better and worse conditions than ours. Through all seasons, the enchantment never failed.

Above us, the skies were often stormy and clouds went scudding by in the strong arms of the wind. At other times when the air was still, the clouds might become languorous white fleecy puffs floating in blue heavens, while near us butterflies drifted gracefully among bright-colored flowers. Blending with nature's beauty, whether placid or turbulent, the immortal music seemed to say to us, "This is eternal; all else is passing. Dream great dreams, and those dreams will become your life."

One of Van's shanty neighbors, a man named Van Voorhees who was vice-president of a large American motor corporation, often accompanied us in the evening to the campus front lawn where we listened to the music. About six-foot-three and husky, Van Voorhees was known as "Big Van", while my Van, a mere five feet eleven, was called "Little Van". Handsome, with snow-white hair and clear blue eyes that sparkled when he smiled, he had weighed a portly 300 pounds until an illness which had kept him outside camp for a year trimmed down his figure to a respectable 230-odd pounds.

Upon his return to camp, he had purchased from a Los Baños-bound internee one of the prettiest shanties in camp, a small cottage with rock-paved veranda, bedroom, kitchen, storeroom and combined living room-dining room. After my Van had built his screened cage, Big Van, not to be outdone, screened his bedroom also. A nature lover, he had hired men to plant

182

and care for a pretty garden of flowers and shrubs, enclosed by a white picket fence with an arbored gateway leading from his flagstone walk to the public path. A birdhouse and weathercock in the form of a girl beside a tiny windmill completed the effect of suburban rusticity.

Having heart trouble, Big Van made it a point to lead as relaxed a life as possible in order to survive the ordeal of internment. Fortunately able to borrow all the money he wanted, he paid a man to do his work assignment of weeding in the camp garden. For personal convenience, he had engaged a secretary to type material for a book that he was writing, and a housekeeper to run the shanty. The latter, a remarkable girl named Eleanor Stone, was his greatest find of all.

Before she started working for Van Voorhees, Eleanor had earned money to support herself and to help care for her mother and younger sister by peddling candy in the evenings. Her husband, a military prisoner at Cabanatuan, had worked for a large gold mining company whose representatives in camp either could not or would not borrow a cent for their people. Big Van had immediately liked Eleanor when she came to interview for the job, and she quickly proved herself a jewel worthy of his esteem and well worth the high salary he paid her. I marvelled at her energy and cheerfulness in accomplishing the endless chores of housekeeping: cleaning, marketing, cooking, serving, washing dishes and doing anything else that needed to be done, besides handling her own camp work.

Big Van had invited us several times to his shanty for dinners that were, under the circumstances, a gourmet's delight: succulent dishes garnished with pickles, olives and all manner of delicacies, served on a table graced with dainty linens. In such an atmosphere, one could almost forget for the moment the stone walls that held us captive.

Farther along the path from Van's and Ralph's shanty lived some friends we had known at Santiago Hospital, the Phillips. Howard Phillips, ill with amoebic dysentery, had been sent out early in the autumn of 1942, and was later joined by his wife, Eleanor, and their two-year-old son, Howie.

During the early months of the Occupation, Ellie Phillips, a rather delicate and high-strung young woman, whose pretty babyface belied a strong determination and a wealth of practical common sense, had resolutely evaded internment. When the Japanese arrived at the Phillips' apartment on January 5th, 1942, little Howie was choked up and running a high temperature. Ellie, fearing diphtheria, announced firmly to Howard that their baby was *not* going to any concentration camp. A Spanish neighbor kept Howie while Ellie hid in a closet, and Howard departed alone for Santo Tomás.

As soon as the Japanese declared mothers with children under two eligible for release, Ellie, who had spent weeks popping in and out of closets, secured an official pass from Santo Tomás. She then turned her energies to begging and borrowing money and to acquiring a large reserve of tinned food — never, however, neglecting Howard, to whom she sent in home-cooked meals each day.

Hauled back from the hospital during the big roundup in May, 1943, the Phillipses had immediately bought a shanty large enough for Howard and little Howie to sleep out comfortably. They found a loyal and devoted old man to wash dishes, haul water, clean the shanty, empty Howie's pottie and serve as general handyman, in exchange for his meals and a good salary.

On her birthday in July, Ellie had invited eight or ten friends to drop in for cake and coffee. Wishing aloud that she could have offered us rum instead, she had remarked on how easy it would have been to smuggle in a few bottles. "The Nips never even looked at our medicine bottles. I hear there's liquor in camp," she added, "and believe me we're going to get some if it's to be had."

Van and I had heard the rumors also, and several months later we decided to make discreet inquiries. Extreme caution was essential, as camp prohibitionists and sadists delighted in nothing more than to see someone else go to jail. Admittedly, liquor in the wrong hands could have endangered the entire camp, as any incident between the Japanese, who had recently forbidden intoxicating liquors in camp, and a drunken intern-ee might have brought on mass retaliation. However, drunk-ards the world over caused trouble, and were no more a deter-rent here than elsewhere from moderate indulgence, if such indulgence were possible. Disobeying Japanese orders caused us never a qualm.

Van first approached our nightly supplier of peanuts, Duke, with whom he had recently transacted some reasona-bly large-scale business to their mutual satisfaction. Duke had supplied Van with several dozen cartons of matches at two pesos a carton, and with cigarettes made from locally grown Virginia tobacco at one peso to 1.50 pesos a package. Van needed the matches to light his asthma powder; and, because of asthma, he could not smoke native tobacco, which was cheaper and more plentiful but stronger than the Virginia leaf, and as different in taste as green tea is from black. When Van asked him if he knew how to procure a bottle of rum, Duke replied, "Sure. I'm not in the business — it's too risky — but I buy it for myself and I'll get you a bottle next time."

A few evenings later, he carried a bayong to our patio space. Eyebrow raised and grinning broadly, he handed the bayong to Van. "Here are the cigarettes you wanted."

"How much do I owe you?" asked Van.

"Cost price. Six pesos."

"You ought to make something out of it."

"Naw, I'm glad to do it. You're a good customer."

"Thanks, Duke. Come back later for a sample."

"Okay, but be careful. There's an awful lot of missionaries around this patio."

Duke brought us several bottles, and was quite willing to continue supplying us indefinitely. However, Van was reluctant to let him take the risk on our behalf, and soon found a bona fide bootlegger, a man named Stew Raab who lived in his shanty neighborhood. Nearly everyone in Santo Tomás knew of Stew Raab as one of the camp's best baseball players; somewhat incongruously, he was one of our best cake bakers as well. He sold his cakes to help support a wife, small daughter and mother-in-law. Far more profitable than cake baking was the rum smuggling which Stew carried on in conjunction with a neighbor and fellow ballplayer named Wally King, whose legitimate camp business was the highly remunerative occupation of contracting for building supplies. Wally's shanty, situated on an isolated spot by the northern corner of the wall, provided an ideal cove for rum-running.

Since both Stew Rabb and Wally King were poker lovers and gamblers by nature, it was not strange that the lure of danger and rich gains should have attracted them to smuggling. Rumors of their bootlegging activities had reached Van's ears, yet for a time he hesitated to approach them directly about such top-secret monkey business. His opportunity came one night when he was invited to sit in on one of their poker games.

Although gambling was forbidden, its devotees had found means from the very beginning to indulge their fancy. One of the men's rooms in the main building had been kept locked in the early days so that its occupants could play poker uninterrupted. Shanties offered even greater seclusion, and practically every night Stew and Wally would meet somewhere for a game with two or three cronies. Usually among them was Hank Parfit, owner of a large-scale canned goods buy-and-sell booth which he operated with stock market technique, chalking up prices bid, last price paid, and articles in demand. His profits were reputedly so high that profiteering came to be known in camp as "Parfiteering." Less astute than Wally King as a poker player, he was no less addicted to the game.

Van, who seldom played, welcomed the chance of wangling some rum, and during the course of the evening he casually remarked to Stew Raab that he wished he knew where he could buy a bottle.

"Did you say rum?" queried Stew. "I can't get any rum tonight, but if you could use gin, I know where to find some." He strolled down the path, returning in about five minutes with the gin tucked under his sweater. Thereafter, Van needed only to mention to him ahead of time that he would like a bottle.

One day I poured some rum into a small bottle which I wanted to give to Ellie Phillips. When I found her, however, I forgot all about the rum. Frantic and distraught, she was flinging clothes helter-skelter into a suitcase.

"What on earth —" I began.

"Howie has pneumonia," she gasped without pausing in her frenzied packing. "I'm taking him out to Santiago Hospital."

"Good Lord! How long has he been ill?"

"He's had a cough for days. It turned to pneumonia this morning. I went to the Japanese office and called our doctor — he fixed everything. I was going to get Howie out somehow, even if I had to kill a couple of Nips with my bare hands — it's his only hope of pulling through."

Little Howie did pull through, but no sooner had Ellie brought him back to camp than another crisis arose: this time, big Howard was found to have a spot on the lung. Ellie, at her wits' end, did not know where to turn. "What on earth can I do, Emily? I've always insisted that we eat well. We buy all the fresh food that's available: eggs, meat, vegetables, everything. We've been using canned food besides. I replace what we use — buying from Hank Parfit is expensive but who cares, if we come through alive? But now, Howard needs a quart of milk a day. Where am I going to get it? What am I going to do?"

I tried to calm Ellie, but what could anyone suggest? She told me that the doctors thought possibly several months of bed rest might cure him.

"That sounds encouraging," I responded, voicing more

optimism than I felt in my heart. "By staying in bed, he'll conserve his energy and can assimilate the full nutriment from his food. Probably he won't need milk — think how lucky it is you can get meat and eggs!"

Ellie departed somewhat less distraught, but I felt sick at heart myself, wondering what the end would be for Howard — and for all of us; especially Van, whose asthma had grown progressively worse: so much worse, in fact, that Dr Fletcher had advised him to interview Dr Cho again with the object of getting another release. Van, however, refused.

I had not been feeling well, either, and had recently consulted Dr Allen, an interned woman doctor who specialized in women's ailments. My old trouble had started again soon after my return to camp, and, while I was not actually ill, I felt weary, heavy, dull-witted and so logy that it was an effort even to move. Dr Allen tried a new series of injections which brought no results. Recently, Van had insisted that I hire someone to do my camp vegetable work, a suggestion that I had at first rejected because it seemed a miserable thing to shirk a job, however disagreeable, that even older women accomplished without too much difficulty. Never one to give up easily, Van finally convinced me that I owed it to him to forego my loathsome vegetables because if my health failed, he would be, as he expressed it, "sunk". "I can't hold up my end and I need lots of help from you," he argued. "Besides, you'll be helping someone who needs the money."

I acceded, albeit sheepishly in the beginning; and I had to admit that it was a relief to be spared the thrice-weekly session at our slime-covered vegetable tables with their floor of mud and rotting debris. I had much to be thankful for, yet how gladly I would have relinquished my privileged status if only Van could have been well!

Never did this thought occur to me more forcibly than on my thirty-third birthday, a steamy day in late October, 1943. Through Fred Guettinger, Van had ordered a feast to celebrate the day: turkey, potatoes, Brussels sprouts, cake and ice cream. After waiting several hours under a torrid sun for the provisions to arrive, he finally loaded his little wagon and was pushing it back to the shanty when he collapsed in a dead faint. Some kind neighbors who rushed to his assistance carried him home and put him to bed. I was summoned, and when I reached the shanty Van was ashen-faced, clammy and cold as ice. Waves of nausea and dizziness swept over him. Dr Fletcher said that he was suffering with heat exhaustion. What price birthday feast?

Although he felt somewhat better in the afternoon, the mere idea of food was still repulsive to him. As for me, I hated the thought of that turkey and ice cream, but I tried to muster a semblance of pleasurable anticipation when Van told me that he had asked Big Van to play host for him. Before dinner, I poured drinks for the two Vans and myself. Big Van commented, "You're a couple of damn fools to share this liquid gold with me, but I suppose I'd be as big a fool myself if I had any." My Van perked up enough to taste a bite of turkey, and later to eat a small dish of ice cream with us.

And so the days passed, and usually the events that set one day apart from others were the kind that afterwards made us thankful they were past.

Chapter Fourteen

On the 14th of November we wakened to a day of torrential rains and high winds: typhoon weather. All day long the violence of the storm increased. When we ventured outside, rain swept around us in blinding sheets and we stumbled through knee-deep pools of water that pitted the campus. After our seven o'clock shanty curfew, the wind raged more furiously than ever. Shanties began to collapse; lights in the building went out; anxiety turned to near-frenzy as the sleepless night hours wore on. When it became light enough to see, we found that the water level had risen alarmingly while wind and rains continued unabated. We were told that seawater was backing up through sewage pipes: the typhoon happened to strike when Manila tides had attained their yearly high, which meant that a real flood was upon us.

People rushed distractedly to their shanties, and many returned with piteous tales of roofs and sides torn away, or of shanties blown down. Food losses were appalling, especially of sugar, which had dissolved by the hundred kilos in flood waters. Substantial quantities of rice, cassava flour and cornmeal were damaged beyond recovery, and many a can of kerosene, important both as fuel and light, had floated away during that horrible night. To add insult to injury, we learned that the Japanese had advised our committee of the approaching storm so that internees could be warned, but the committee, fearing a panic, had agreed among themselves to withhold the information. "It will only worry everyone," declared one of the conferring officials. "They'll find out soon enough anyway."

Through needless stupidity, therefore, precautions were not taken. Provisions which could have been stored away at a safe level were left on the floor to be ruined by rising water. Shanties that could have been braced and tied were wrecked by the wind. And this at a time when our losses might be irreparable.

As the water level climbed, filters for drinking water stopped functioning and we were told to boil every drop we drank. I was thankful for a kerosene stove which Van had recently bought at the personal service office, because our charcoal, drenched in the eighteen inches of water that covered the patio's sub-sidewalk level, could not be made to burn. No food was on sale, as the flood had halted all transportation. Van, however, had waded early in the morning to the main building with a bayong full of canned goods from the shanty. For lunch we had chile con carne: Van had grabbed the first tins in sight, and they all happened to be chile. He took several to friends who could not reach their own shanties without swimming.

While he was gone, Ellie Phillips and little Howie turned up, tired and discouraged. The Phillips' shanty was low and water had come in during the night, forcing Howard to wade back to the building (Howie had stayed with Ellie). He had found scores of other shanty refugees wandering through the halls; having no place to go, they curled up, soaking wet, in whatever benches or chairs they could find to snatch a few hours of rest. Ellie was sure that Howard would develop galloping consumption from exposure. After borrowing dry clothes for Howard in the morning, she had set out for the shanty in a makeshift raft to salvage what food had not already been destroyed. Five or six hours later, having struggled against time and tide to stow away canned goods, sugar, flour, and kerosene on shelves high enough to escape flood waters, she gave up, famished and exhausted, and returned to the building.

"Sit down and relax," I told her. "I'll heat up some chile.

Where's Howard? Has he eaten?"

"Yes, someone brought him some food about an hour ago. I carried over some cans, but I have no way to heat food here. I'm just worried sick about Howard, sleeping all night in his wet clothes. He has a bed now, thank God. But Emily, this is really grim!"

"It's no picnic," I agreed. "I wish I had something to offer you besides chile. It's not a very good diet for Howie."

But Howie hungrily gobbled the improper fare. After a meal of steaming beans and boiled drinking water — horrible flat stuff that it was — they both felt more cheerful. "That was pure heaven," Ellie assured me. "You have no idea how a little hot food can brighten up the world."

After they left, I boiled more drinking water and cleaned dishes and pots as best as I could, wading through water a foot and a half deep to reach the dishwashing faucets. Drains were stopped, and I noticed that the camp garbage cans were overflowing with debris. The next disaster, I reflected gloomily, was sure to be an epidemic of typhoid.

In mid-afternoon, I went up to my room to rest awhile. All windows were tightly shut and the air, foul almost to the point of asphyxiation, reeked of dampness and stale clothing. A slime of watery mud coated the concrete floor. Outside, wind lashed the trees into a wild dance: the dance of death, it seemed to me. As I peered through the window, their waving branches took fantastic shapes before my eyes, and there loomed suddenly the gaunt skeleton of a horse riding the wind, the jaws of its hollow-eyed skull opening and closing in ghastly grimaces, keeping rhythm with long, bony legs that rose and fell in an endless gallop of death. Surely, Death himself was the unseen rider of this weird monster. I heard the wind's monotonous accompanying chant: "Storm, Famine, Pestilence; War, Famine, Pestilence."

The macabre fantasy did not calm my nerves, nor did the sad tales of shanty damages and lost food raise my spirits. I decided to clean up and go back to the patio. A shower was out of the question: water pressure, normally maintained by electric pumps, was practically nil. Water, water everywhere, but not a drop to bathe in! After a sketchy wash, I donned dry clothes, pulled on my rubber boots and a "Sou'wester"-type rubber hat, then wrapped myself in a Japanese-made raincoat purchased from the personal service. Advertised as manufactured from American army airplane cloth, the coat was a tacky olive drab affair which tore at the slightest touch and stuck together wherever one piece of material overlapped another.

The pelting, wind-driven rain had made a sieve of our patio roof; no matter where we sat, we could not escape streams that spouted through. However, a bamboo shade hanging from the roof's edge deflected the worst of the oblique rains. The sidewalk lay under about ten inches of water, with torrents still gushing from building drains. We had often watched rats play hide-and-seek around a drain which opened in front of our space, but now the rats were no longer in evidence: either they had sought shelter inside the building, or they were drowned out. And we were in practically the same situation ourselves!

Van had brought over more provisions and two-thirds of a bottle of rum which we had been saving for the usual "rainy day." On this far from usual day of rain, a stiff shot of rum was the best available substitute for sunshine: it warmed the chill in our hearts as well as in our hands and stomachs. The coolness of typhoon weather reminded us once again to be thankful that we were in a tropical land instead of in China, Manchuria or Japan. After a toast to a speedy end of the storm with no further loss or misfortune, we drank another that was a prayer: let them never move us until home shall be our destination!

Van returned early to the shanty so that he could see his way. One of two bridges over a ditch that he had to cross was washed out, and the handrail of the other was already submerged. I had urged him to stay in the building, because the water was still rising and the wind and rain showed no sign of subsiding; but he was afraid of looters, both in camp and outside. "Our shanty is well braced," he reassured me. "It won't fall or blow apart. Ralph and I are both going to stay there. If the water rises too high we'll head for the building."

"Groping around in the dark is dangerous. Suppose you miss the bridge?"

"Now don't worry. We'll be all right. We have kerosene lanterns to see our way."

When I went upstairs again, I carried a lantern from our patio space into the dark, congested hallway outside my room, where flickering flames from kerosene and coconut oil lamps cast strange shadows over internees huddled along the walls. Now and again a sudden burst of white light from a high-candlepower pressure lamp would dispel the dim shadows, but quickly as the lantern had swung by, the eerie gloom leapt back to accentuate the haggard look of faces lined with worry and bodies sagging with fatigue.

Through the corridors, squads of men were hauling buckets of water for sanitation, for water pressure by now had failed completely on the second and third floors. Bathroom waiting lines, long and slow-moving, extended far out into the halls. Squads of women maintained a constant patrol to keep toilets flushed and to mop up the worst of water pools that collected on the floor. Nearly everyone pitched in to help in the struggle for cleanliness and sanitation; but it seemed to be a losing battle, and we wondered how much longer we could go on.

Tuesday the 16th showed no letup in wind, rain or tide, and by evening our final remaining utility, gas, had failed. It was during that night that we witnessed a job of unselfish labor in a common cause that I think none of us will ever forget. Immediately upon learning of this latest disaster, a group of men volunteers set to work to build outdoor stoves in the dining shed behind the main building. All through the night they toiled, hauling great rocks which they hoisted and piled up tediously, one on top of the other, until they had fashioned three huge stoves. Just before dawn, three blazing fires proclaimed more eloquently than words what victory their titanic effort had won. Kettles and cauldrons were simmering in no time to furnish our usual hot coffee and mush.

Van and Ralph, flooded out of their shanty at about four o'clock that same morning, reached the main building in time to witness the finish of the stupendous night's labor. Volunteers who were passing around a bottle of rum offered them a drink. "Just a minute," Van replied. He rushed to the patio and brought out our half bottle. "I only wish it were more," he said as he gave it to the tired workers.

There are times that the dignity of man asserts itself in never-to-be-forgotten acts that stimulate pride in the hearts of all beholders: pride in the human race itself, which, with all its failures and inadequacies, is yet capable of rising on occasion to heights of glory through sacrifice and service. All of us who survived the ordeals of Santo Tomás must pay eternal tribute to those heroes of the storm who pitted their strength and ingenuity against the wild forces of nature itself, and through their achievement brought hope and comfort to their discouraged fellow prisoners.

Emily Van Sickle at home
circa 1940.

Charles Van Sickle in Hong Kong.

Emily and Charles Van Sickle in Asia
circa 1940.

Charles Van Sickle
in Hong Kong circa 1940.

Until the Japanese turned Santo Tomás University into a concentration camp, it was best known as "the oldest university under the American flag."

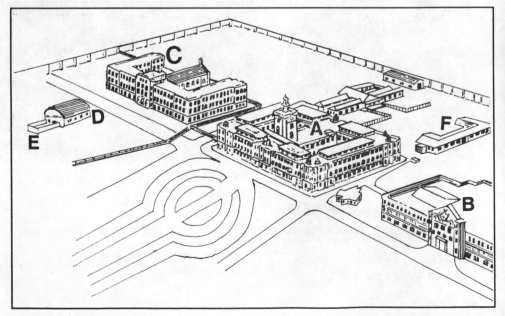

An aerial view of Santo Tomás.

A. Main Building
B. Education Building
C. Parish House and Chapel
D. Gym
E. Pool
F. Hospital

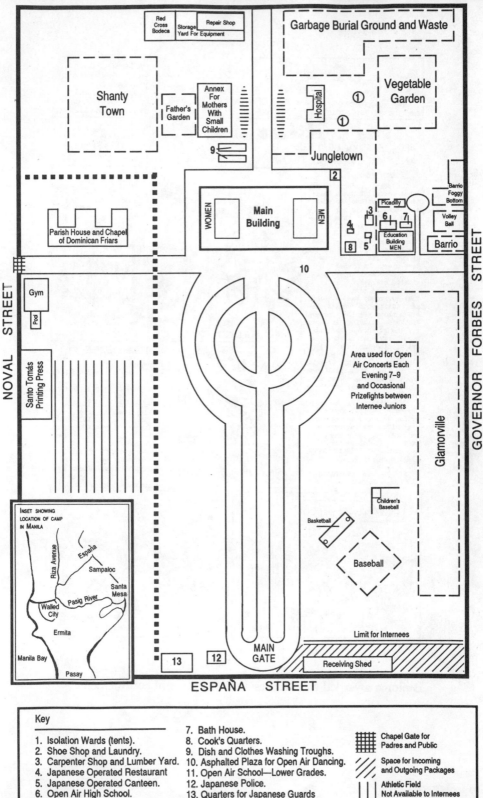

Red Cross Bodeca

Storage Yard For Equipment

Repair Shop

Garbage Burial Ground and Waste

Shanty Town

Father's Garden

Annex For Mothers With Small Children

Hospital

① ①

Vegetable Garden

9

Jungletown

2

WOMEN

Main Building

MEN

Picadilly

3
6 7

4
Barrio Foggy Bottom

8 5

Education Building MEN

Volley Ball

Barrio

Parish House and Chapel of Dominican Friars

10

Gym

Pool

Santo Tomás Printing Press

Area used for Open Air Concerts Each Evening 7–9 and Occasional Prizefights between Internee Juniors

Glamorville

NOVAL STREET

GOVERNOR FORBES STREET

Inset showing location of camp in Manila

Riza Avenue

España

Sampaloc

Santa Mesa

Pasig River

Walled City

Ermita

Manila Bay

Pasay

Children's Baseball

Basketball

Baseball

Limit for Internees

13

12

MAIN GATE

Receiving Shed

ESPAÑA STREET

Key

1. Isolation Wards (tents).
2. Shoe Shop and Laundry.
3. Carpenter Shop and Lumber Yard.
4. Japanese Operated Restaurant
5. Japanese Operated Canteen.
6. Open Air High School.

7. Bath House.
8. Cook's Quarters.
9. Dish and Clothes Washing Troughs.
10. Asphalted Plaza for Open Air Dancing.
11. Open Air School—Lower Grades.
12. Japanese Police.
13. Quarters for Japanese Guards

Chapel Gate for Padres and Public

Space for Incoming and Outgoing Packages

Athletic Field Not Available to Internees

Map is not to scale. Actual campus is 250 square meters.

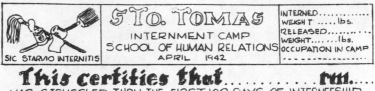

Diploma awarded to internees after 100 days of confinement.

Page two of diploma.

CHEER UP EVERTHING'S GOING TO BE LOUSY

from the

Santo Tómas Show   March 21st 1942.

Our lot is getting better and the country's getting wetter,
So I'm no longer sad and pessimistic.
Conditions are chaotic, but, I'm very patriotic
And I want to show that I am optimistic. -
I wouldn't say a word to make you blue - oh no,
I've come to bring a word of joy to you.

CHORUS
Cheer up everything's going to be lousy.
You'll still be eating cracked wheat every day.
You may have built a shanty, but it won't be there for long,
'Cause the sides are going higher every day.
You eat your mush without any milk in the morning,
But, the prune juice works in the same old fashioned way.
You may have been the president of Manila's leading store,
But you still've gotta haul the garbage from the third and
                                                    highest floor.

You may grumble now at beans and peas,
But wait till you start on the bark of the trees.
Cheer up everything's going to be lousy.

PATTER
I've plenty to be thankful for although it's hard to bear.
Things could be a darned sight worse, although I don't know
                                                    where.
Don't think that I'm complaining, 'cause it's really not the
                                                    case,
And, if I look disgusted, why, it's just my natural face.
I haven't a pot to cook in, but, at least I have a bed.
It may belong to the Red Cross, but, it's a place to lay my
                                                    head.
So smile and show your dimples, they're worth their weight in
                                                    gold.
You may as well my friends before you know it you'll be old.
CHORUS
Cheer up everything's going to be lousy.
The rules are getting longer every day
You can't do this, you can't do that, you can't even romance
                                                    in your shack.
I know because I tried it yesterday.
You think the Flit is decreasing mosquitoes in numbers,
But, they're going in mass production any day
The lines are getting longer just like the ones in your face,
But, wait till you're five years older and you're still in the
                                                    same old place.
The rumors may be all that you need
But you'll soon begin to believe what you read.
Cheer up everything's going to be lousy.

From *Internews*, March 21, 1942.

SANITARY INSPECTIONS

Room inspections in the weekly sanitation contest will be at unannounced times, beginning next week, the sanitation committee said. Inspections will be held any time between 10 and noon on weekday mornings, without prior notice.

The committee also announced that the sanitation report now prepared by the room monitor will be discontinued. Instead, the inspection committee will prepare a report, furnishing the monitor a copy.

TUBERCULIN TESTS

(continued from page 1) quarters be secured to alleviate overcrowding, that milk and fats be increased in the diet of growing children and that active open cases of tuberculosis be isolated. He reported three of the latter.

SCHOOL BOOKS WANTED

Fourth year high school students would appreciate about two weeks' loan of the following books: "Dark Lady of the Sonnets," G.B. Shaw; "Caliban Upon Setebos," Robert Browning; Moffat's translation of the New Testament; "Elizabeth & Essex." Leave books at education desk.

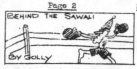

BEHIND THE SAWALI
BY GOLLY

Facing each other with a yawn were two hard-punching boxers of the new storkweight division (7 pounds, 7 ounces). One-Punch Danny vs. Slugger Bill.

The gong! And again the gong. One-Punch had not heard it, being engrossed in conversation with a girl near his corner. "You betcha I'll wallop 'im," he said. "You betcha."

They came out fighting. One-Punch was cagey; he stayed near the girl, trying to get her telephone number. Slugger regarded him idly, then waved to a friend in the gallery. Finally Slugger began his famous double-barrelled attack. He put both hands in front of him, followed them with bowed head and sent the whole cargo, special delivery, into One-Round's eye.

There was a moment of silence. Then One-Round began to blubber. He slapped at Slugger like a mosquito. The fight was stopped and Slugger's hand raised. TKO for tears. Something new in boxing.

Such is life in the Annex

SOFTBALL LEAGUE TIED

Going into the homestretch of the morning softball schedule, the Independents and Polo 1 were deadlocked today at the top of the standings.

The Poloers retained their position today by downing Shanghai, 18-11, in a free-hitting tussle. The losers tallied three runs in the last of the 7th, but failed to knot the count. The Poloers held a slight hitting advantage, 18-17, with Doyle and Brines leading the pack, each getting 3 for 4.

Another All-Polo, All-Star tussle is scheduled for Wednesday at 5:30 p.m. The All-Stars hold two consecutive wins.

Other recent morning results: Independents 12, Polo Two 6; Shanghai 5, Polo Two 4.

FIGHT PROGRAM

Nine bouts are scheduled for the 2nd internee boxing smoker Wed. at 6 in front of the restaurant. Buddie Myers will meet Tom McKinney in the main event. Promoter Johnnie Burk reported that fans contributed ₱51.10 after last week's show but further funds are needed to complete the ring.

Fight and Conditioning Gym. It goes on like that every afternoon among the four-year-olds.

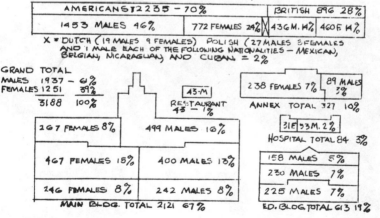

POPULATION GRAPH OF STO. TOMAS AS OF MARCH 28, 1942.

The following charts, illustrating the distribution of camp population, were compiled by Fred Comings, roll call chief, from reports received last night. Stencil prepared by Jim Stuart. The population on March 1 was 3266; a week later, 3241.

AMERICANS 2285 - 70%		BRITISH 896 28%	
1453 MALES 46%	772 FEMALES 24%	436 M. 14%	460 F 14%

X = DUTCH (19 MALES 9 FEMALES) POLISH (27 MALES 3 FEMALES AND 1 MALE EACH OF THE FOLLOWING NATIONALITIES — MEXICAN, BELGIAN, NICARAGUAN, AND CUBAN = 2%

GRAND TOTAL
MALES 1937 - 61%
FEMALES 1251 39%
3188 100%

43-M
RESTAURANT
43 - 1%

238 FEMALES 7% | 89 MALES 3%
ANNEX TOTAL 327 10%

267 FEMALES 8% | 499 MALES 16%

31F 53M. 2%
HOSPITAL TOTAL 84 3%

467 FEMALES 15% | 400 MALES 13%

158 MALES 5%

230 MALES 7%

246 FEMALES 8% | 242 MALES 8%

225 MALES 7%

MAIN BLDG. TOTAL 2121 67%   ED. BLDG. TOTAL 613 19%

Page from *Internews* showing population graph, March 28, 1942.

Drawing by internee showing the cramped quarters in Room Five, which housed twenty-two women.

Washing up in Santo Tomás.

Chapter Fifteen

By noon of the 17th, the typhoon was over and lakes covering the campus had begun to recede. Electricity came on during the afternoon, tap water was pronounced drinkable, upstairs plumbing slowly improved. It seemed nothing short of a miracle that we had come through without epidemic or even serious illness. Next day we had a fleeting glimpse of sun, and on Friday the 19th there were actually chickens on sale at the cold store, the first meat in five days to come into camp. By Monday, things were more or less back to normal, except for twisted and roofless shanties awaiting repairs. Several hundred eggs, priced at fifty centavos apiece, sold out in a flash. People will pay dearly for food they have been denied even for a single week.

Thursday, the 25th of November, was Thanksgiving. On that day, two loyal and generous friends, Juan Elizalde and Enrico Pirovano, sent into Santo Tomás a feast of stuffed roast turkeys, chickens and potato salad, enough for every internee in camp to have a portion. It was no easy task to procure such quantities of food, especially since poultry stocks had been depleted by the storm. However, they found a way, and thanks to them, friends and strangers alike who dwelt behind the bars celebrated Thanksgiving Day with a full stomach.

But our day of feasting ended all too quickly. The typhoon had dealt us a staggering blow from which we never fully recovered, for although most foodstuffs soon trickled back into camp, the supply never again was adequate. Meat we

197

could buy in limited quantities: cold cuts, chickens and later on carabao meat, at the cold store; steaks and pork chops at the Japanese store. Eggs were on sale only about twice a week, first come, first served as long as they lasted. Fruits and vegetables continued to be scarce because the flood had ruined many gardens. Days passed before we could buy roasted peanuts, and weeks before peanut butter was again on sale. Peanuts and peanut butter, rich in vitamin B, satisfied some lack in our diet: many of us had a real craving for them. As soon as I could buy it again, I filled all my empty jars (two quarts and three pints) with peanut butter to store away for the future. Our greatest shortage of all, predictably, was sugar. Tons had been lost outside, and weeks went by before any came into camp. When it did come in, prices had skyrocketed. The Japanese no longer issued it on the breakfast line; furthermore, they announced that no more soap or lard was available for camp use.

To furnish our monthly laundry soap ration of one small cake per internee, the camp began to manufacture a substitute of grossly inferior quality from what meager ingredients were on hand. Although the cakes melted away like spring snow, we could with care stretch them over the month to wash dishes. Clothes often were laundered by an overnight soaking in cold water, with or without "go-go" bark (a dried native fiber frequently used in camp for shampoos). The sun and wind helped to freshen, if not to cleanse, our garments and linens.

Certain staples which had been sold at the canteen were now vanishing overnight. Two signs warned us of pending disappearance: first, exorbitant price jumps, then rationed sales, one unit per customer.

Early in December, cocoa and a local product called "Tam's Cake Flour" (blended from cassava and rice flour mixed with cornstarch) showed signs of following the recognized pattern. The flour I had found excellent for pie crust, which I baked in a glass-doored oven (purchased at the personal service) that fitted over any conventional charcoal or kerosene stove.

Cocoa and sugar, combined with coconut milk and a little cornstarch, made a luscious chocolate filling for the crust. I tried to buy cocoa and flour enough for occasional pies through-out the internment, but by the time I had accumulated five and one-half pound tins of cocoa and five packages of flour (about a pound and a half each), both were off the market.

Well-meaning friends counselled me against "throwing my money away" on such perishables as flour, cocoa and peanut butter. Cocoa, they said, would mildew; weevils would ruin the flour, peanut butter would turn rancid. Nevertheless, we had to chance it: money could never be eaten, while food, even if deteriorated, might avert starvation.

Another unpleasant aftermath of the typhoon was a sharp increase in shanty looting, chiefly by Filipinos who climbed the wall. Under the leadership of an internee named Norris Wadsworth, shanty owners banded together to form a nightly "wall path patrol" of volunteers, whose work was recognized as a camp assignment. Norris asked Van if he would be willing to serve as captain of the Foggy Bottom and Jerkville squads ("Jerkville" being the elegant suburb where Van and Ralph lived). Van agreed gladly. On call in case of trouble at any hour of the night, he did no actual patrolling himself, but merely supervised the squads at intervals. Patrols worked two-hour shifts in pairs, staying always together to assist each other in case of attack from would-be marauders.

Most shanty owners welcomed the protection of nightly patrols. The few who objected were smugglers, and they had reason to be skeptical, as smuggling was considered a crime not only by the Japanese but by our central committee — a crime punishable by jail sentence. Naturally, smugglers cast leery eyes at an accredited camp patrol. However, the volun-teer guards wanted no part of policing internees, and Norris Wadsworth assured his men that smuggling was strictly an af-fair for the camp police.

One night in mid-December, Van met the two a.m. patrols

coming up the path by his shanty near the eastern wall, and joined them as they walked toward the northern wall. Near the shadowed juncture of walls, they spied a crouching figure, which quick investigation proved to be the figure of Wally King. Wally muttered something — probably curses — and returned to his shanty a few feet away. It required no great powers of deduction to guess that Wally had been awaiting a rum delivery. The following day, Van sought out Stew Raab.

"Stew, when are you going to get me that bottle of rum?" he demanded. "I want it in time for our wedding anniversary on the eighteenth."

"You'd have had it today," Stew retorted, "if those dumb patrols of yours hadn't walked into Wally last night. He got cold feet and postponed the deal."

"That's all I wanted to know. I saw Wally last night myself, and you can tell him for me that next time all he had to do is tip us off ahead of time and we won't patrol his corner while he's busy."

"I hear you talking, Van. That's swell of you. But how about the other fellows?" Stew asked dubiously.

"They're all okay. We signed up to catch thieves, not to stop internees from making a living."

Stew delivered the anniversary rum on schedule. Also in time to celebrate the day, we moved to a brand-new shanty, built of property acquired from an internee selected in the second group to go to Los Baños.

It was early in December when at long last the "Los Baños widows" (including the Duchess) were allowed to rejoin husbands and sweethearts, and great was the rejoicing as they rode away, sped by the lilting strains of Wagner's "Wedding March." A number of other internees, chosen by lot, went not so gaily along with the volunteers.

One of the reluctant selectees lived across the path from Van and Ralph Baskerville in a dilapidated shack which Van, convinced now that we probably would remain at Santo

Tomás, bought for 2,000 pesos. The value to us was not in the building, which we planned to tear down, but in the grounds, luxuriantly landscaped with flowers, and large enough to build a shanty that would accommodate both of us; we hoped that the Japanese, to make space for new internees, might eventually allow family living in Santo Tomás as they had already at Los Baños.

Van designed a shanty thirteen by twenty-eight feet, with a six-by-seven-foot wing in back for a kitchen. A good-sized bedroom, enclosed by screening and tight-woven petate panels, opened onto a side hallway leading from a small sitting room in front to a tiny dining nook and dressing room (separated by cabinets) in the rear. Bamboo latticework formed an open partition between kitchen and dining nook. The shanty was to be constructed principally of nipa, with wooden floor in front and bamboo strips for ventilation in back. So much for the blueprint; now to find materials and a builder.

No longer were individuals permitted to have materials sent in from outside, nor were contractors allowed to bring them in, with one exception: Wally King, whom the central committee had appointed sole and exclusive camp building materials contractor, was privileged to resell materials to other contractors. This monopoly was created ostensibly to prevent profiteering: because a few contractors had sold shoddy goods for exorbitant prices, all except Wally were penalized.

After the typhoon, there was a great demand for materials to repair damaged shanties. At the same time, the former steady flow of nipa, sawali, bamboo and lumber had dwindled to a driblet, partly because of necessary repairs outside, partly because of our socialist Commandant's prejudice against the "privileged class" of shanty owners — many of whom had earned with hard work and enterprise their "privileged" status. It was soon evident that certain contractors stood a much better chance than others of obtaining scarce materials from Wally King. Some who had undertaken to rebuild shanties were forced to bow out when, due to "previous orders," Wally found himself unable to supply them. Camp authorities ignored charges that Wally accepted kickbacks from favored "inner circle" contractors.

Although we had engaged a henchman of Wally's to build our shanty, we ran into the usual snag: no materials. Van dropped in to have a chat with the boss himself; a fifty peso "bonus" did the trick: on December 18th, we were in our shanty, as sturdy, spacious and conveniently designed a little house as there was in camp. Set on four-foot bamboo poles, it cleared by several inches the area flood level, and was protected from rain and prying eyes by low-hanging eaves and shutters that swung upward to form media aguas over the windows. Tall cannas and hibiscus bushes helped to veil the open sides required by law. One side, facing a path that crossed the camp garden, we kept closed at all times. The windows opposite opened onto ginger flowers bordering our walk to the kitchen entrance, and a ten-foot strip of yard beyond. A canna hedge hid the front path, which passed our gate about fifteen feet from the front doorway.

There were shanties architecturally more beautiful than ours; but not to our eyes. For above all, this was a spot we could call our very own, a blessed haven of privacy in that walled-in world where our lives were anything but our own to live as we chose.

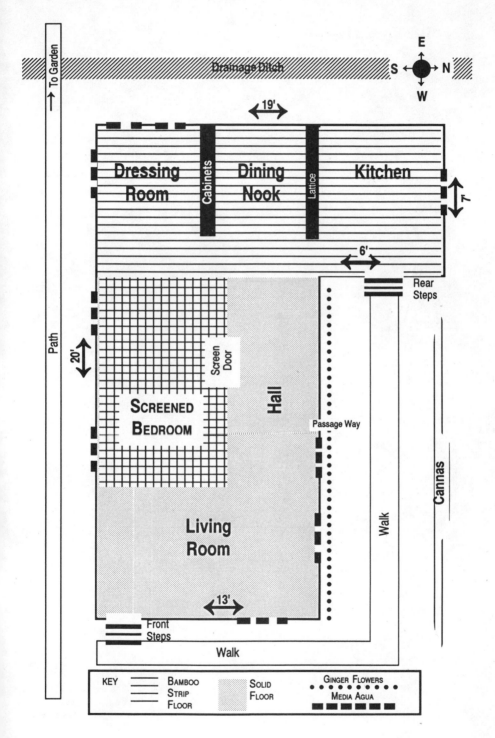

203

Chapter Sixteen

A few days before the great typhoon, the Japanese had brought into camp a shipment of American Red Cross packets, sent to us on the exchange ship *Gripsholm*. These they had kept securely locked away in a barred room of the main building until about ten days before Christmas, when they dragged them out and dumped them for inspection onto the road between main building and restaurant, now occupied by Japanese officials.

Our diplomat-Commandant, a pint-sized man decked out in full military uniform with trailing samurai sword, climbed over the piled-up cartons, stumbled, kicked three or four boxes, then stepped back and peevishly watched the inspection through heavy, horn-rimmed spectacles. His Chaplin-type mustache wiggled comically as he grunted remarks to dusty-booted soldiers who were ripping open our packets. After they had emptied out the contents of a dozen kits, the soldiers began jabbing bayonets through tins of meat, jam, milk and other foodstuffs. "Looking for bombs or propaganda, I suppose," jeered an internee onlooker.

Fury surged up inside us as we watched that needless despoilment of food. For weeks practically no meat had been served in line chow, yet now, before our very eyes, our wanton gaolers were destroying pounds of Red Cross meat intended for internees. The sight of Grinnell, grinning like a hyena as he sauntered around with Japanese inspectors, enraged us still more.

After all the kits had been checked and reassembled, distribution finally began, each internee receiving a carton of four "comfort kits," full except for what the Japanese had ruined or removed. They had confiscated for the time being all cigarettes because one brand label bore an offensive reference to the war. Eventually they issued thirty-five or thirty-six packages to each internee. We estimated that the quota should have been a carton per kit, or forty packs a person.

Our kits contained a masterly assortment of nourishing foods: corned beef, Spam and other canned meats, many of them vitamin-enriched; ham-and-egg loaf; tins of butter and jam; powdered milk; Kraft cheese; prunes and raisins; white sugar; biscuits, bouillon and soup powders; instant coffee; chocolate bars; and one quarter-pound tin of cocoa for approximately every eight kits.

Van and I traded most of ours for cigarettes, to non-smoking mothers whose children needed milk. Since our days at Santiago Hospital, Van and I had been saving stubs to re-roll in cigarette papers bought for us by the nurses. Recently we had been breaking open fresh cigarettes: we found that one fast-burning original made three slow-burning rerolls, plus butts. Even after the fresh windfall, we continued rolling our own.

In the evening, our camp broadcaster urged us to conserve our food. Warning that worse times were coming, he begged us above all to save the chocolate bars, which, he explained, were vitamin-loaded emergency rations. Each of the 600-calorie squares which formed the bar could sustain life, he told us, for a whole day; if hastily consumed, all those calories and vitamins would tie up our insides in knots. Many heeded the well-timed advice; others landed in the hospital, full of internal knots. Not all of the latter were line chow dependents, whose craving for nutrient could be well understood.

After acquiring our kits, Van and I checked, listed and

repacked all our canned goods. We set aside for early use some spaghetti and beans which had puffed, but all other food we stored away to be opened only when we began to feel the pinch of starvation.

Gradually the Japanese portioned out non-edible supplies which the Red Cross had sent: bath towels, women's playsuits and men's shorts, materials, underclothes, shoes and shoe repairs, pipe tobacco, cosmetics, soap, face cream, toilet articles and a variety of other things, including Tampax (until that small shipment of Tampax, many women in Santo Tomás had used cloth napkins, issued and laundered by the camp). We especially welcomed the shoes: nearly all of us found one pair of shoes that fit reasonably well, and a few were lucky enough to find two.

After inspecting and thoroughly "sampling" Red Cross medical supplies, the Japanese turned over what was left to the camp hospital. We felt certain that they had helped themselves liberally, as our doctors received only token quantities of critically needed medicines, such as adrenalin. Camp authorities soon distributed multiple vitamin tablets, each containing "half the necessary vitamins" for a day, and advised us to begin taking at least one a day. At that rate, we had enough for about ten months.

The influx of Red Cross goods started such a trade boom that new camp-sponsored booths opened up, some for exchanging goods, some for buying and selling. Hank Parfit did a staggering business, although camp authorities now eyed him with partial disfavor: they actually suspected him of profiteering! "Parfiteering" Hank, however, paid no attention to the eye of authority. Because he paid more than the camp booths did, he acquired a wider range of marketable goods, which he managed to dispose of rapidly and profitably. Demand, ever greater than supply, caused prices to soar perpetually higher: a three and one-half ounce tin of butter sold for twenty-five pesos, corned beef for fifteen pesos a can — and up and up.

Along with the buy-and-sell fever, a fresh rash of smuggling broke out, this time smuggling goods out of Santo Tomás. Some of the smugglers, oldtimers with children and Filipina wives living outside, could scarcely be blamed for sending food to their families. Big-time operators, however, bought quantities of Red Cross supplies to sell outside for fabulous profits.

One of the smugglers, who was caught and jailed, had a piteous tale to tell: a tale of sorrow, hatred and vengeance that had led him to the very brink of insanity. Before he became a smuggler, he had been able to look up from his shanty near the wall into a second story apartment window across the street, where his wife lived. Every evening and many times during the day, she had stood in the window so that he could see her. Then one day, she was not there. A friend, who had sent in a message to tell him that she was ill, signalled to him thereafter with candles by night. When he tried to get a pass to see his wife, camp authorities would do nothing to help him. Finally, the candles told him that she had died.

Almost out of his mind with grief, he brooded night and day on how to get even with Grinnell and his committee, and finally vowed to avenge his wrongs by breaking every rule in Santo Tomás. Soon he discovered a malevolent pleasure in smuggling: it became an obsession with him, a remorseless, perverted thrill, to listen in the darkness for the thud that signified another can thrown safely over the wall. Even in jail he repented nothing except that he had not climbed the wall himself in time to see his wife before she died.

What to do about this type of smuggling puzzled Norris Wadsworth and the wall path patrol. Sending Red Cross tins outside would, to a greater or lesser degree, affect everyone when food became really scarce. Yet, unless the goods were stolen, smuggling lay outside the jurisdiction of the wall path patrol. Norris instructed his guards to try to stop smugglers peaceably. "But don't report them to the police," he added. "Your job is still to catch thieves."

Chapter Seventeen

Christmas, 1943, was a time of good cheer, as jolly and festive as such a season could possibly be in a concentration camp. Gay trimmings decked the halls: silvery spiral icicles and other ornaments fashioned from bits of Red Cross tins. To delight the children, men fabricated toys of wood, while women stuffed rag dolls and animals with button eyes. After weeks of assiduous rehearsal, an internee chorus sang Handel's magnificent Oratorio. The all-pervasive spirit of Christmas shone in every eye and on every smiling face, betokening hearts full of rejoicing, thanksgiving and prayer: rejoicing that the November storm was past, thanksgiving for our comfort kits, prayer that this might be our last Christmas in enemy hands.

Quantities of rum came into camp for the holidays, enough for every internee who wanted a drink to have one on Christmas Eve. I drank a toast in the patio, after shanty hours, with Tommy Pratt, Howard and Ellie Phillips and several other friends. Van treated some of his shanty neighbors, and the next day we had rum enough left for an eggnog.

Big Van had invited us, along with half-a-dozen other guests, to dine with him. After an exchange of cordial greetings, he passed around drinks of rum tinkling with ice; everyone commented on the ice, which now had become a greater novelty in camp than rum. His shanty looked almost like a bit of homeside Christmas. A huge red candle, about four inches in diameter, burned cheerfully on the buffet, and on the dining table stood a fluffy, star-studded artificial tree, complete with powdered snow and bright baubles. Decorative colored match folders served as place cards for a dinner that was super-abundant. Big Van had ordered a veritable feast from out-side: our plates were heaped high with turkey, dressing, gravy, baked ham, potatoes, several vegetables, cranberry sauce, pick-les, and more that I do not remember. Rice bread and butter were on the table; for dessert, ice cream and cake. It was too much: I could not help thinking of others in the camp to whom a taste of meat in the food line was an infrequent treat.

After dinner, the conversation turned to Grinnell and the central committee. My Van wondered aloud why, when for months the Japanese had consistently cut our food and privi-leges, Grinnell still refused to resign. "He can't possibly believe now that he's doing a good job for us," Van remarked.

"Now, now," chided Big Van, "it isn't Grinnell's fault. The Japs would have done the same thing no matter who was in charge of the camp."

"My point is," Van retorted, "that Grinnell knows he is hat-ed. He announced two reasons for staying on when he wasn't wanted. First, the Japs wouldn't let him go. Since he made that statement, the Japanese administration has changed more than once. Even Grinnell can't maintain that each new ad-ministration refused to let him resign. Second, he said he understood Japanese psychology so well that he could do a better job than anyone else. Since then, release privileges have been practically stopped. Some of our people have been sent away to Los Baños. Food has grown consistently scarcer. If that's what a knowledge of Japanese psychology accomplishes, give me someone who never saw a Jap before!"

"Come, come, Van," Big Van remonstrated. "Why are you sore at Grinnell? You have nothing to kick about. You have a nice shanty. You have plenty to eat. *I'm* not complaining. Any administration is all right with me when I can sit in my comfortable shanty and eat a Christmas dinner like this in the clink!"

"But Van," I interposed, "what about people with no money, who can't afford a dinner like this, who can't even afford an occasional piece of stew meat at six pesos a kilo? Besides, even the food we can buy is getting scarce. Eggs come in about twice a week — if you're lucky, you get some. You wait two hours in the meat line and find nothing left but bologna."

"That isn't Grinnell's fault. Food is scarce outside, too."

"I'm not arguing about that," my Van continued. "This is what I mean. We can still buy food. We may not be able to for long, but as long as *we* can eat meat, why doesn't the camp administration see to it that internees without funds get meat every day in the line chow?

"Grinnell makes a big to-do about the money he has borrowed for the camp at large and for private loans. Sure, he's borrowed money, and he's loaned it to some people who couldn't have gotten it otherwise. So have you; so have I. But the man who runs this camp should borrow on a scale big enough to provide food for everybody as long as food can be bought. "Why doesn't he consult with all the men in this camp who *can* borrow money, like you and me and a hundred others? Collectively, we could bring in a lot more than he can borrow on his own. But no, he wants to be the big hero and do it all himself. He won't even go to Tommy Wolfe, who could borrow plenty under Red Cross signature. He's an egomaniac, and he's made an awful mess of his job.

"He could have avoided the Los Baños move if he had been smart enough to suggest building barracks here. He's never even built a decent eating place for the poor devils who have no place of their own. There's nothing much to do about it now that building materials are scarce. But if we, through individual effort, can manage to live fairly decently and comfortably, why couldn't the man in charge of the camp have provided reasonably for the comfort and decency of all of us? It could have been done; he simply didn't do it. If I were in good health, I'd fight him until he was forced out. At least, it would bolster the camp morale to get a new leader!"

"Quite a speech!" remarked Big Van. "But now you listen to me, young man. There's no use getting so wrought up about the thing. I think we're going to be in this place for a total of about five years. Just take it easy if you want to live through it. That's what I've done, and what I plan to continue doing. I have a weak heart, and I don't think getting excited over the way the camp is run would help it a bit!"

"But you do admit it's bad, don't you?" my Van persisted. "Take your own case. You are vice president of a big company. The supposition is that you have plenty of sense to get where you are. You have good contacts outside. In other words, you're the kind of man we need to help run the camp. But when you came in, were you ever consulted about camp affairs? Were you ever asked for advice or offered an administrative job? No, and neither were a lot of other outstanding businessmen. I think you were offered a job in the kitchen, weren't you?"

"Yes, and when I turned it down, they gave me a garden job. I put my 'shadow' to work out there: it's money in his pocket, and makes life much more pleasant for me." Big Van chuckled.

I broke into the discussion again to remark to Big Van that, had he been selected to help run the camp, he could have done a lot to help all the underdogs of Santo Tomás.

"My dear," he replied, "I am not interested in how the other half lives. The only important thing to me is to get Van Voorhees out of this place alive some day. If I can help a few friends and others whose existence is important to my comfort, well and good. As for the rest, it's every man for himself."

"I don't believe you, Van!" I gasped.

Big Van smiled at my shocked expression. "It's the truth," he replied. "And you'll find out before this thing is over that it's a necessary philosophy if you want to come out alive."

There was no use arguing about an unknown future. My thoughts turned instead to the past, the distant past when a

Child came into the world to give His life for us. This Christmas holiday, so named because it was His birthday, had been for nearly two thousand years a day of feasting, of rejoicing because He had been born; a day of giving, because He had given the greatest gift of all.

I thought of Christmases at home: the holly and snow and mistletoe, the Christmas trees, the jolly Santas dressed in red; the packages wrapped in fancy tissue, trimmed with bright stickers and tinselled ribbons elaborately bowed; the turkey and plum pudding; the faces of children, wide-eyed with wonder and anticipation as they tumbled downstairs to behold the miracle wrought by "Santa," whose magic touch transformed the familiar home scene into a fairyland filled with toys of every description, spread out beneath a tree all aglitter with lights and baubles and spangle-dust. Above all, I thought of the warmth and the love, the spirit of giving and sharing, which carried out the meaning of Christmas, the birthday of Christ.

And here we were, imprisoned far from home on Christmas day, sharing a friend's bounty, a feast with Christmas trimmings reminiscent of home; yet how flat, how empty was the celebration! Turkey and tinsel: hollow symbols of a spirit that was not there, a spirit locked out somewhere in the free world. What appalling power had prison bars that they could deprive the heart of humanity?

And what of the "other half." They, too, fared well on Christmas day: beef stew from the line, and a feast for all, as on Thanksgiving, of turkey and chicken sent in by Juan Elizalde and Enrico Pirovano. Outside, life was not easy, nor was there much more freedom than within our walls. Yet it is the mark of great souls that sympathy for others is nourished by the very adversities that wither in lesser men the generous impulse to share. If Juan Elizalde and Enrico Pirovano ever feared for survival, they gave no sign: theirs was a very different philosophy from Big Van's announced way of life.

Chapter Eighteen

Just after the New Year, on January 2nd, 1944, internees from Davao and the Southern Islands arrived at Santo Tomás, the last of a number of groups from all parts of the Philippines to be transferred to our camp. As soon as the new arrivals were released, Van looked up an old friend from Davao, a man named Umpstead.

I remembered Umps, whom I had met just before the war, as a middle-aged man of medium height and husky build, in the peak of physical condition except for cataract blindness, corrected by thick spectacles. When I saw him again in camp, his appearance shocked me: a loss of some fifty pounds had robbed his frame of all robustness, and had left him a haggard, almost feeble, old man.

Van brought him to the shanty for a dinner of carabao pot roast smothered in native onions and vegetables, with fried white camotes on the side, topped off by ice cream which, ordered for New Year's, had opportunely come in a day late. Except for the ice cream, the meal was not an exceptional one for us, although pot roasts were now scarce. But when Umps sat down at our table, he gasped and his eyes filled with tears. "I haven't seen such a meal as this since the war began — I just can't believe it!" He took off his glasses to wipe away the mist.

He told us that Davao internees, half-starved from the beginning, had tasted no meat since internment. The Japanese had forced their civilian prisoners, often beaten and abused by sol-

215

dier guards, to work on the road. "Once I was digging a ditch for them," Umps related, "when my glasses fell off, and I couldn't see a thing. As I reached for them, a Jap soldier came over and hit me. I tried to explain what I was doing, but he began to beat me over the head with his rifle butt. I was stunned pretty badly for a while. There was nothing to do about it, though — I just had to keep on digging. Things like that were not unusual in Davao. We got very bad treatment."

"What about the civilian Japanese you knew there?" Van asked. "Didn't they do anything to help you?"

"Some of them tried to in the beginning," Umps replied. "They brought us eggs and bread until the Army stopped all contact. You couldn't really blame the Army, in a way. When American troops pulled out, they ordered the release of all interned Japanese; but instead of releasing them, some Philippine soldiers bayoneted a number of the prisoners. Half-a-dozen of those Japs had been cooking breakfast for the rest of the camp. The Japanese Army moved in and found them slumped dead over their boiling pots. Naturally they thought the Americans had done it. I'm surprised they didn't kill all of us."

After dinner, Van set up a bed for Umps inside the screened room, and poured him a drink of rum. There was enough for a second drink, but Umps declined, saying that he did not trust himself after so long a period of abstinence. Next morning, I found the two men sitting down to a breakfast that Van had cooked: bacon, fried eggs and fried white camotes. Once again, Umps choked up. "Please excuse me," he apologized. "If only you knew what it means to have food like this again!"

Van invited him to stay on with us, but he was eager to move into a shanty that friends had bought him in December, when we first had word that Davao internees were to be brought to our camp. We gave him a mosquito net and bed — the same that Daré had used; also a lamp and some household utensils. Other friends chipped in with donations to help him get started, so that by evening he was fairly well set up in his own place.

Van urged him to relax for at least a month or two until he regained his strength. However, the newcomers from Davao had a laudable, albeit under the circumstances a foolish, spirit of insisting on doing their share of camp work from the beginning. Instead of resting and allowing their better-fed Santo Tomás compatriots to take care of them for awhile, the Davao group volunteered immediately for work assignments. Umps, half-sick from malnutrition and fatigue though he was, undertook a grueling job in the camp carpentry shop. Far be it from our amazed authorities to discourage anyone who actually *wanted* to work! Many of us, deploring as much as we admired the excessive zeal of our Davao friends, thought that the work assignment board should have refused their services until they had recovered from their arduous trip and the previous rigors of imprisonment. Although we knew little as yet of how far the limits of human endurance could be extended, we feared that needless exertion might rob them of an ultimate chance of survival.

Already we had learned of one death caused, we believed, by strain beyond mortal capacity. Our old friend Joe Yetti had dropped dead in Los Baños of a heart attack. As sound and strong in the beginning as any man who had entered camp, he must surely have received his death sentence when the Japanese strung him from the ceiling by his thumbs at Fort Santiago and bound his arms and legs until the circulation stopped. Although the excruciating torture did not kill him at the time, it had undoubtedly so weakened his heart that he could not last out the rugged years of prison life.

Everyone who had known Joe mourned his death. We remembered the services he had done for all of us: dishing out our mush and stew, bringing in money and messages when he worked as a censor, cheering us with his quick smile. We missed him, and we saluted him for the gallantry that had saved many lives, and in the end had cost him his own.

I sometimes wondered how long the rest of us could hold

217

out, for already the specter of starvation, like lengthening shadows of the evening, was creeping towards us. The Japanese repeatedly warned us that food would become scarcer and exhorted us to plant more vegetables; and each night our camp administration spokesman earnestly besought us to save canned goods for hungry days ahead. Yet many found reason to hope that the worst might never befall us. The war news was good: our forces were moving ever closer along the island steppingstones to the southeast. Even the weather conspired to make us optimistic: January, normally clear and dry, was a capricious month of showers and muggy sunshine, clearly indicative, we persuaded ourselves, of heavy fighting nearby. Only war smoke, we theorized, could cause such freakishly unseasonable storm clouds to materialize over Manila. Perhaps we might be free in another three months — four months — six months — ?

Although Van still predicted another full year, I found myself dreaming the infectious dream of an earlier liberation. Partly, perhaps, I was able to dream because I was in better health, thanks to a thyroid prescription from Dr Allen, than I had been for many months. Partly, too, the dream was due to fear, specifically the fear that Van, whose health was badly impaired by continuous asthma and a recurrence of beriberi, might not survive another year. Then, too, there was always a longing to be free, and rebellion against the indignities of imprisonment.

I used to think, as I waited my turn for a shower in line with a dozen other women — many of them older women whose wasted flesh hung in sagging, scar-marked folds — how unmerciful it was that those women should be forced to expose their pitiful nakedness to public view. What would happen to them if we were not soon liberated, and to others already weakened by illness or undernourishment?

What, for that matter, did the future hold for any of us? If power were given us to penetrate the mist-shrouded Unknown that lay ahead, most of us would recoil in horror from the palpable future manifestation of dimly-perceived present dread, and some would turn away in desperation, giving up hope and ready to die rather than meet their destiny. It is one of God's blessings that we are not given this power, for in the struggle to survive privation and sorrow, one draws strength from living each day in the hope that some tomorrow soon to come will bring better things.

PART IV: THE SHADOWS DEEPEN

Chapter One

Our dark year began in February, 1944, when the Japanese Military discharged most of their civilian deputies and took direct control of our camp. Two civilians whom they retained — release man Ohashi and a repatriated ex-consul from Brazil named Hirose — tried to resign in protest, we were told, against the military prisoner-of-war regime inaugurated by the Army. Disdainful of civilian recommendations, the Army ignored their disapproval but forced the unwilling civilians to remain at Santo Tomás.

Soldiers with fixed bayonets now patrolled the campus night and day, especially around the wall. Our new Commandant, a lieutenant colonel, delegated full authority over camp affairs to a handful of lieutenants, chief among them Abiko, swaggering captain of the guards, and Shuraji, fat and pigeyed, who doled out our food. The military abruptly commandeered for their offices the entire first floor of the Education building. Ousted internees crowded into the gymnasium and the Ed building's second and third floors.

The first announcement portended worse times ahead: the gate was to be permanently closed within days; no more communications with the outside, no more passes except for emergency operations, which would be performed at the Philippine General Hospital only. All other hospitals were closed to internees except Remedios for the aged and chronically ill (our friends the Stevensons were now there) and San Juan de

Dios for tuberculars.

Learning of the impending shutout, Manila vendors rushed their wares to us; but unfortunately internees generally were not allowed to deal with them. All transactions had to be consummated by canteen buyers who, mobbed by internees with last-minute requests, purchased only what they could pay for, turned back the rest. When Van, aghast that food was being hauled away, asked why the camp did not solicit loans to finance supplies for later resale, he was told by a buyer, "If we bring in too much, the Japs might confiscate everything." Scarcely a satisfying reply for those of us who believed the old adage "Nothing ventured, nothing gained!"

Van at least had bought what he could for ourselves and several friends: dried lima beans, cooking fat, kerosene, sugar, eggs for preserving in lime; everything, in fact, that we could think of except charcoal, which we failed to acquire through a misunderstanding, and rice, which we foolishly supposed the Japanese would always furnish in sufficient quantity.

The Commandant had announced that our daily per capita rations would include one hundred grams of fish, four hundred grams of cereal (rice, corn, beans, camotes), two hundred grams of vegetables (if and when available), twenty grams of sugar, twenty grams of cooking fat, one gram of tea: for children under eleven, half-rations. In actual fact, our daily allotment between February and June, 1944 averaged less than 1500 calories (required calories for an average-sized man doing light work: 3000).

We had rice or cornmeal mush for breakfast, with tea and sometimes coconut milk or a banana (no sugar). Lunch: thin bean soup and rice; dinner, invariably vegetable stew or boiled vegetables with rice, tea and perhaps a few calamancis (native limes). The "available vegetables" proved to be a monotonous round of squash, camotes, green onions, chayotes, eggplant and three spinach-type greens called talinum, pechay and kang-kong. For a time, the Japanese sent in fish once or twice a week.

When they closed the gate, the Japanese also evicted all Filipino and Japanese stallkeepers. However, they promised that the vegetable market would continue as a camp project, operated by internees, and that the camp laundry, canteen and cold store would go on as before. The canteen had so little to sell that very soon buying on "canteen cards" for groups of six replaced the former haphazard rationing of "one to a customer." We could purchase what was available — seasonings, cornstarch, baking soda, cassava flour, black beans — only on days when our card number was posted.

Despite their promise, the Japanese very soon closed the cold store. It happened just at this time that Van learned from a neighbor how to preserve pork by "frying down" and sealing it with melted fat. With his help, I spent five days chopping and frying some twenty pounds of fresh pork, salt pork, bacon, and sausage meat, which we sealed for storage in cracker tins. We felt like blobs of grease ourselves, but it was a good thing we had kept on with it, for on the fifth day the cold store shut down for good.

The Japanese said they would send in chickens each day, which we could buy in alphabetical order, half a chicken per internee. However, after once around the alphabet, no more chickens came in. For a brief time they brought in eggs, rice bread and carabao milk. The trickle of milk, reserved primarily for the sick, soon dried up entirely. Eggs at first came in several times a week, bread every other day; each internee was allowed to buy one egg (eighty centavos) and half a loaf of bread. As weeks passed, the intervals grew longer, and by mid-March there was no more bread. Eggs lasted a bit longer: one (1.45 centavos) apiece every ten days or two weeks — then no more eggs.

The internee-operated market opened in such pandemonium that many a first day customer vowed (briefly) never again to brave the mobs for the sake of a few fruits and vegetables. A large crowd had gathered while marketmen were stacking produce in roped-off stalls. When the ropes were pulled away, a sudden stampede of internees, shoving and pushing their way to the stalls, almost overwhelmed the vegetable sellers and created a near-riot. Those who did not push were forced forward by the crush behind. Men brushed women aside and pounded the stall counters, shouting, "I'm first. Serve me!"

One simple fact explained this wild scramble: there was not enough for all. Since the Japanese declined to increase our allotment, the camp soon issued group ration tickets (four to twelve internees per ticket). Thereafter, we purchased in rotation, taking turns by card number at first and last choice.

Almost daily, the military issued new restrictions and regulations. Shanty building was halted, the Japanese allowing us to keep only what materials were essential for immediate repairs. Those who had planned shanty enlargements had to forego the idea. Most of us had a few extra nipa shingles and a piece or two of sawali for repairs in case of damage by future typhoons; what we could not hide was confiscated as "superfluous."

One of the military's most unpopular proclamations was a line-up roll call twice a day, at eight a.m. and six-thirty p.m. Building residents were ordered to assemble by room, shanty residents by area (A, B, C, and D), to be counted by monitors who passed along the totals to floor and area supervisors. The latter handed in their completed lists to the Japanese for checking with the official record.

Early each morning we were awakened by bright, cheerful (and to most of us, odious) music over the camp loudspeaker. In the evening our summons came at six-twenty-five. How long we waited at each roll call depended on whether or not our monitors counted us correctly the first time. If all was well, the Japanese usually dismissed us in about twenty minutes; but often the records did not tally: internees ill at the hospital or working on special jobs might be counted twice, or omitted entirely. When such errors occurred, we waited, sometimes as long as an hour and a half, while a complete recount was made. The Japanese allowed us at first to take chairs with us, to be placed evenly in a double line. In case of inspection, we were instructed to rise and bow when officials passed by.

Internee reactions to Japanese "get tough" policy shaded, predictably, from ultra-optimism to extreme pessimism. We all believed that American successes in the Gilberts and Marshalls had precipitated the crackdown, but our guesses differed widely on how soon the wave of victory would sweep Philippine shores. To most of us, those tiny islands in the Pacific seemed very far away.

Van Voorhees, most pessimistic of the pessimists, berated himself for having been caught with little food when the gate closed. To make up for his oversight, he was buying canned goods hand over fist from Hank Parfit. It was Howard Phillips, a middle-of-the-road moderate, who best expressed the uneasiness that most of us shared: "I knew the Japs would close the gate a few months before the end," he said, "but damn it, this is too soon!"

Before the end of February, Japanese Kempei-Tai officials scandalized the camp by arresting five men who had served, while the gate was open, as buyers. Four of them, charged with smuggling news transcripts, were taken for questioning to the Japanese guard house by the main gate. Kempei-Tai guards brutally beat one of the four, a man named Blair. After hours of pommelling with a rubber hose across head and kidneys, he was bound and held until evening, so badly hurt that when released he could scarcely stumble back to his quarters. Next morning, friends carried him to the camp hospital.

A day or two later, the other three buyers and a fifth not previously questioned were transported from camp and held incommunicado. They were allowed to take nothing with them. Although Japanese authorities in camp subsequently accepted a few parcels of food, clothing and medicine for them, we felt no assurance whatsoever that the supplies had been delivered.

After several weeks at the hospital, Blair, still in a wheelchair, was pushed into the Commandant's office for further questioning. When he was barely able to walk, he, too, was taken out and held incommunicado.

To compound the tragedy, a dark rumor spread that it was the "girlfriend" of a buyer who had tipped off the Japanese. This girl worked as secretary in the administration office, where, like other internee government workers, she associated with Japanese officials. Whether the charge was true or false I never learned, but I have always discounted it as a product of that mass fear which mesmerized many an internee mind with the spy bugaboo.

From outside came news of further Kempei-Tai activity: Juan Elizalde and Enrico Pirovano, along with half a dozen other loyal friends of Americans, had been imprisoned incommunicado. Exactly why, no one knew at the time: perhaps because of help they had rendered American prisoners, civilian and military alike; perhaps because the Japanese had discovered that they were aiding guerrillas.

Grief for our suffering friends and associates colored our thoughts each day, and by comparison made our own hardships unworthy of mention. Hoping and praying always, we could not help fearing the worst for those who had fallen victim to the implacable Japanese Gestapo.

Chapter Two

With the advent of the Japanese military regime, our internee administration underwent an alteration of form which, however, effected little actual change in operation. The central committee, stripped of its last tattered illusion of power, was disbanded and in its place a three-man "internee committee" was set up, with a British vice-chairman, Earl Carroll as financial vice-chairman, and none other than Carroll Grinnell to head the committee.

Although we were unable to curb Grinnell's power, we made the most of an opportunity offered by the committee itself to express disapproval. Because of clamorous demands to know what was discussed in conference with the Japanese, our committee proposed an election of three men, to be called "agent for the internees," who would serve as liaison officers between the Japanese and ourselves. The committee then bid for a vote of confidence by asking us to elect its members as our agents. Marvelling that Grinnell had the gall to put himself up for popular election, we promptly stamped disapproval on our ballots. Each of the three committee members gleaned about one hundred votes. By a landslide, we elected agents of our own choice: a wealthy Manila business man, a retired British consul, and Clyde DeWitt, a lawyer who had smuggled into camp a copy of Geneva Convention laws.

Our agents wrote scathing letters of protest to the Japanese regarding maltreatment of internees, specifically citing the cases of Blair and the four other camp buyers who had been seized by the Kempei-Tai. Quoting from Geneva Convention rules, they declared that "No civilized nation ever countenances such treatment of unarmed and defenseless men and women who are its prisoners, especially when they are held merely in 'protective custody'."

As to what went on in Japanese-internee committee conferences, our agents, who were not allowed to attend, were as much in the dark as the rest of us. Only from committee-issued edicts did we learn, belatedly, what probably had transpired. Dissatisfaction with the committee, specifically with Grinnell, inevitably brought about further disregard for our never widely respected camp laws. Two of the offenses most frequently committed in the past, thieving and refusal to perform camp work, increased progressively as food grew scarcer and resentment against internee authority more bitter.

From the beginning, certain internees had sought jobs that offered legitimate compensation in extra rations or, occasionally, illegitimate opportunities for graft. Among the former were kitchen and heavy duty workers; the latter, a much smaller group, included one of our early buyers, a Manila businessman of good standing, who had purchased food to resell at a profit in camp: a fine racket until he was caught and dismissed.

Since more and more internees were now reluctant to work unless they could earn extra food, inducements were sometimes offered: for example, a share of fruit and vegetables for garden workers. When the market became a camp project, many volunteered to work four or five hours at the stalls for no other reward than first choice of the day's produce, an advantage which ration tickets soon eliminated.

Always, there had been those who pilfered. Kitchen crews had been changed time and time again because of thieving. Now, several market workers were caught and reprimanded (but not dismissed — workers were too hard to find!) for hiding away what they wanted before the stalls opened.

Of all thefts attempted at this time, probably the most notorious happened in the unlikeliest spot: the fish-cleaning detail. The squad supervisor, another prominent Manila business man, one day whispered to a fellow-worker, "Stick a couple of the biggest ones under your apron. I'll split with you later." The man he had selected as his partner-in-crime chanced to be an Englishman of impeccable honor and dignity, the prewar manager of a British banking firm in Manila. Outraged and insulted, the Englishman ripped off his apron, flung it on the table and resigned on the spot, declaring emphatically as he strode away, "I refuse to work with a scoundrel!"

The crassly conniving supervisor became a camp laughing-stock. Whether or not he subsequently approached a more willing co-worker, his fish-stealing days were numbered, for the Japanese soon eliminated that item from our diet.

To round up ever-growing numbers of internees who shirked jobs that held no recompense of extra food, the director of work assignment made a determined effort to enlarge his roll of camp workers. Although well-intentioned, the campaign accomplished little that was constructive, and resulted in such absurdities as posting over-aged men beside wash troughs to tell other internees how much water they could use. Water in those days being plentiful, no one paid the slightest attention to elderly checkers, who soon gave up in disgust.

The director's personality did not help him to gain general cooperation. Our minor camp officials, and indeed all camp workers, could be classified roughly in three categories: the obliging and helpful, who were in the majority; the arrogant snarlers, who appeared to believe that any service rendered was a favor for which the rest of us should be duly grateful; and the pompous gauleiter-type, who liked to throw around the weight of their wee bit of authority. The director of work assignment belonged to the third group.

One day as Van was crossing the garden path, the director accosted him. "You're captain of the wall path patrol, aren't

229

you?" Van replied that he was, and the director continued, "Well now, look here, that isn't listed on the work assignment."

"It's a voluntary job," Van explained. "I have a medical certificate exempting me from camp work, but I want to do what I can as long as I'm able to."

It happened that quite recently I had implored Van to give up his job, much as he liked it. Not only was it dangerous to prowl around in the dark looking for Filipino thieves who were sure to be armed with knives, but also his health had declined so steadily that he needed all possible rest to recover his strength. However, he explained that when he wakened with asthma, as he did each night, it was helpful to have something to do until he could sleep again. After a series of vitamin B injections had diminished recurrent beriberi symptoms, I stopped protesting.

The director of work assignment, who had been fully informed of Van's state of health, sputtered, "Well now, see here, fellow, we don't honor those doctor's certificates any more. Too many faked ones. We want everybody on the work assignment rolls — looks better that way. You're doing the job anyway — might as well get credit for it."

"And suppose I have to quit next week?" Van retorted. "I'm not going on the work assignment roll, and if there's any question, Dr Fletcher will back me. I assume you don't question his work or reputation as a doctor?"

"Now don't get mad," the director replied. "We're starting a new system — want to get everybody to work. Harrumph! What does your wife do, now?"

"She's assigned to vegetable duty."

"Well now, we've got too many vegetable workers. How'd she like to work in the garden, fellow?"

At that, Van exploded, "My wife is *not* going to work in the garden, and *don't* call me fellow!"

Still in a blind fury, Van found me in the shanty and related the details of his encounter.

"He probably doesn't like my hiring someone to do the vegetable job," I remarked.

"It's none of his damn business!"

"Well, anyway, I think it's time to look for another job. Maybe I can get office work."

After he had calmed down, Van agreed with me. If the director of work assignment said there were too many vegetable workers, then that was that; nothing could be gained by trying to buck him.

That same afternoon, Norris Wadsworth dropped by the shanty to tell Van about changes on the patrol schedule. When we mentioned the director's conversation and my decision to scout around for an office job, Norris exclaimed, "You don't say! I've just applied to the work assignment board for a typist, someone who can come to my shanty — that's my only office, you know. You'd be perfect for the job."

I told him that I had my own typewriter, and could work wherever it suited him best . "Then you can work right here, on your own time," he replied. "I'll stop by and tell the director I've hired you."

Soon after I began my new job, the Japanese ordered camp officials to lock up all typewriters not in use for camp business, as they suspected that news transcripts were being typed in Santo Tomás from broadcasts over a hidden radio. Those used for camp work were registered and listed with type samples. I blessed the lucky chance that made it possible for me to keep mine.

Typing schedules, memos and instructions was routine and not particularly interesting work, but Norris Wadsworth's reports, on the other hand, often read like cops-and-robbers thrillers. Although the night chases frequently ended in escape, sometimes Filipinos were caught red-handed and turned over to the Japanese.

At this particular time, Santo Tomás was a lodestone for robbers. Not long before, we had dressed in threadbare rags:

women had cut off worn slacks to the knees, had made skirts and blouses of old dresses, had knitted socks and panties of coarse string. Then came our treasure chest of clothing, materials, canned goods and other Red Cross gifts. Filipinos, ragged and hungry themselves, risked punishment from the Japanese to ransack our comparative — and temporary — opulence. Poor devils, one could not blame them too much; like us, they had every day less and less food, less and less freedom. When they managed to escape empty-handed, most of us were glad; it meant no loss to us, and only the most vengeful could have wished them exposed to the mercies of the Japanese.

Chapter Three

Almost unnoticed in the upheaval of camp affairs under the military, a new decree brightened life for some of us: the Japanese finally allowed women to sleep in shanties. As Van anticipated when he built our shanty, they needed more space for the steady tide of internee flowing in from hospitals and homes in Manila. When the announcement was made, eager wives began hotfooting the shanty trails — "almost indecent haste," someone called it. Be that as it may, most of us who tarried a few days or weeks did so only because of alterations needed to accommodate us in our shacks. During the day, the 600-odd shanties that sprawled over the campus housed some 2000 internees. The new rule made it possible for approximately 1200 of them — men, women and children — to sleep out.

An amusing side-effect of the wives' sudden exodus: overnight, beards disappeared from the faces of the few stalwart males who had clung all this while to their hirsute decoration. Ribald laughter rippled through our prison air as face after face came up clean-shaven, and many a man went for days unrecognized by camp acquaintances. Brave men, to endure snubs and ridicule for the sake of the "little women" who came to share their bed and board, but evidently not their beards!

Bed and board naturally did not include built-in toilet facilities, which, for men in our area, were a block away in the Education building. Women used two toilets in a wooden shack behind the Ed building. At night, the going was difficult, as the path to the "little house on the hill" was dark and uneven.

We walked even farther for a bath: to the main building, or, at certain hours, across the garden to open air showers normally reserved for men. Van soon conceived an ingenious plan for my convenience: he enclosed a corner of our dressing room so that I could "dip bathe" myself from an earthenware jar, using a dipper made by nailing a tin can to the end of a bamboo stick. Bath water cascaded through the slat floor and trickled off into a ditch which marked the rear border of our grounds.

After so many months in a room with forty other women, nice women though they were, the blessedness of living privately with one's own husband eludes description; although privacy in a shanty, it must be added, is a relative term. The nipa walls which partially secluded us from view did not in the least exclude, or even diminish, sound, especially the sound of voices from nearby shanties. Loud conversations overheard often reminded us to lower our own voices.

Although no thought of our comfort had motivated their shanty edict, the Japanese soon afterwards performed several consciously "magnanimous" acts for our benefit: first they brought in personal packages from home. Van and I received three, two of them addressed in my father's handwriting. For moments before I made a move to open the parcels. I stared at the beloved, familiar script, until finally Van remarked gently, "There might be something worth looking at inside, too."

There was, indeed: an assortment of priceless necessities and luxuries — vitamin tablets, cheese, cocoa, dried soups, razor blades, soap and toilet articles, towels and clothing, and many other things. Ours had come through in good condition; some internees were less fortunate. One luckless man received an empty box, broken open so that the contents were either lost or stolen en route.

Next, there were cables from home: ours read, "Overjoyed receive message. All well. . . ." Although the cable was undated, we knew that the "message" was the letter that Daré had smuggled in, and we blessed the day we had met that strange but remarkable woman. And finally, at long last, the Japanese delivered letters from home. In the first batch, I received two from my mother, one dated May, the other August, 1943.

We never solved the mystery of why the unpredictable Japanese had relaxed their ban on correspondence (they now also allowed us to send home each month a twenty-five-word typewritten postcard) — at the very time that they were clamping down the lid more tightly over us in other respects. There is no doubt that adverse war news precipitated their toughness. Although they admitted no defeats, we sensed their worry in each new restriction, each cancelled privilege, each exhortation to plant more vegetables because food would become ever scarcer.

The camp had opened a second public garden in a field that fronted the Seminary, and, like most of our neighbors, Van and I also heeded the admonition to try our luck on the land. A camp gardener whom we had hired to help us transplanted six banana trees to our front yard; then, poor man, he was jailed for having sent out Red Cross supplies to his Filipina wife and children. His trees flourished — which was more than we could boast of onion and string bean beds we had planted ourselves.

A few internees began to raise chickens. Those that thrived — and not all did — brought their owners a small income from the sale of eggs.

The war news that so disconcerted the Japanese gave us plenty to cheer about, and plenty to laugh about, too, as told by the *Tribune*. One story, for instance, depicted invincible Japanese soldiers annihilating foolhardy Americans who had attempted a beachhead on a certain island; several days later, Japanese planes were reported bombing *our* positions on that very same island! Our army's morale, they claimed, was shattered;

our soldiers quavered and shook with terror at the mere thought of a Japanese soldier. But through all the fables, we followed the steady, tireless progress of our armed forces. Although they ridiculed the notion that American troops would ever return to the Philippines, the Japanese began in March to hold practice air raid alerts and blackouts.

Howard and Ellie Phillips became so encouraged — or apprehensive — about the proximity of our planes that they hired construction men to dig them an air raid shelter. Ellie, the perpetual worrier, could no longer center her anxieties on Howard, who had miraculously recovered from TB; hence she focused them on a new target: namely, "What will happen to us all when the Battle of Manila begins?"

The Phillips' shanty was near the east wall, where Japanese patrols passed regularly. As the shelter neared completion, a soldier, pointing to the freshly sodded bamboo roof, stammered in broken English, "Very nice, but no need." He waved his arm skyward. "No danger. No come back."

Ellie recounted the incident with obvious glee. "I told him it would be a nice, cool place to sit in the hot season anyway. I don't think our planes are coming back quite yet, but at least we're prepared when they do."

"You don't think that they're going to bomb Santo Tomás, do you?" I asked her.

"Who knows? Maybe the Nips will say they've taken us all out of here just so our planes *will* bomb us. Or maybe they'll bomb us themselves and say our planes did it. I'm taking no chances."

Whatever might have been their intentions about bombing Santo Tomás, the Japanese presently discommoded the Phillips and many other internees by decreeing that shanties be moved back at least fifty feet from the wall. Trying thought it was, the ultimatum was scarcely unreasonable, for the Japanese caught Wally King and helper, Maxie Brummett, trying to smuggle out canned goods.

236

Our legal board sentenced both men to a month in jail and confiscated their shanties, to be later returned or not as the court saw fit. Maxie Brummett pleaded with them not to evict his wife and small daughter. "I deserve my sentence," he admitted, "but don't punish my wife and baby for something they had nothing to do with."

Many of us felt sorry for Maxie, a former building contractor who, we believed, had assisted Wally King only because he needed money to feed his family. After due consideration, the court promised to grant his request; then, when Maxie was safely locked up, they reversed the decision.

Meanwhile, the Japanese ordered internees to build a barbed wire fence around the top of the wall, an order which our internee agents immediately protested on the grounds that forced labor was illegal in a civilian prison camp. In the end, the Japanese paid a few pesos to each internee worker so that the labor could not be considered "forced."

Far more disastrous to those affected was the shanty-moving edict. Frenzied measuring began all over camp, and dozens of shanties were condemned: our own was safe only by inches. Big Van's was caught behind the line; also Ralph Baskerville's, Stew Raab's, the Phillips' and, of course, Wally King's.

The committee on shanty sites opened up new plots of ground at the edge of the garden, and those who had to move drew lots for locations. Shacks that were not too heavy or too dilapidated were transported intact from the old spot to the new. As shanty owners pitched in to help one another, we witnessed the strange spectacle of houses marching slowly across the garden, propelled by men who strained under their load like ants with a giant beetle in tow.

Within a few days of the shanty moving order, the Japanese announced a new move to Los Baños. As before, those who wished to go could volunteer and other lots would be drawn. To our surprise, Ellie and Howard Phillips decided to volunteer. "Our shanty is too big to move," Ellie explained, " and parts of it are old and rotten. We can't get building materials to repair it, so what's the use of going to all the trouble of tearing it apart and reassembling it, only to end up being uncomfortable?"

When I reminded her that living quarters in Los Baños were cramped by shanty standards, she replied, "We plan to build a daytime shanty in the woods. Lots of people have done it. Besides, even if we could fix up our shanty here, we couldn't move the air raid shelter. I'm not worried about bombings in Los Baños, but Emily, it's going to be bad here. Besides, the food situation is getting grimmer every day. They say Los Baños is better."

I asked her whether she planned to take all her food supplies, and she said, "Everything but the limed eggs. We'll sell those and buy fresh ones in Los Baños where they still have plenty. If you want any, you're welcome to about a hundred. I've already promised the rest. Another thing, if you'd like our man to work for you, I think he'd be glad to have the job. We want to take him, but he doesn't want to leave because his friends are here."

We bought the eggs, but we did not see our way clear to feed the Phillips' man. Since no one else did, either, he decided after all to go to Los Baños: three meals a day transcend casual companionship, especially in a concentration camp.

When Ellie and Howard left, they sold their old shanty to Big Van. His own being too heavy to move all in a piece, he dismantled both shanties and had a new house built from the useable parts. Although it lacked the homey attractiveness of his little cottage, Big Van's composite shanty preserved most of his comforts, including the screened bedroom.

It often seemed that the Japanese sharpened their wits thinking up new restrictions. In April they imposed a particularly trying one on shanty dwellers: no more cooking in shanties until adequate fire protection was assured and communal cooking sheds were built for all. The fire hazard was a real one, especially now that charcoal shortages had forced many of us to burn high-flaming wood and bamboo; and there was no doubt that community cooking facilities were long overdue.

Nevertheless, all of us who lived in shanties cursed the Japanese as we hauled pots and pans, mixing bowls, knives and forks, fuel and food to makeshift open-air "kitchens," which were nothing more than benches to set stoves on. Frequently three or four of us prepared meals at the same time. April's hot winds fanned our fires to infernos that leapt up to scorch our faces and singe our eyebrows. Then, just as the flames subsided enough to make cooking possible, the wood would burn out, and back to our shanties we would trek for more fuel. Meanwhile, ants and flies crawled happily over our half-prepared meals. By the time we finished, smoky-eyed, dripping with perspiration and reeling from the heat of the fire and sun, we no longer had any appetite for the food we had cooked.

Some of us began surreptitiously to cook in our shanties, and soon there were few who regularly used the outside "kitchens," although we all did so on occasion to avert suspicion. Van hid our kerosene stove behind the screens that enclosed my dip bath, and there I boiled or baked food with little risk of detection: no smoke to attract attention, no sizzle as with frying, no coals to smoulder if a sudden inspection should force us to extinguish the fire.

What consideration for fellow internees and threats from our former Commandant had failed to accomplish, the Japanese military edict achieved in a hurry. Our committee members, who naturally wanted to cook in their own shanties, promptly organized camp workers to build outdoor kitchens: rude, open-sided structures of bamboo and nipa which contained several charcoal stoves, not very conveniently arranged, but better than nothing for those who could find and afford anything to cook.

Shanty owners speedily complied with minimum safety regulations. Our own kitchen was well prospected: when Van designed it, he had incorporated safety measures along with many conveniences. Our stoves stood in a metal-lined niche under a ceiling of sheet iron which shielded the nipa roof. Conveniences included a fawcetted, five-gallon water tank, bought from the personal service; a galvanized iron drainboard; and a sink which emptied itself through a bamboo pipe into the ditch. Nearly all the conveniences of home: no wonder I rejoiced when the ban was lifted!

Chapter Four

The months of the hot season passed slowly, each new day forging another ponderous link to an interminable chain of days. Time was a vast grey sea, and we in Santo Tomás were tiny bits of flotsam tossing wearily on its surface. Anxieties of an uncertain future magnified a hundredfold the irritations of daily existence, except when serious trouble numbed the senses to all but pending problems or tragedies of the day.

Life often seemed an endless succession of standing in line. Up at six-thirty, line up for the little house on the hill, line up for breakfast, then for roll call (our shanty area assembled in front of the Education building); after roll call, line up for market, for the canteen, for this, for that, until day finally ended with the evening line up for roll call. Yet at least there still were occasionally things worth lining up for: a few fruits and vegetables, from time to time an egg or a bit of cassava flour.

Leisure hours were frequently devoted to perpetual pitched battles against omnivorous insects, from cereal worms to bedbugs. We had hoped that the shanty would escape bug infestation, but soon I discovered a bug on Van's pillow. I checked the mattress: not a sign of them; then I looked at the springs and was horrified to discover literally hundreds of vermin crawling among the steel coils. To kill them off in a hurry, Van lighted a kerosene-soaked asbestos torch and burned them out of their ill-chosen nests. Fascinated, we watched a rain of frizzled bedbugs plummet to the floor.

When someone told us of finding bedbugs in the bindings of library books, we concluded that ours must have emerged from such a source — which might explain why Van's bed harbored a surfeit while mine had none: I always read outside the screened room because the light was brighter.

The bugs never again took up residence in Van's bed, but we found them in our wooden furniture, where they could not be so easily exterminated. Boiling water killed them, but their eggs, buried deep in the wood, survived to hatch another day. Hence the intermittent warfare continued for weeks, and the vigilance always.

With the advent of rain came the usual plague of ants on the march, attacking our scant sugar reserves; and mosquitos; and flies which buzzed maddeningly in our ears, swarming over food and bare legs.

Second only to the insects, our most incessant irritant was the noise: exclamations, arguments, shouts, buzzing conversation and in shanty areas, record players. An ebullient little Syrian named Phil Shaouy, who lived across the ditch from us, owned a record player which often clattered on from morning to night, through meal hours, work hours and quiet hours. Favored numbers he would play for himself and his various girlfriends over and over and over again, until our heads throbbed to the repetitive beat. The recording of a brittle, peppy, masculine voice singing, "I'll take the train, you can go by boat!" topped my list-for-smashing, and not far below it was "Tomorrow is a *Lovely* Day!"

We were amazed one day to hear several brand new, patriotic American records which Phil said a friend outside had sent him — a gift, perhaps, from some American submarine? We advised a degree of caution in playing such obvious propaganda songs as "Any Bonds Today?" and "The Man Behind the Man Behind the Gun."

Phil shrugged. "Why be careful? The Japs are too dumb to understand them. Anyway, if they want to get tough — I'm a little man, but I can lick my weight in wildcats!"

His ability to "lick his weight in wildcats" was Phil's favorite boast. I noticed, however, that he did not play his new records when guards wandered close to our shanties: Japanese soldiers, unlike wildcats, carry guns.

The wet season brought new noise to shanty areas: the croaking of a million frogs. Soothing in the distance, even soporific like a lullaby, their chorus boomed up loud as a brass band from the swamp-mud just below our windows.

It was in this season of mud and mildewing clothes that the Japanese shut down the camp laundry; we wondered only that they had not done so earlier. During the ensuing months, the sun, our only bleaching agent, seldom shone; but by now we scarcely noticed such trivialities as garments that were spotted and "tattle-tale grey."

My greatest anxiety as the dank, humid weather settled down upon us once again, was Van's health. Weakened by recent sieges of flu and dengue fever, he had little strength to combat the ever more acute assaults of asthma. There came a day — the 25th of May, 1944 — that haunts my memory like a nightmare. On that day, he suffered an attack so tenacious that asthma powder gave no relief. Alarmed, I called for help to our next door neighbor, Don Keiffer, who rushed immediately for assistance and, with three other men, carried Van to the men's ward at the camp hospital.

A nurse gave him a shot of Japanese adrenalin, then went off to find a doctor. I stayed by his bedside, helplessly watching his struggle for breath; the weak Japanese adrenalin was ineffectual.

Suddenly he reached for my hand. "I — can't — make it," he gasped. "Goodbye, darling."

He closed his eyes and stopped breathing. I tried to find his pulse. His heart, I thought, had stopped beating.

I ran to the hall, screaming, "Get a doctor quick! I think my husband is dead."

243

The nurse was coming up the stairs. "I've found the doctor," she said. "He'll be up in a minute."

"Oh, please tell him to hurry," I implored her. One glance at Van's clammy grey face sent her dashing downstairs. I began to cry. Later, I remembered that men who were patients in nearby beds looked silently on with sad, compassionate eyes. At the time, I was conscious only of Van, stretched out so still on the hospital cot.

After what seemed a century, but was actually only a few minutes, the nurse came back with a missionary doctor. He felt Van's pulse and assured me that he was still alive. Dispatching the nurse for more adrenalin, he began to administer artificial respiration. Van rallied for a moment, then after a few breaths, gave up again. The doctor resumed artificial respiration. At last, Van's tired lungs responded, and he dropped off to sleep, breathing evenly and regularly now. The two shots of adrenalin had finally taken effect.

I stayed at his side until he awakened two hours later. Although he looked pale and weak, he insisted that he felt all right, and he wanted to go back to the shanty. With Don Keiffer's help, we left the hospital, Van supporting himself on our shoulders. As soon as we reached the shanty, he collapsed on the bed, exhausted from the effort of moving. Almost immediately, another asthma attack started.

While I feverishly lighted asthma powder, Don rushed off for Dr Fletcher. They returned soon, and with them came a friend who looked to me like an angel bearing heaven's greatest gift: a vial of American adrenalin. The bearer was the wife of Leonard Self, a dry season asthmatic whose allergy usually lasted from January through April. Leonard had bought quantities of adrenalin, which his wife, a former nurse, injected as he needed it.

Torn between gratitude and a feeling of guilt at accepting so precious a gift, I asked her whether her own husband might not later need it. She replied that Leonard himself had sent her. "He has enough adrenalin for another full season," she continued. "If we're here longer than that, we'll be dead from starvation, anyway, so he won't need adrenalin."

A few moments after the injection, Van's muscles relaxed their vise-like grip on his chest; he began to breathe freely and after a short rest, he felt all right again. To this day, I bless Leonard Self and his wife in my prayers.

Chapter Five

On Emperor Hirohito's birthday, April 29th, the Japanese "magnanimously" accepted for us some meat sent in by the International YMCA — the first fresh line chow meat since Christmas, when beef stew was served. No steak at the Waldorf had ever tasted better than the three dinners provided by our hosts of the Y: beef stew for the Emperor's birthday, vegetable stew with beef the following day, fried rice with ham to finish off the third day. Although Y officials tried repeatedly to duplicate their gift, never again were they successful: the Japanese thereafter neither accepted nor provided a single smidgeon of meat for their prisoners at Santo Tomás. The scarcity of food alarmed everyone. Internees were not yet starving only because they were using up comfort kits and other food reserves. In May, the height of the mango season, our market ration was one mango for two persons, three times a week. By the end of May, our staple bulk was cut off: no more camotes.

As long as we could buy local produce, Van and I, like many others, had not claimed our share of line chow; but now gradually we were forced back onto the line, at first for bananas and calamancis, or for breakfast mush to substitute for eggs as a "binder" in hot cakes or muffins. Finally, when we could buy no more camotes, we had to go onto the dinner line for rice. As the line lengthened, rations became proportionally shorter.

In a desperate last minute attempt to stave off starvation, Earl

Carroll called together a group of Santo Tomás business men and proposed that those who could raise funds outside sign notes to be cashed through the Japanese, who could then use the money to buy more food. The plan fell through, because the Japanese refused to honor internee-signed notes.

At that critical moment, there came to our rescue a courageous young Filipino, Luis de Alcuaz, a professor at Santo Tomás who was allowed to maintain in camp a liaison office between University administrators and the Japanese. When he learned that Earl Carroll's proposal had been rejected, Professor Alcuaz volunteered to smuggle our internee notes, countersigned by Tommy Wolff in the name of the Red Cross, to be cashed in Manila. Earl subsequently white-lied to the Japanese that he had raised funds from internees who had money in camp.

We observed with interest that Van Voorhees signed a substantial note. Doubtless he would have pooh-poohed as pure humbug the conclusions we drew as to his true sentiments toward "the other half!"

Earl Carroll's only mistake was not borrowing enough. The hundred-thousand-odd dollars signed for by public-spirited internees was soon sucked up the chimney in a draft of vaulting prices; but at least for a few months our daily ration was slightly better than Japanese issue.

Partly to blame for the tasteless messes dished out each night as vegetable stew was an unimaginative kitchen crew. When Earl Carroll brought in protein-rich peanuts and mongo beans, new cooks were chosen, who created crisp patties that tasted almost like meat cakes. Another palatable innovation was hominy made from dried corn furnished by the Japanese as part of our cereal ration — previous cooks had stewed it, which turned it into a very, very tough and indigestible substance. Any change was welcome, except the consistent change of less and less food.

The acute need for food brought about the resurgence of smuggling which had waned after the conviction of Wally

King and Maxie Brummett. Both men now were free again, and their shanties restored. No longer did anyone attempt to send out canned goods; instead, hams and sides of bacon trickled in to us over the wall. Because the risk of detection by Japanese patrols was great, smugglers lay low for several weeks after each haul.

Twice we shared in the contraband: for 175 pesos, we split a slab of bacon with Stew Raab; and we divided a ham, for 237 pesos, with Big Van. Two hundred and six American dollars was a fabulous price indeed for four pounds of bacon and half a ham; but money balanced against hunger weighs light in the scales.

As food became ever more persistent a topic of thought and conversation, a mild form of madness began to attack internees. To compensate for gnawing gastronomical cravings, many pored over tempting food advertisements in old magazines, copying and trading recipes for succulent dishes far beyond the realm of possibility in our present world.

Recipe trading was wholesome and helpful when internees worked out substitutes for ingredients that we did not have. Someone discovered, for example, that a type of hot bread could be made from sour mush and soda, which required no eggs and only half the flour called for in the original recipe. In chop suey, we found that we could substitute for water chestnuts a root vegetable called cincamas, available in the market, which tasted approximately like an apple crossed with a raw turnip. We learned to bake in banana leaves, to rub our skillets with salt to save shortening, and to reboil leftover beans that were on the verge of souring.

Exchanging dream recipes, however, denoted near-insanity. The very thought of such foods made one hungrier. Many of us tried hard to eject from our minds the food images that haunted us. When lobsters and steaks were mentioned, we changed the subject; yet we could not always control our thoughts, or even our conversation.

Hunger caused more and more internees to refuse camp jobs that offered no compensation in extra food. In July, facing a shortage of vegetable peelers, the work assignment board found it expedient to rule that helpers could take home camote skins and other refuse from which they might salvage a morsel of edible stuff. To prevent over-thick peeling, no one was permitted to carry away her own leavings; those who wanted them received a portion of scraps swept together in large baskets.

It so happened that the Japanese had recently disbanded Norris Wadsworth's night patrols, which ended my job of typing reports and schedules. I had been assigned once again to vegetable duty, on call whenever produce came in. As soon as the refuse reward was offered, internees began clamoring for vegetable work — and I gratefully exchanged, for typist work with the special activities committee, a job which, however distasteful to me, had now become a plum eagerly sought after by many.

Early in August the Japanese struck two vital blows: they closed the vegetable market, and they ordered us, individually and collectively, to turn over for deposit in the Bank of Taiwan all money in our possession. Each adult internee, they stated, would be permitted to withdraw fifty pesos a month; for children under ten, twenty-five pesos a month. The Commandant would allow our committee such sums as he deemed essential to run the camp. The new order, they informed us, was promulgated "to protect us from robbery, to increase our money through interest, to prevent needless or wasteful expenditures, to curb gambling and to steady the camp's economic position by making our money last as long as possible."

It was not difficult to make the money last, for the edict had rendered virtually worthless our "Mickey Mouse" currency. Fifty pesos would buy next to nothing — and, except for smuggled wares, there was even less to be bought in camp. No longer was it possible to hire services for cash, although many internees were willing to work for food and a few for credit. Van and

I lost our helper, a lad who had hauled water and done chores about the shanty; but his two younger brothers agreed, for twenty-five dollars (gold) a month in promissory notes, to bring our food from the chow line. Often we gave them a part of our ration.

A wild splurge of buying and selling preceded the currency call-in date, and when the day arrived, many of us ignored the order because we hoped that later we might have a chance to buy smuggled hams or bacon. Our hopes were dashed when smugglers refused, for a time, at least, to deal in "hot" Mickey Mouse: for good reason, because the Japanese began searching rooms and shanties for hidden currency. During their first spot inspection in the main building, they discovered two internees who possessed more than the allotted fifty pesos. The Commandment confined the offenders for a week to their rooms and forthwith issued a second notice to Carroll Grinnell:

"In my order of August first requiring that all money in the possession of internees be turned in to your committee for deposit in the Bank of Taiwan, it is provided that internees found in possession of money in excess of the authorized amount will be punished. The cases just discovered of violations of this order have been dealt with lightly because there was some excuse, but the monies illegally possessed are turned over to your committee for safekeeping. There may be other internees who have more money than is allowed this month, and also in currencies other than Japanese Military Notes. Internees are ordered to turn in your committee any money stilll in their possession. . . ."

Van and I heeded this warning by turning in for ourselves 500 pesos of the more than 4000 pesos Mickey Mouse in our possession; the rest we donated to the committee for camp use. However, we kept 200 pesos in good Philippine bills. Current rate of exchange: twenty pesos Japanese to one peso Philippine. Van hollowed out a stick of wood, stuffed the 200 pesos inside, then nailed across the opening another piece of wood. This unlikely treasure chest we tossed carelessly

251

into our woodbox, fingers crossed that it would never attract a second glance.

Many internees retained sizeable sums of money, some burying it in the ground near their shanties. Phil Shaouy, who had amassed wads of Mickey Mouse from the sale of Philippine embroidery factories he had owned before the war, banked under a bush what cash he had not already lent to Earl Carroll and others. Whenever we saw him digging near his shanty, we knew that he had discovered a good loan risk, or possibly something edible to buy — for it was not long until smugglers again wanted Mickey Mouse.

After the vegetable market was no more, hunger stalked us relentlessly. Line chow, including supplemental food bought by the camp, contained less than half the calories we needed. Our diet lacked vitamins, minerals and all proteins except what few could be found in cereals. We remembered with longing the pittance that had been in the end our weekly market ration: half a papaya, a few tiny eggplants and bananas. How we had complained about paying twelve pesos for a papaya, 1.50 pesos apiece for bananas; yet now, we would have given our entire monthly allowance, or more if we had it, for that same small allotment.

In July, statistics were compiled as a basis of protest to the Japanese: average loss of weight for men from the beginning of internment, 31.4 pounds; for women, 17.7 pounds (percentages of original weight loss: men, 18.3%, women, 13.4%). In August the rate of loss accelerated sharply.

Parents, unable to buy supplemental food for their children, wrote a letter of protest through the Commandant to the Commander-in-Chief of the Imperial Japanese Army in the Philippines. The letter pointed out that more than fifty percent of the children were underweight, some of them seriously so; that more than fifty percent had defective teeth; that the Japanese food allowance had been reduced "from a bare maintenance to a starvation level," and that the children's allowance was only half that of an adult over ten.

They requested that "children be given an adequate ration which will include sufficient quantities of corn, vegetables, fruit, meat, and the following essential supplementary items: one egg per day per child; one pint of milk per day per child up to six years of age; one-half pint of milk per day per child from six to eighteen years of age; three bananas per day per child; one-half kilo of peanut butter per child per week."

The letter continued: "In requesting the above, we believe we are asking for nothing which present conditions make impossible. All these items are produced in or near Manila in large quantities. . . . From information given to the internees in this camp by a Japanese official who had been interned in the United States, we know that the Japanese children there are being especially well cared for. Therefore, we request that steps be taken immediately to provide reciprocal treatment for our children. We cannot reconcile the traditional Japanese love for children with the treatment being accorded to the children in this camp."

The Commander-in-Chief did not acknowledge the letter, nor did the Japanese provide more food for the children. To the contrary, they cut fruit, vegetable and cereal rations. Camp food committees saw to it that children shared at least equally with adults; but that share was far less than their growing bodies needed. The Commandant declared in speech after speech that food was hard to obtain in Manila, that he was trying to get more for us (which we did not believe), that the only solution was to plant more vegetables in our gardens. Internees growing weaker each day from insufficient food must work twice as hard to escape starvation tomorrow!

From time to time, the camp threw open talinum patches which already had been plucked for the kitchen. Although a few miserable leaves they gleaned made it hardly worth the effort, internees searched diligently among rows of bare stalks, grateful if an hour's labor netted them a quarter-cup.

253

During those months, we learned to relish as rare delicacies the buds of banana stalks. It was shortly after the market closed that Van and I first sampled a bud, which came from one of our own trees. Day by day we had watched the unfolding of slender green fingers clustered near the top — twenty-seven bananas in all; then we had cut the bud so that the tree's strength would nourish the fruit. We shared it with a neighbor who showed us how to cook it with garlic and dried onions which we had bought during the last days of the market. The result tasted to us at the time as exotically tempting as any dish our imagination could conjure.

As soon as the bananas matured, we cut them and brought them inside to ripen. With perfect timing, two or three turned gold in a day, more precious to us by far than replicas in solid gold.

After bananas are harvested, the tree must be chopped so that new trees can spring up from its roots. When Van cut ours, he gave the trunk to a friend who had helped him. What was edible made three meals for his family: anything to fill the hollows.

Stranger things were eaten to stay the gripping pangs of an empty stomach: cats and rats, which at least provided nutriment; bulbs of canna plants, leaves of bushes, roots of trees, which provided only bulk. Although camp officials warned that canna roots were poisonous, and urged us to eschew such harmfully fibrous stuffs as leaves and tree trunks, many were too hungry to care how ill they became from eating outlandish vegetation never intended for human consumption. It surprised no one, least of all the doctors, that an epidemic of intestinal disease swept the camp. The Japanese, who had recently vaccinated and inoculated us against smallpox, cholera, typhoid and bubonic plague, constantly denied us the nourishment that would have helped to prevent most of our intestinal illnesses. Improper sanitation afforded fertile breeding grounds for a host of parasites which preyed the more easily on tissues already weakened with hunger and often damaged by coarse food substitutes.

To eliminate one possible source of infection, the doctors

inaugurated the pasteurization of coconut milk and ordered that coconut water, impossible to sterilize, be discarded. Always before, graters had freely given away the nutritive and refreshing coconut juice, which could not be used in milk because it turned rancid overnight. Now that dietary supplement was banned. Next, the doctors declared our drinking water impure and strongly advised us to boil every drop we drank. For a while, most of us complied; but boiling water consumed more fuel than we could spare.

During past months, the camp kitchens had been burning trees, for want of gas and charcoal, to prepare three so-called meals a day for all. Short rations cut fuel needs very little, for even the tasteless broth and ginger tea served at noon required cooking — and gas pressure had dropped so low that the tiny blue flames dotting the burners would frequently snuff out long before the food was even warmed through, much less cooked. One noticed now a growing barrenness in the once-verdant campus lanes as branch after branch, finally tree after tree, was felled for firewood.

Yet even this was not enough. As a fuel-saving device, the food committee offered semi-weekly allotments of raw rice, rice flour and cornmeal to all who preferred to cook their own cereals. To preclude cheating, "raw" ration meal tickets were stamped with a large "R", signaling chow line servers to ladle out only non-cereal foods.

Despite individual fuel shortages, many of us jumped at the chance to prepare cereals as we chose. Only twice after the closing of the gate did the Japanese allow us to buy minute portions of charcoal, which we eked out with wood and bamboo. After cooking, we doused our burning coals with water and dried them for re-use, yet no measure of conservation could replenish the fast-dwindling piles. It was a toss-up which would run out first, fuel or food; we could only pray that the dilemma would not be finally resolved in a total disappearance of both. Awaiting the outcome, we struggled to keep going from day to day, and tried to banish worry about the future, over which we had absolutely no control.

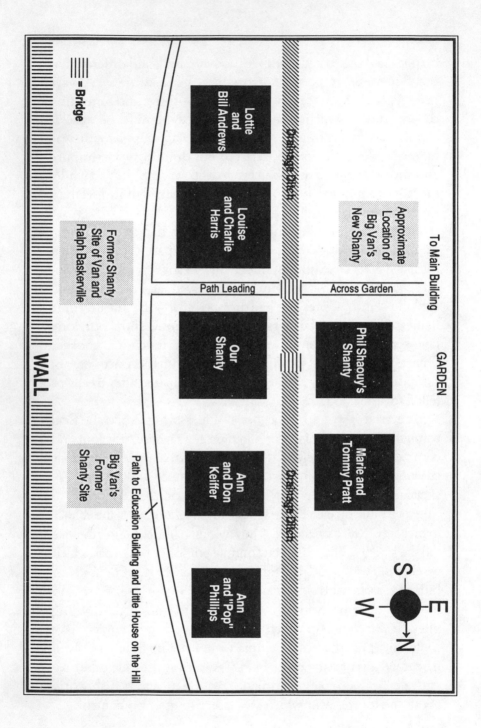

= Bridge

Lottie and Bill Andrews

Louise and Charlie Harris

Former Shanty Site of Van and Ralph Baskerville

Approximate Location of Big Van's New Shanty

To Main Building

GARDEN

Path Leading Across Garden

Our Shanty

Phil Shaouy's Shanty

WALL

Marie and Tommy Pratt

Ann and Don Keiffer

Big Van's Former Shanty Site

Path to Education Building and Little House on the Hill

Ann and "Pop" Phillips

N
W — E
S

Chapter Six

As the cheerless weeks went by, Van's ill health continued. Scarcely a day passed without some revealing notation in my tiny diary: "Van ill today; Dr Fletcher came to see him. . . Van worse. . . . Van a little better. . . Worse again today. . . To hospital for adrenalin shot. . . ."

We were only two among thousands; all over camp there were the sick and the troubled. Of our neighbors, none were free from anxiety except possibly the exuberant little Syrian, Phil Shaouy, who had fine health, reserves of rum and food which he shared liberally, and plenty of money and girlfriends.

Across our side path lived Louise and Charlie Harris with their two small boys. Because Charlie had been ill with tuberculosis several years before the war began, the Japanese had released him, with his family, in 1942. Early in 1943, Louise was purchasing food in a Manila market when Japanese soldiers suddenly seized her and incarcerated her at Fort Santiago. They arrested that same day dozens of other released Americans, some of whom they had found in forbidden restaurants, movies or bars; others, like Louise, had been shopping legitimately. Sitting on the floor with only a bit of rice to eat, they were locked away incommunicado for two days and nights. After that experience of Japanese whimsicality, the Harrises had voluntarily returned to Santo Tomás.

Although his tuberculosis had not recurred, Charlie was too weak and emaciated to be of much help to Louise, who labored weak and emaciated to be of much help to Louise, who labored without end to perform such daily chores as cooking, washing dishes and clothes, hauling water, scrubbing floors and children. Their two boys, four and six, ran wild, as did many other youngsters in camp whose parents, exhausted from the effort of keeping them fed and clean, had little energy left over to train them.

On the other side of us lived Don Keiffer with his wife and three-year-old daughter, and the shanty next to theirs belonged to "Pop" and Ann Phillips and their fifteen-year-old son. The specter of hunger had long haunted the Phillipses, because they had no money: Pop's company was one of those that had borrowed nothing for employees in camp. Since they could not buy local foods, they used up canned foods which they had brought in with them. However, they had the foresight to save their Red Cross kits.

When ration-cutting began, Pop Phillips, a former camp policeman, took a job in the kitchen, where he worked long hours at night for his morsel of extra food. Ann served on the chow line, dipping out portions three times a day for several thousand internees who, as rations shrank, would often execrate the men and women who served them.

During the summer of 1944, the Phillips' son, seemingly a healthy lad, began suddenly and rapidly to fail. His energy almost visibly melted away, leaving him so listless that his parents consulted Dr Fletcher.

"Your boy has pernicious anemia," was Dr Fletcher's diagnosis. "There isn't much we can do for him, beyond giving vitamin injections. Have you any food of your own?"

They told him about the Red Cross kits they had been saving.

"If you want your son to live," Dr Fletcher advised, "start opening those cans immediately. Feed him every last ounce of meat you have, if necessary."

The boy picked up amazingly as soon as his diet was enriched by good, substantial tinned meats. When he had gained

sufficient strength, he took a job of hauling huge food cauldrons from kitchen to serving line — a job that paid extra food,
but how long would he be able to continue such heavy work? No
meat reserves were left to restore his health next time, if there
was a next time.

Behind Don Keiffer's shanty lived Tommy Pratt and his wife
Marie, one of the loveliest women I have ever known. She had
been ill for two years, in outside hospitals for a year. Back in
camp since February, she was now so frail that one scarcely dared
hope that she would not fade away to the land of no return.
Tommy had a small food reserve, but there was little that Marie
could eat, either of tinned meats or line chow, that did not make
her ill, with resultant loss of strength and weight.

Few diversions disturbed our companionship, constant and
intimate, with worry, work and hunger. Along with the laundry
and vegetable market, the Japanese had cut off the occasional
movies formerly permitted us, and had banned nightly music
broadcasts during the now frequent blackout practices. A
Dave Harvey stage show about "The Lost Tribes of Luzon"
struck too close to home to seem very funny.

No longer was war news permitted us: the Japanese had
stopped *Tribune* deliveries soon after the opening of Europe's
Second Front. However, we still saw copies smuggled in by
Filipino garbage truck drivers on their nightly rounds; also,
there were radio transcripts, aglow with tales of American
triumphs. However skeptical we might have been of the
transcripts, we never doubted good news when we read it in the
Tribune — and in August, 1944, the *Tribune* said that Davao had
been bombed!

Rumors spread that our forces had landed in Davao, which
cheered some and depressed others who thought Davao too
distant and too strong a Japanese fort to serve as a base for our
liberation. As one internee put it, "By the time our men clear the
place out and fight their way up to us, island by island, we'll all
be dead!" Van did not believe that our troops had landed, or

Many, however, were wildly optimistic. Davao, in the southern part of the Philippines, seemed almost next door to Manila; surely our island-hopping army could free us within a month or two!

About that time I saw Dr Allen on the plaza, and stopped to ask her whether I should ration my thyroid medicine to make it last longer.

"How much have you?" she inquired.

"Full doses for about three months – through November."

"Through November!" Dr Allen was unfeignedly astonished. "Why, how long do you expect to be here? Haven't you heard the news?"

When I mentioned Van's reaction to the Davao bombing, Dr Allen was unimpressed. "I'm sure you have plenty for the duration," she responded. "My advice is not to change the dose. Even if you run short, it's better to take full doses as long as it lasts. I don't think you have a thing to worry about, though!"

It was a heartening sign that the Japanese were patently becoming concerned. On August 20th, they announced the camp's air raid routine: in case of attack, we were to seek shelter immediately and stay under cover until the all-clear was sounded. Under no circumstances were we to watch the planes, whether from windows or the ground. A few days later, the Japanese army launched intensive anti-aircraft drills. As we listened to the rat-tat-tat of enemy guns and watched tiny white smoke puffs burst from the sky, our hearts lifted – for surely it could not be much longer now.

At the end of August, the Japanese rounded up the remnant of their released prisoners and re-interned in Santo Tomás all but a few emergency and tubercular patients. Remedios Hospital was closed. American Catholic sisters and priests were hauled into camp, then packed off the following day to Los Baños.

Along with others came our friends the Stevensons, who were convinced that liberation had all but arrived. "It can't possibly take longer than a month," they predicted jubilantly. "The news outside is simply marvelous! Dragging us back here is the Japs' last move. My dear, we'll be free in no time — just no time at all!" Van cautioned them to ration their food, in any case, to last at least six months. But the Stevensons turned a deaf ear; it simply could not be more than a month!

On September 1st, 1944, a strong rumor buzzed through the camp that Germany had surrendered. Wishfully, Van and I half believed it. The following day, which happened to be my parents' wedding anniversary, Van suggested that we have a drink to toast what we hoped was a dually happy occasion. Before the military took over, we had bought from Stew Raab a few bottles of rum (thirty to thirty-five pesos a bottle) which we had later hid away behind a false-fronted kitchen work table. Between illnesses and rare celebrations, we had already used most of it; was it worthwhile depleting it further, or should we save it for future emergency? While we vacillated, Van suddenly recalled that someone had told him Edgar Kneedler had a five gallon tin of pure alcohol.

"I don't know whether it's true or not, but you might find out," he suggested. "You know him better than I do. Perhaps he'll trade a pint for food. We can spare a can or two for an occasion like this."

I found Edgar in his shanty. He had alcohol, but was not interested in trading. "Maybe later on," he said, "but right now I have plenty of food. I'd like to toast your family's anniversary, though," he continued. "I'll bring a bottle to your shanty and have a drink with you."

We mixed the alcohol with calamancis and sugar to make warm, psuedo-Tom Collinses. Edgar left us the rest of the pint he had brought over, and later gave us another half pint. Some time afterwards, we found another source of supply: part of the alcohol that internees had bought months before at the canteen to prime pressure lamps had proved to be absolutely pure and drinkable. Two technicians tested it, one at the hospital, the other in the main building's fourth floor laboratory. Fee for testing: a stiff drink, if the stuff proved drinkable. We pried open our kindling wood "treasure chest" and purchased three quarts from internees who lamented the previous waste of valuable liquor for priming lamps. By experiment, Van and I had found that Philippine alcohol, slightly sweet because it was distilled from sugar cane, tasted best when poured into lukewarm coffee, which gave it a brandy flavor. Or had we forgotten what brandy tasted like?

Although the announcement of Germany's capitulation was disappointingly premature, signs on the prison front looked more and more encouraging. The Japanese, who were building themselves an air raid shelter on the front campus, advised shanty owners to do the same. We needed no second suggestion. Some built private shelters; others joined forces in community projects. The men of our section erected on Big Van's former homesite a shelter for some twenty-six or twenty-seven persons who declared that they wanted to use it. Everyone contributed labor or materials, or both. Van, unable to work, donated bamboo poles which we had hidden away for possible shanty repairs. Someone else donated a piece of heavy sheet iron to cover part of the roof. Work progressed slowly, as our men had little energy left after the day's chores were finished to carry on the heavy task of digging mud to pack onto bamboo scaffolding they had erected for the shelter. Yet, spurred by daily developments, they struggled to finish the job.

On Saturday, September 9, we had a practice alert which later that same day — thrilling announcement! — became a real alert. Although nothing happened, the alert lasted two days. Rumors of Mindanao landings buzzed through camp. Again on the 12th we were alerted, and at seven-fifty a.m. on the 14th came an air raid alarm — which saved us from roll call, the Japanese having specified that we were not to move from cover. Even though the all clear sounded soon afterwards, we knew that now, surely, our planes must be close. But when would they come?

Time passes most slowly when one is waiting, and we were all waiting, waiting, waiting. After unbearably long days, there followed nights that were restless with yearning as we listened to the lonesome, stirring call of train and boat whistles — Japanese trains, Japanese boats — and remembered days of yore when we had traveled afar by train and boat. How soon, how soon would our own ships sail in to carry us safely back to the trains in our beloved homeland?

On Wednesday, September 20th, I wrote in my diary, "Just another day. . . ." I went in the afternoon to work for Mr Nolting, head of the religious and special activities committees. A pleasant and kindly missionary who devoted many hours to helping his wife run the children's hospital, he found relaxation in the relatively undemanding job of handling his committees. For me, work had its ironically entertaining aspects, although I am sure that Mr Nolting did not share my amusement. The minutes of religious meetings which I typed sounded often like tales of naughty, squabbling children: intolerant bickering between Protestant groups who, in one case I remember, refused even to attend the same conference. Heaven knows we needed divine guidance in Santo Tomás, but how could we expect to learn of God's all-embracing love from men so preoccupied in disagreeing amongst themselves?

Yet, prison bonds are hard to bear, and who was to criticize anyone for human faults and failings? Doubtless the missionaries prayed sincerely, in their way, for all of us — and we needed all the prayers that were offered up, from within the walls of Santo Tomás as well as from loving hearts at home.

On this particular Wednesday, it was my duty to type the weekly schedule of special activities. When he handed me the list, Mr Nolting said, "You know, I have a feeling. . . I wonder how many more weekly schedules we'll be getting out?"

That evening Phil Shaouy's record player ground out, "Tomorrow is a lovely — a lovely, lovely, lovely — tomorrow is a lovely day!"

Chapter Seven

At nine-thirty on the morning of September 21, 1944, I was standing on the front steps of Marie Pratt's shanty, facing the garden. As we exchanged the latest war news, we gazed southwestward across the garden at Japanese anti-aircraft shells bursting in the sky over Manila Bay.

"The Japanese are really getting worried," Marie commented. "They've been practicing all day for the past week."

Suddenly we heard a roar of planes. Automatically, our eyes turned skyward again. To our utter amazement, we saw planes from the south flying directly into the white smoke dots near the horizon. Anti-aircraft fire intensified.

"Good Lord! What a realistic practice!" I exclaimed. At that very instant, our camp air raid gong sounded. Tense with excitement, the voice of our loudspeaker announcer told us, "This is an air raid. Seek shelter immediately!"

I rushed back to our shanty. Van said, "We'd better get the hell over to the air raid shelter."

Although the entrance to the shelter was not more than thirty-five feet away, bombs began dropping into the bay before we reached it. We ducked under cover, but we could not stay put. Hearing the bombs was not enough — we wanted to see our planes! Cautiously, we squeezed around the shelter's two entrances to watch our bombers peel off into their dives, then zoom back again into the sky. They shifted formation like players on a football field. Never had we seen, or even dreamed of

265

anything like it. What grace! What perfect timing! What joy to watch their well-planned destruction!

Our shelter filled up quickly, its twenty-six-odd occupants squatting on cushions or sitting on folding chairs that lined either side of the tunnel. The passageway was so narrow that our knees touched, yet we climbed over one another a dozen times to peer at the fireworks. When Japanese guards shuffled down the path, we scurried inside: we were not supposed to watch the show.

Japanese shells and shell fragments soon began to fall in camp. As anti-aircraft shells explode in the air, we did not at first understand several close explosions — until someone deduced that, along with anti-aircraft, the Japanese were using pom-poms which burst only on contact. With our shelter only partially finished, we did not feel very secure. Although the front and sides were well packed with earth to within a foot of the top, the rear was protected solely by bamboo scaffolding.

Suddenly a deafening report, like a pistol fire at close range, nearly bowled us off our chairs. It seemed for an instant like a direct hit.

"Everyone okay?" someone asked when we caught our breaths. Everyone was. Van and several other men crawled out to see where the shell had struck. About three feet to the right of the shelter, they found a deep hole torn in the ground. "Lucky it *wasn't* a direct hit," one of them commented. "Our roof is only about four inches thick!"

At that point, a small boy announced that he had to wee-wee. "But you can't," his mother remonstrated. "It's too dangerous with all those shells dropping around. Besides, Japanese soldiers don't want people wandering outside the shelter."

The child still insisted that he had to go. His younger brother then averred firmly that he, too, had to wee-wee right away.

"Oh, for God's sake!" the exasperated voice of the father spoke up. "Can't you wait till the air raid's over?"

"No!" chorused the brothers.

"Oh, all right. I'll take them over to the shanty," conceded the father, resigned but thoroughly irritated.

After more than two hours of steady bombing, we heard our planes drone away in the distance.

"Going home for lunch, I guess," Don Keiffer remarked. "Which reminds me, I wonder how we're going to get ours?"

Half an hour later, the loudspeaker announced that we could move across the campus to get our chow from the line. No one was to walk around unnecessarily, and all movement was to cease after one hour.

While I was fixing lunch, Van returned from the Education building with news that a pom-pom shell had burst through the roof of the top floor men's bathroom. Miraculously, a man who had been shaving at the time escaped without a scratch.

To celebrate the long awaited coming of our planes, I opened a tin of crackers that we had been saving since 1942. No sooner had we finished the hasty meal of Spam on crackers than the planes returned. Joyfully, we all paraded back to our mud shelter.

"Boy, they're really plastering these Japs," exulted Charlie Harris. "It won't be much longer now!"

Every one of us was elated. In December, 1941, we had watched the Japanese bomb Manila without a single plane of our own to challenge them. They had chased out our army in less than a month. Now, after two years, eight months and sixteen days in the "clink," we saw our planes in the sky again — dozens of them. That one day's bombing wiped out all the rankling humiliation of defeat. Now, our boys had things *their* way, and we in Santo Tomás had the unique pleasure of watching our own planes bomb our own territory while we were prisoners of the enemy.

That "tomorrow" *was* a lovely day!

Our planes were back again the next day to blast various military strongholds. Knowing the relative positions of Nichols Field, Nielson Airport, Fort McKinley, Zablan Field, Grace Park, Camp Murphy and other nearby army centers, we could guess with reasonable accuracy what target the planes were hitting each time they dived.

After two straight days of bombing, most of us were sure that our troops would soon be landing on Luzon. It might take time to fight their way to Manila — but surely by Christmas we would all be free!

On the 23rd, the raid alarm sounded. Planes flew over us, but no bombs fell. All day long we waited hopefully. Nothing happened. We consoled ourselves with the thought that they were bombing nearby.

On the 24th, same story. That night we read in our smuggled newspaper that the Philippines had declared war on the United States. Could this mean that our soldiers had landed in Philippine territory?

Still nothing happened. On the 26th, the all-clear signal was given. No longer were we even under an alert!

The lull gave our men a chance to complete the air raid shelter. They worked at it every spare moment, driven by the memory of shells exploding close around us. Already shell fragments had wounded several internees; nothing serious yet, but why take chances? Day by day, the sod thickened on the roof, and finally the open backside was completely covered. The shelter was finished; and still day followed uneventful day. An occasional alert was sounded, soon to be canceled out by the all-clear. How difficult it was to tread the old ruts again, after soaring for a brief two days to the clouds! On everyone's lips was the question: "What has happened to our planes?"

A few mornings after the bombings, our reveille broadcaster was inspired to awaken us with the strains of "Pennies from Heaven." We had smiled appreciatively. Now, it was raining only rain, a sodden token of our own bogged down spirits. As one week of silence became two, then three, our broadcaster was moved to echo our depression in the plaintive melody, "Lover, Come Back to Me." Cheerlessly, we dragged ourselves out of bed to line up for roll call and to pursue our tedious chores.

Chapter Eight

Ah, what can ail thee, internee,
With hollow eyes that search the sky?
The smile is withered from thy lips,
And no planes fly!

Jubilation over the bombings aroused in most of us an over-confident expectation of early deliverance from starvation and the Japanese. Many shanty owners, after plucking their daily greens from beds of fast-growing talinum, began to be careless about replanting. "The boys will be here by the time this stuff grows," they stated with assurance. Then gradually, exhilaration gave way to gloom, and people plodded back to their gardening.

Those of us who had food reserves now began to fear confiscation by the Japanese, although thus far they had seized only maps, money, written and typed material, and food which obviously had been smuggled in. On several occasions they had impounded large quantities of sugar in the possession of a single internee, but each time had returned it after the owner had submitted proof of acquisition prior to the gate's closing. However, one could never be sure what would happen as American forces moved closer; the Japanese might decide to appropriate our canned goods to feed their fast weakening army.

Many internees buried their tins, but Van and I chose drier and more accessible hiding places, concealing as many as possible in our rum cache behind the secret panel in our kitchen table, and distributing the remainder among false-bottomed chests and a wall pocket where petate panels overlapped beside my bed. The half-dozen that we left exposed would scarcely excite unwonted attention from the Japanese.

We were lucky indeed to have food supplies in those days of dreariness and hunger. The nightly dinner menu, chalked up on a blackboard near the serving line, invariably read: "Rice and Vegetable Stew." One evening, in place of the usual legend, we observed the notation: "Hebrews XIII:8." Someone produced a Bible; the verse in question read, "Jesus Christ, the same yesterday, and today, and forever." Mr Nolting, my missionary boss, was not amused; but most of the camp chuckled for days — although we could not help wishing that "the same today as yesterday" were literally true: for now the evening stew comprised little more than greens, boiled radishes and an occasional camote, while the cereal diminished steadily, week by week.

As shortages grew shorter, tempers followed suit; nerves overwrought with worry and frustrated hope snapped like taut violin strings on a humid night. Often the most trivial request would provoke an explosion — such as my request for new monthly meal tickets after a field rat had invaded our shanty and nibbled away the greater part of our current ones.

It scarcely surprised me that the internee in charge of issuing meal tickets was not overjoyed to behold the mangled pair I presented for replacement: paper of every variety had long been in short supply. Drains were daily clogged with unsuitable substitutes for toilet paper, which had run out months before; typing paper gave double and triple service, both front and back; and meal tickets were fashioned from old posters, properly stamped and cut to size. Posters, too, had all but vanished. Hence the skeletal remains in my outstretched hand justified a certain annoyance; but I did rather resent the indignant inference that I had enticed rats into our shanty with meal ticket bait.

"I'm terribly sorry," I apologized contritely.

"Well," snapped the ticket issuer, "I don't know what you expect *me* to do about it. We *have* no more meal tickets."

She busied herself about other jobs while I cooled my heels. Finally she yanked out of the drawer two meal tickets, on which she wrote our names.

"There!" She flung them across the desk at me. "But see to it that it doesn't happen again!"

We borrowed a trap from Big Van and caught our marauder, a poor little fellow not much bigger than a mouse. I hated to kill him — but he should have stayed out in his fields, away from our precious meal tickets and still more precious food.

The alarming deficit of line food forced internee officials to make a grave decision: should corned beef stored in the camp warehouse be added in minute portions over a period of months to our nightly vegetables, or should the tins be distributed direct, six ounces a week per internee? If the latter course were chosen, reserves would be depleted at the end of October.

Camp officials turned for advice to our doctors, who, before making up their minds, proceeded to line up all internees for a physical examination. As we waited our turn to be prodded in the ankles and tapped on the knees, an English girl named Valentine Masefield remarked, "This is like trying out for the chorus! I almost expect the doctor to call out, 'All right, girls, swing it now. That's nice, girls — that's pretty nice!'" Daumier might well have immortalized that weird chorus line of dull-eyed, hollow-cheeked, skinny-shanked girls, whose concerted efforts to "swing it" might at best have produced a wicked wobble of knobby knees and a jerky ripple of ribs and vertebrae, rudely revealed through skin that should normally have been their disguise and protection.

The doctors found all of us suffering to some degree from lack of protein. Dr Fletcher strongly recommended that the corned beef be made to last as long as possible. Some of the other doctors disagreed just as strongly. One of three army doctors who

271

had been sent to Santo Tomás from Cabanatuan (Prisoner-of-War Camp) at the beginning of 1944, to replace the three doctors repatriated from our camp, took the lead against Dr Fletcher. This doctor's dissenting opinion — that infinitesimal portions of corned beef would benefit no one, while six ounces a week would build up a sufficient strength to enable us to do without meat for a short period afterwards — won by a single vote.

Accepting the recommendation of the doctors' committee, our Internee Committee started issuing corned beef twice weekly on our canteen ration cards: three twelve-ounce tins for every two tickets. To prevent the sale or hoarding of issued corned beef, each can was punctured before distribution.

While the doctors' consultation was going on, internees argued the subject among themselves. Some thought a camp-wide vote should decide the question; others wondered why the committees made no effort to find out which internees needed meat and which had reasonable personal supplies. Had we been asked, Van and I would have refused the camp corned beef. As it was, there was no choice: the punctured tins were passed out by group, to all alike. We earmarked an equal number of our own cans as a minimum to turn back in case of a call for donations later on; but no call ever came.

Since the Japanese continued cutting rations, the extra corned beef allotments did not prevent October's death rate from shooting up. First to succumb were the older men. Never was starvation listed as a cause of death, yet we knew that most of those who had died — from "heart disease," "old age," "myocarditis," "operation," "unknown," — would have survived, had their latent ailments not been aggravated by malnutrition.

An ever-increasing number of internees who had stored away what they had considered plentiful food stocks were now running short. I remember one couple who had deliberately rationed their reserves to last through the end of July. From the time the gate closed until the end of July, they had lived well, opening several cans a day, sharing pies and cakes with friends, baking cookies for neighborhood children; but at the end of July, there was no more food. Thereafter, they scraped along meagerly with a few kilos of smuggled beans that they managed to buy at fabulous prices.

Stew Raab, who had bought twenty-five pounds of cocoa and so much sugar that in February he had generously baked a cake for Van's third birthday in camp (inscribed, "Three Strikes — and Out?") and had confidently promised me one in October, now realized that he had left less than enough to satisfy his own family's wants. When my birthday came around, we furnished a bare minimum of essentials — cassava flour, shortening and sugar (no cocoa: after receiving our packages from home, we had a total of a pound and a quarter, which we rationed for chocolate pies — one every two weeks — figuring it to last through February, 1945). Stew added fresh eggs from his own chickens and turned out what was, for the times, a very acceptable cake.

The Stevensons, entering Santo Tomás in August, had brought in several cases of canned goods, and could have brought more. However, they undertook to feed a family of five with whom they had lived for a year outside, and in little more than a month, all their food was gone. They came to Van for help. "We thought the war would be over by now," they ruefully admitted.

The days of easy buying were long past. Although a number of internees sought exchanges, few were willing now to sell their food. The exchanges often became complex four- and- five-way deals; a relatively simple three-way barter resulted when an internee with milk, for example, wanted corned beef, while another had corned beef to trade for coffee, and a third had coffee and wanted milk. To buy was less complicated but far more difficult. However, Van finally located two dozen tins of corned beef, priced at forty Philippine pesos a tin. He advised the Stevensons to give up trying to feed five extra mouths.

Until August, Van and I had opened very few tins of meat, having first used up our limed eggs (about a quarter of them had gone bad) and fried down pork. Van then had budgeted the canned meat to last for ten months, which allowed each of us two ounces a day. After the bombings, we had increased our rations to three ounces; then, when the planes stayed away, we cut back to two. Using our canned vegetables, mostly green peas, at the rate of twelve ounces a week, we had enough to last through February. In addition, we found ourselves blessed with wild seguidillas, a local vegetable of the bean family which grows into long, edible pods. Every other day for several months we harvested pods enough for a small serving, from a vine of mysterious origin which had entwined itself amongst our cannas.

As cautious friends had predicted, we had bad luck with certain foods we had stored away. I discovered that two packages of Tam's cake flour were teeming with small worms. To throw away the flour was unthinkable. Painstakingly, I began to sift it, almost grain by grain, picking out and destroying the tiny worms that fell through the sieve. As a final precaution, I baked or toasted the flour after each day's sieving. The task required a good four hours a day for three weeks, but I counted the eye-straining hours well spent, because we saved our flour.

We opened a tin of American saltine crackers which we had bought at the Santiago Hospital, only to find them a mildewed and sodden mess, quite unfit to eat. Our unsalted crackers, locally made, had stayed bone-dry, but the saltines had soaked up like blotting paper the dampness of three rainy seasons. They remained inedible even after prolonged slow-baking, and we were on the verge of discarding them as a total loss when I suddenly thought of scraping off the mildew and pulverizing them into flour. Mixed with rice flour, they made passable hot cakes; by a stretch of the imagination, we fancied that the slightly mouldy flavor resembled the taste of buckwheat!

Van and I disagreed only once about food rationing: I had been surviving nicely on a quarter of our cereal until he insisted that I increase my portion to a third of our allotment. He

274

maintained that I needed more cereal because I ate no beans, dried or tinned, as he did, and turned a deaf ear to my valid contentions that beriberi victims required far more than average quantities of cereal and other foods containing vitamin B, and furthermore that men needed considerably more food than women — this was proven over and over again in our camp. (In our own case, Van dropped from 190 to 125 pounds, while my lowest weight was 108 pounds, only twenty-three below my maximum in camp and twelve below my normal weight. Doubtless part of Van's loss was due to ill health, but the principal cause was a natural difference in metabolism.) However, he was adamant and I finally yielded against my better judgement, although I cheated as much as I dared by making his hot cakes and muffins slightly larger than mine.

I had reason to regret my weakness when soon afterwards Van again developed beriberi symptoms. At the same time, his groins swelled with a double hernia caused, so Dr Fletcher told us, by the pressure of the a constant asthmatic cough against abdominal tissue weakened by malnutrition. Another series of vitamin B injections arrested the beriberi; for the double hernia, nothing could be done.

All round camp, the ghastly handiwork of starvation began to show plainly in dragging footsteps, gaunt faces, emaciated bodies. For the sick, there was little help; those of us who were stronger could only watch and pray that our loved ones would manage somehow to hold on until we were free.

Chapter Nine

Our planes returned full force about mid-October: the wait that had seemed forever was little more than three weeks. During one of the raids, an earsplitting crash caused us instinctively to duck, arms protectively crossed over our heads. "Thank God for the roof!" someone in the shelter exclaimed. "Must have hit the same spot again."

Pop Phillips peered out from the entrance. "It hit my shanty," he called back. "There's a big hole in the roof and nipa flying all over the place. I'm going over — it might catch fire." Several other men joined him. They returned in a few minutes, Pop proudly displaying a pom-pom shell. "No fire, but wow! What a skylight!"

Half-a-dozen shanties in other areas were hit that same day. As a precaution against fire, we were now warned never to leave stoves burning when we sought shelter outside: a necessary regulation, but inconvenient for those of us who cooked beans and other foods requiring prolonged simmering. Since the raids usually began about seven forty-five a.m., I solved the time problem by starting Van's noonday meal the previous night, although night cooking under blackout restrictions was not easy. The difficulty resolved itself all too soon when our beans ran out a month or so later.

In the midst of the October fireworks, we read in the *Tribune* that convoys had landed at Leyte. The Japanese papers chided our armed forces because, they claimed, our fleet had tricked the Imperial Japanese Navy by sneaking into Leyte harbor under a sheltering cover of fog!

Over the camp loudspeaker, our newscaster made an ingeniously audacious comment on the good news. It happened that for some time no rice had been sent into camp and each nightly broadcast had warned us to ration carefully what we had on hand. Then, on the very day that we read of our convoys at Leyte, the Japanese brought in rice. That evening, the announcer duly noted its arrival, adding casually, "This has come a little late. . .but better Leyte than never!"

Soon afterwards, our paper stopped coming in; the Commandant had discovered the smuggling route. Thenceforth, papers were sneaked in very infrequently, and we missed them. However, our planes were the most important news — news good enough, Van and I thought, to again increase our meat ration, this time permanently.

Life now took on a sustained excitement: liberation surely would come soon! Each day we waited breathlessly for our planes; sometimes sirens wailed when nothing happened, but often enough to keep spirits high, our fliers would return: every four or five days unless bad weather lengthened the intervals.

However bright our hope, its light nevertheless silhouetted dark dangers still lurking in the shadowy path of our future, for the fear of Japanese treachery haunted us always. Already the army had dumped quantities of military supplies on the front lawn of Santo Tomás, and had buried huge drums of gasoline outside our wall and in the hospital garden. The camp bristled with soldiers, who slept at night in a pavilion beyond the plaza which had been built for internee class and lecture rooms. This influx of troops and matériel alarmed us. Were the Japanese turning Santo Tomás into a military headquarters, safe from attack by reason of its status as an internment camp?

In reply to an internee committee protest, the Commandant stated that no classrooms in the pavilion were to be used by soldiers, who would sleep in the "woodshed" portion only and would use no camp-owned property. He went on to say that the committee's letter "expresses a feeling on the part of the internees which is most unexpected and may be construed as *an insult to the Imperial Japanese Army. The Japanese do not use internees as a shield.* It should be remembered that all of Manila and the Philippines is actually an objective in this war. The Government of the United States had not been officially informed that the Santo Tomás University was to be used as an internment camp. Therefore, officially it has no protective status. However, everything possible will be done to protect the internees of this camp to the fullest extent."

At roll call that night, someone echoed Eleanor Phillips' dire prediction: "Maybe the Japs have spread word we've all been taken out so our own planes will bomb us. If a bomb ever hit one of those gas tanks, Santo Tomás would burn up like a box of match sticks."

"Maybe the Japs will bomb us themselves," responded another echo.

"If they aren't using us as a shield, then I never saw a shield," replied the first.

Where our committee had failed, the Catholic fathers of Santo Tomás surprisingly succeeded. The Japanese yielded to their vehement protests against using the university as a dump for war matériel, and promptly removed their equipment.

With every American victory, the Japanese became tougher with us. They began to pick up people who walked across the campus during lulls between raids. Technically, we were not supposed to move until the all-clear sounded, or an announcement was made that we could go to the meal lines. Yet sometimes it was imperative to rush to the "little house on the hill" or one of its counterparts. The Japanese attributed those urgent calls to an overwhelming desire to watch our planes. They grabbed several men crossing the campus, along with a few who were spotted actually watching raids from windows of the Education building, and stood them by the gate for hours in the hot sun. One man was forced at gunpoint to stand all afternoon on an ant hill where he had unwittingly stopped. By the end of the day, his legs were swollen masses of fiery red bites.

One night at roll call, we were informed that the Commandant desired all of us to sign the following:

OATH
The Commandant of Internment,
Camp of P.I.

I, the undersigned, hereby solemnly pledge
myself that I will strictly comply with orders of
Japanese Military Authorities and will not,
under any circumstances, attempt escape.

Signed_____
Date_____

Our internee agents battled doggedly with the Japanese and a few days later, we were offered this alternate:

"OATH
To His Excellency
The Commandant of the Military Internment
Camps of P.I.

I, the undersigned, hereby solemnly pledge
myself that I will not, under any circumstances,
attempt to escape or conspire directly
or indirectly against the Japanese Military
Authorities, as long as I am in their custody.

Signed_____
Nationality_____
Date_____

Although there was little difference between the two, our agents advised us to sign the second oath, since it did not pledge us to comply strictly with Japanese military orders. How could the Japanese suppose that we would be bound by an oath that we, as prisoners, had been forced to sign? Perhaps they wanted our sworn statements as face-saving evidence to present to their government in case we *did* escape and conspire against Japanese military authorities.

Every internee in camp signed the oath except one American-born Chinese, who flatly refused. "I am an American citizen," he maintained resolutely. "I won't sign any oath to the Japanese." When persuasion failed to alter his decision, the Japanese threw him into our camp jail.

Another champion who had fought for our rights, not as Americans but as internees, was banished for his boldness: internee agent Clyde DeWitt was deported to Los Baños. Although it was said that the Japanese had sent him away because they were tired of his constant protests on our behalf, some suspected that Grinnell might have engineered the transfer. Clyde DeWitt had had many run-ins with both the Japanese and Grinnell. No matter who had got rid of him, he left, not too reluctantly, in a blaze of glory.

Grinnell seldom opened his mouth that tactless words did not tumble out. Van passed him one day in front of the Education building just as an elderly woman called, "Oh, Mr Grinnell, I'd like to talk to you a minute." Without a word of apology, Grinnell brushed her aside. "I can't talk to you now. I'm busy." And away he strode into the Japanese office.

Another incident attracted camp-wide attention. Arrangements had been made for Dr Allen to move from her tiny office in the annex to a larger room in the main building, which had formerly served as a first-aid station. Some confusion arose over the change, and when Dr Allen tried to take over her new office, the first-aid nurse refused to move out. What the details of the misunderstanding were, or who was in the right, I never found out. The next we heard about the matter was that Grinnell had arbitrarily barred Dr Allen from practicing medicine in camp, a move which outraged not only her many patients but nearly everyone also in Santo Tomás. A group of incensed internees deputized a representative to ask Grinnell by what right and for what reason he had forbidden Dr Allen to practice; to which Grinnell retorted, "It's none of your business."

Although Dr Allen was reinstated at the end of a week, abhorrence of Grinnell's high-handed methods did not abate. More and more frequently one heard the query, "Why doesn't the s.o.b. resign? He knows we all hate him."

Earl Carroll, who managed to get along with Grinnell even though he often disagreed with him, repeated an interesting conversation to us:

Grinnell to Earl: "Do you think I ought to resign?"

Earl to Grinnell: "You know what I think."

Grinnell to Earl: "Well, I'm not going to do it!"

On one public occasion, Grinnell introduced the Commandant with ill-chosen words: "The Commandant is going to speak to you" — (not "to us") — "in a few moments. When he comes onto the stage, you will all please bow to him." Thereafter, internees often referred to "Grinnell and the other Japs."

There were some who surmised that Grinnell's ultimate goal was to become a delegate to a postwar international peace conference; others guessed at the fortune he might have been piling up by lending money to internees. Few in high places were spared accusations of graft, and suspicion was sometimes justified. However, oppressive though his leadership was, I sincerely believe there was no reason to question Grinnell's integrity; the flaw in his character was something approximating egomania, not dishonesty.

On the first day of November, 1944, the Japanese inaugurated standing roll call, forbidding chairs to all except those too weak to stand. We had ourselves partly to blame for this latest inconvenience, for despite frequent orders to line our chairs evenly in double rows, it was no uncommon sight to see chairs scattered at random while internees lolled against trees behind the roll call lines.

A few days later, the Japanese commanded us to bow whenever and wherever we encountered any Japanese. Shanty area supervisors and monitors were trained in this special Japanese etiquette, so that they could pass on to us at roll call the art of bowing from the waist, feet together, arms to the side, eyes front. Day after day the Commandant's lieutenants inspected our lines, calling out for special, on-the-spot instruction those who did not bend low enough.

Bowing irked us, independent Occidentals that we still were, even though the Japanese returned a military salute. However, our obstinate occidental sense of humor helped us to bear up. Since proper bowing required an empty-handed, arms-to-the-side posture, we entertained ourselves with mental pictures of perpetually laden internees suddenly dropping, with great clatter and racket, their dinner buckets, plates, bayong, and other paraphernalia to stand at attention whenever they chanced to meet a Japanese.

In practice, we could usually mark the enemy far enough in advance to turn aside before we had to bow. Those who openly defied the new rule were lined up and made to bend at the waist for fifteen or twenty minutes, or longer if the guard was not satisfied with their performance.

Rebels against the internee high command delighted in bowing to Grinnell "along with the rest of the Japs." No threat to his power, Grinnell ignored the taunts.

Along with Grinnell and the Japanese, November's capricious weather disturbed us. Bad storms had halted all air activity, and we wondered, as the wind snarled and ripped at our nipa shingles, whether our roofs would hold together until we needed them no more. As the storms waned, flaming sunsets ignited low-riding clouds in the west, transforming the darkly massed rolls into blazing colorbursts of crimson, cerise, smouldering rose and golden-edged purple, which spread like prairie fire across the entire sky: a glorious spectacle that mirrored as in a celestial pool our own burning hopes for the Day of Liberation, which we earnestly prayed was not too far distant.

On December 13th, a clear day, we observed that a new moon trailed the setting sun. Hopefully, we whispered of possible troop landings, for we had often read of beachheads secured by the "dark of the moon."

On the 14th, our planes attacked all day, and all through the night. When they returned the next day, and the next night, and again on the 16th, we were sure that our dreams were coming true. Never before had we seen such sustained, intensive bombing.

By evening of the 16th, word electrified the camp that our forces had landed at Polilio, on the east coast of Luzon. An internee interpreter had glimpsed the headline in a Japanese newspaper. To verify the rumor, Van, always a doubter, checked personally with the interpreter. Yes, he assured Van, he had seen the headline about a fight at Polilio; the Japanese had folded up the paper before he could read the details.

For a few hours, we were jubilant. We might be free by Christmas; surely by New Year's!

But the night of the 16th was too quiet. No bombings; no indication of excitement on the part of the Japanese. Van immediately lost hope in the Polilio story. I did not give up so easily. Perhaps nothing worth bombing was left in Manila. Four days went by — still no bombings. Then we read the real news in one of our rare smuggled copies of the *Tribune*. Our forces had landed on Mindoro. The "Polilio" fight had taken place at Peleliu in the Palao group: Peleliu and Polilio are written with the same characters in the phonetic Japanese language.

For those of us who had believed in the Luzon landing, the Mindoro story came as an anticlimax. My spirits felt horribly deflated. But Van, innately realistic, thought that the situation looked excellent. "Even when I half-believed the Polilio story," he said, "I didn't understand how we could land on Luzon without land-based planes to cover Manila. All the planes we've seen so far have been carrier-based. Now we'll begin to see Army planes. We're really getting somewhere!"

My own reaction was less sanguine. How long would it take? From Leyte to Mindoro, almost two months. Another two months from Mindoro to Luzon — then how long to Manila? How many more would perish from starvation while our long-awaited help was still on the way?

Chapter Ten

As the battlefront moved closer, we had more than enough time to reflect on the gruesomeness of war. Japanese soldiers just outside our walls bellowed hideous, blood-curdling war cries as they practiced bayoneting dummy targets. We wondered whether those barbaric shrieks were calculated to strike terror in the hearts of the enemy, or, more subtly, to reassure the attacker of his own strength and ferocity, like whistling in the dark to convince oneself of fearlessness. What brutalization of human beings! But how else could a man be induced to disembowel a fellow wayfarer on this earth, a stranger, yet a man like himself, who dreamed of home and the quiet comfort of family and friends at his hearthside, once the nightmare of war was ended?

Day after day, explosions rocked Manila as the Japanese destroyed military installations before the anticipated American assault became a reality. Hopeful of an early Japanese evacuation, our morning broadcaster wakened us with an appropriate song called, "Why Don't You Get Out of Town?" The Japanese were not amused and prescribed thenceforth only wordless records for Reveille. Shortly afterwards, they cut off all shanty area loudspeakers; regular music broadcasts had long since been banned. So now we heard only the percussion noises of war: thunderous drum-rolls of blasting, shrill war cries of soldiers, staccato pings of gunfire.

Although our announcer's bravado spurred our spirits, we could not live long on hope alone. Almost as intense as the spiritual yearning for freedom was our physical yearning for food. In mid-November the camp had stopped issuing breakfast allotments of raw cereal when it was found that the tiny portions could be stretched farther in a watery gruel called "lugao."

As time went on, deliveries of rice and cornmeal became more tardy and uncertain. To tide us over when the cupboard was bare, the kitchen crew worked out a formula for "emergency biscuits" of rice flour, baked hard and dry so that they would keep indefinitely. More and more frequently, biscuits were passed out in lieu of rice, which meant shorter rations day by day. Remembering a time when platefuls of rice had been dumped into garbage cans, one wished futilely that the cooks had dreamed up their biscuits a year or two sooner.

Even those of us who still had canned goods ate meagerly. My breakfast was black coffee — we blended our dwindling supply of fresh coffee with retoasted grounds and considered ourselves lucky indeed to have coffee of any kind. Van ate a small dish of lugao for breakfast and usually another — my portion — for lunch, while I had talinum broth, watery as weak tea, from the line. About twice a week we varied the luncheon menu when I made pseudo-hotcakes by mixing lug with cornmeal or rice flour from the dinner quota of raw cereal we still received. Very occasionally, Van opened one of our few remaining tins of beans.

Dinner was the same unpalatable vegetable stew, fibers and often full of peels. At this meal we fared considerably better that those who were without food reserves, for our canned meat and occasional vegetables added flavor as well as calories to the tasteless mess.

On Thanksgiving, the kitchen served extra-large portions of a stew made with cassava root, a good camote substitute when properly prepared, but poisonous otherwise. Through inexperience, the cooks bungled their processing, and three-fourths of the camp suffered reactions ranging in severity from simple stomach ache to acute indigestion.

A few weeks before Christmas, we read in a smuggled copy of

the *Tribune* that American Red Cross comfort kits had been delivered to Japan for trans-shipment to prisoners in Manchukuo and other camps farther south. Although Philippine camps were not specified, most of us longingly inferred that they must surely be included among others "farther south."

Shortly thereafter, Shuraji, the pig-eyed lieutenant in charge of camp food supplies, made a speech abruptly ordering us, as he periodically did, to plant more food. The Japanese Army, he said, did not believe that we were trying to help ourselves. Food everywhere was scarce, but the Japanese might reward us, he promised, if we would do our part. What could Shuraji mean, we wishfully asked each other, if not comfort kits?

An internee claimed to have read in a smuggled copy of a Spanish newspaper that comfort kits had arrived in Manila. When days passed and no kits appeared, our internee committee tried to pump the Japanese — who disclaimed knowledge of any kits allotted to Manila.

While hunger vied with hope, Earl Carroll and his resourceful friend, Professor Luis Alcuaz, undertook a bold and risky new venture to procure more food for the camp. Through a hole in the wall of the gymnasium where he maintained an office, the Professor passed in to Earl several thousand cans of meat and many kilos of kidney beans. That such a daring plan could be executed without detection is a tribute to the discretion and cunning of those two intrepid men. Undoubtedly the food helped to save lives — but it was a mere pittance for 4000 starving internees.

Only the frequent sight of our planes broke the dull, hungry monotony of those times. Two days before Christmas, we beheld a vision, exquisite and magical, that etched an indelible image on our memories. The sky, a deep blue, was dotted with powder-puff clouds trailing behind them wisps of vapory cloud-dust. We heard a roar of planes — and suddenly, through the streaks of sky mist, there appeared an apparition from fairyland: planes that surely must have been fashioned from spun glass and dainty silver filigree. We gaped in dazzled astonishment as they glided gracefully from cloud into clear blue sky. There were two types: giant, four-motored bombers and tiny, twin-fuselaged fighters. Their silver wings did not flash, hard and metallic, like Japanese planes; rather, they resembled finely wrought lace, or the delicate tracery of foam on a moonlit sea.

One of our neighbors produced a pre-war plane magazine that identified the planes as land-based B-24s and P-37s, the very first we had ever seen. Later, we learned that the B-24s were called "Liberators," a name befitting their beauty and promise.

Tragedy marred the vision a few days later when one of those fairy-winged planes was shot down in a burst of flame. The stricken ship veered sharply away from its echelon of planes; then, as we watched aghast, it split into three fiery segments which crashed to the ground in a matter of moments. Three parachutes drifted more slowly earthward, but we held little hope that their occupants would survive: the Japanese reputedly killed American airmen on sight.

Although we had steeled ourselves, we thought, to expect the worst from the Japanese, we were not at all prepared for their next unnerving act. On Christmas Eve, without warning, they arrested Carroll Grinnell, Doug Duggleby and two other internees, locking them up in our camp jail. Why, no one knew, for charges were never proferred. Although Grinnell and Duggleby had hoodwinked the Japanese many a time to bring in food and money, and had allegedly sent help to military prisoners and guerrilla forces, the other two men, so far as we knew, had done nothing more than the rest of us who had committed such offenses as borrowing money illegally.

Had it been Grinnell alone, we might have wondered whether in the end he had not antagonized the Japanese as he had a majority of internees. Much as we had wished for his downfall, its extent and the manner of its coming shocked and saddened us.

The four men were held prisoners in camp until the last day

of 1944, when a group of absurdly disguised Japanese shuffled into Santo Tomás. In a different setting, one might have mistaken them for a band of strolling, third-rate comedians; here, they were instantly recognizable as members of the dread secret police. Their mission was no secret: they removed the prisoners from our jail and marched them away to an unknown destination.

We wondered who would be next on the Japanese list: Earl Carroll, perhaps, who had now taken over Grinnell's job – or anyone at random? What would happen to the men already marked by the Japanese, those newly abducted and those who had been taken away months before; and to Juan Elizalde, Enrico Pirovano and dozens of other neutrals whose loyalty to us had doomed them to foul Japanese prisons?

The shadow of fear that darkened our Christmas Eve was not mitigated by carols played over the loudspeaker, which reminded us only of how different this Christmas was from the joyous, remembered ones of years past. Our evening newscaster announced a Christmas morning bonus for each of us: half a cake of native chocolate (less than one inch square) and two teaspoons of jam. For dinner, a larger than usual serving of fried rice.

During the night, a lone plane flew over us. We made a half-hearted stab at jesting about Santa's preference this year for planes.

On Christmas morning, however, glad tidings flew through camp: a message had been dropped from the skies! It bore a reproduction of the Nativity, and the leaflet read: "The Commander-in-Chief, officers and men of the American Forces of Liberation in the Pacific wish their gallant allies, the people of the Philippines, all the blessings of Christmas and the realization of their fervent hopes for the New Year. Christmas 1944."

Several leaflets had dropped in camp. Although the choleric Japanese ordered us to turn them in immediately, a few internees managed to keep their treasured find. Many saw the actual

291

placard, and all heard its message. Again the light of hope flashed through the gloom.

This Christmas for Van and me was a day of opulence, like our previous one in Santo Tomás, and for the same reason: Big Van had invited his guests of 1943 to dine again with him. The lavish spread of canned meats, vegetables and fruits that he set before us far surpassed our now limited capacity. Amid the starving, it seemed almost criminally wasteful to serve such a feast. Yet, of the food that was left, I am sure that no scrap was wasted; and I am sure that Big Van, no longer big except in stature, had scrimped many weeks for this one splurge. Christmas is supposed to be a day of festivity. Thanks to Big Van, Christmas 1944 was just that for some dozen internees of Santo Tomás.

Festive, but far from happy, for I could not help thinking of those who had little or no food of their own. The knowledge that there were others hungrier than I was often troubled me deeply, and I longed to share with all the less fortunate — obviously an impossibility, because our reserves could not have saved four, far less four thousand, internees. Van and I had helped a few friends, as many as we could, throughout the months; but it was so little, and the need so great.

There was no answer — only a prayer, that must have been in every heart that Christmas Day: please, God let us *all* live to see the realization of our "fervent hopes for the New Year."

Chapter Eleven

Nineteen forty-five opened with the beat of a funeral march as the death toll trebled that of preceding months. Haltingly in the wake of death came a series of births: although hunger and weakness had temporarily deprived many of the power to conceive, nature in some cases had taken its inevitable course after shanty living had broken the barriers of enforced birth control. The anguish of parents barely able themselves to exist on our starvation diet was deepened a thousandfold as they faced the irresolvable problem of how to feed their newborn babes.

The last glimmer of hope for Red Cross kits vanished when the Japanese failed to produce them by Christmas. And if ever there had been a doubt as to their intention deliberately to starve us, no trace remained now, for on Christmas and New Year's Day, sentries barred the entrance of Santo Tomás to International YMCA trucks laden with food for internees.

"Internees have plenty of food," the soldiers lied.

Reluctantly, the drivers turned back. Many a life could have been saved had the Japanese willed it; but saving internee lives manifestly was not a part of the military plan.

Misery from hunger was a sight too harrowing to describe. Children — and sometimes adults — dug in garbage cans outside the Japanese kitchen for whatever partially edible stuff they might retrieve, while Japanese soldiers looked on and laughed: very funny to observe Anglo-Saxons raiding the refuse. Occasionally a "magnanimous" soldier would give some child a banana or a piece of candy.

Long since vanished were the once numerous pigeons that used to nest in stone ledges on the main building; enticed with bits of corn, they had been snared and eaten by internees made crafty by hunger. Dogs and cats disappeared every day, the strays first, then personal pets. There were not many of the latter to begin with: they were patently out of place in a concentration camp, yet the bonds of affection between animal and master are strong, and some took a chance on sharing imprisonment rather than abandoning a beloved pet. In the end, only a handful, carefully guarded, survived the relentless game hunt.

Our daily ration in January averaged less than 700 calories. The food committee made a plea for donations to buy coconuts, "when and if available," at seven dollars and fifty cents per nut. Most of us donated from our monthly fifty pesos allowance, but "available" coconuts seldom appeared in camp. Hot water now took the place of tea on the breakfast line.

There were hundreds of men and women — Van was one of them — whose flesh was drawn taut over ribs and backbone, resembling the hide of starved dogs. Knees, knuckles, elbows protruded in gnarled and swollen knots, while weakened muscles stood out like cords with the slightest movement. Arm and leg bones were scarcely hidden by their parchment-thin covering of skin. And the children — it made one's heart ache to see the skinny limbs and pot bellies that resulted from an inadequate diet.

All of us showed annoying symptoms of malnutrition. Urination was a constant and urgent need over which we had little control; intestinal afflictions, ranging in seriousness from worms to dysentery, plagued us; all of which made the bathroom lines longer and the waiting harder. Our discomfort was in no way alleviated by standers-in-line who insisted on recounting detailed syndromes of their maladies.

Internee volunteers now carried line meals to many of the

older men who were too weak to move from their beds. The hospital, more overcrowded than ever before, had no room for them.

Death from starvation was the most difficult to predict. One man — and there may have been others — died because he gave too great a share of his food to his children. Another, having waited too long to use his Red Cross food, succumbed to starvation with a full comfort kit in his possession. An old man keeled over dead in the Education building, a freshly copied recipe in his hand.

One morning in the breakfast line I saw but scarcely recognized old Mr Gross, the Canadian gourmand who had refused repatriation to spite his wife, now a long-time volunteer resident at Los Baños. The erstwhile glutton rolling in fat now looked like a wizened and jaundiced infant swathed in ill-fitting sacks — sacks of his own sagging flesh which hung in layers about his small frame. His eyes held a look which might have been terror: pitiful to behold and hideous. A few days later, Mr Gross died.

Van's good friend Mr Umpstead had collapsed and died early in December from overwork and undernourishment. We had watched him grow weaker and thinner after his arrival from Davao, and in vain had urged him to work less hard. In Santo Tomás, where every man was his own keeper, Umps had chosen to keep faith with his Maker, performing tasks for his fellow internees at the cost of his health and, ultimately, his life.

Another among the lamented dead was a retired Justice of the Philippine Supreme Court, who for months had prepared special foods for his wife, ill in the camp hospital. With faithful regularity he had trod the dusty road to the hospital, until at last his weary feet would carry him no more. In thoughtful care of his wife, he had neglected caring for himself.

The Commandant's office forbade mention in death certificates of starvation, malnutrition or beriberi — an order protested in vain by our doctors, all but one of whom then shrugged their shoulders and complied. The lone dissenter, a missionary, found himself locked up with other recalcitrants in the camp jail.

There were some who hailed the martyred doctor as a hero, and, in a sense, no doubt he was. Others thought that he could better have served God and his fellow men by ministering to the sick than by futilely rotting in a barred cell.

One thing stands out in my memory during this time of anguish: among the dying and the fast failing, there were no complaints; the starving showed no bitterness that some still had food. As in the beginning, there was mute acceptance of an ordeal in which every man looked out for himself. Those who had never been able to procure money accepted their lot as a gambler accepts his loss in a game of chance.

The deep grievance against Grinnell and his administration had at last faded away. We all knew that, whatever the reason for his imprisonment, he was paying dearly for the power he had wielded so long against our will. Aside from the Japanese, the sole remaining targets for angry scorn were thieves and profiteers. To the dying, even those were unimportant.

Among the living who were still strong enough to move about, the desperate effort to sustain life often entailed new troubles.

One man watched with bulging eyes each evening while Japanese soldiers fed rice and other grains to a couple of horses which they had brought into camp. As soon as the soldiers' backs were turned, he would sidle over to the horses and surreptitiously snatch a few handfuls of fodder from their feed bags. Once, when his startled eyes perceived that a group of internees had observed his pilfering, he sheepishly mumbled that he was procuring feed for his ducks. We learned that the same man had stolen cigarettes from the Japanese office. Entering on some pretext, he had made off so easily with a pack lying on a desk that he decided to try again; but the second time he was not so lucky. A Japanese soldier who spotted him in the act knocked him down and beat him up soundly.

A young Britisher who ground cornmeal for the camp kitchen

was arrested and tried for taking leavings from the grinder. Although his supervisor had assured him that it was all right to scrape out the cornmeal residue for his own use, our legal board tossed him into the camp jail.

Another "offender" was Bradley Fairchild, brother-in-law of the camp chief of police, Gordon MacKay. Struggling hard to keep the breath of life in himself, his wife, and his extremely feeble old father, Bradley was haled before the legal board because he had plucked pigweed from a ditch in the camp garden. Spunkily, Bradley defied the board. "I stole nothing from the camp," he declared stoutly. "I picked ditch weeds that belonged to no one. If you want to try me for it, you'll damned well have to come and get me." So saying, he retired to his air raid shelter dugout.

Since brother-in-law MacKay would have nothing to do with the case, a member of the legal board deputized three strong-armed lads from the garbage crew to route Bradley out of his hole. Bradley, a hulking six-foot-three or -four, still retained strength enough in his emaciated frame to put up a good fight; but three comparatively well-fed men against one half-starved one loaded the odds. The strongarmed gang dragged him into court, where he received a jail sentence, later commuted to hard labor: chopping trees for kitchen fuel.

On the heels of this well-publicized punishment for picking pigweed, a fifty-kilo sack of rice vanished from the camp's locked warehouse — undoubtedly an "inside" job by someone who had access to the warehouse. Since no individual needed fifty kilos of rice for survival, this theft was obviously perpetrated, by a thief or thieves who were never caught, to turn a quick profit from selling.

Some internees eked out their wretched existence by working in gardens which the Japanese had planted for their own use in front of the Education building. The wages: food and tobacco. Those driven by hunger to volunteer for this labor were sharply criticized by certain of their fellow internees. Should a man starve, then, and perhaps allow his wife and children to starve with him, rather than weed a Japanese garden?

Edwin Cogan one day brought us bad news about the Stevensons. Not only were they again out of food, but Walter Stevenson was sinking fast with tuberculosis of the throat. "What in the world are we going to do about them?" Edwin asked. "I can spare a few cans, but they'll need a lot more."

We contributed some of our own tins, enough, we hoped, with Edwin's to tide them over until they could buy smuggled food. Van then called on an American Meztizo named Brooks (nicknamed "Brooksey"), a smuggler, who succeeded a few days later in bringing in rice and beans at one hundred dollars U.S. per kilo, for which Walter Stevenson signed a U.S. dollar note countersigned by Van.

Financing smuggled goods became more and more intricate as time went on. Immediately after the Japanese took away our "Mickey Mouse" pesos, smugglers would accept Philippine pesos or, if they trusted a customer, U.S. dollar notes. Later, however, certain smugglers began to deal with Japanese guards in camp, who stole food from the Japanese warehouse to sell, but only for Mickey Mouse currency. There was enough Mickey Mouse buried around camp to carry on this operation for a time. Smugglers, who borrowed Mickey Mouse, sold their goods for Philippine pesos or U.S. dollar credit. The exchange rate for Mickey Mouse dropped within a few months from forty pesos to one dollar U.S. to sixty pesos to one dollar, and skidded very much lower before the end.

When buried Mickey Mouse became extinct, jewelry supplanted it as a medium of exchange with Japanese soldiers, who coveted diamond rings and wrist watches to take home to wives or sweethearts when the war was over. Internees desiring food or tobacco, which many craved to subdue the pangs of hunger, would carry their treasure to a smuggler for an estimate. A good diamond ring might net three kilos of rice and two kilos of beans, the quantity depending on how much the dealer could entice from the Japanese guard. The dealer's commission, a third or more of the total received, netted several hundred dollars on each transaction when he sold his share on credit to some other internee.

Many who dealt with smugglers condemned their profiteering and announced that they had no intention of paying their debts when the war was over. Whatever the ethics involved, illicit food dealers took a double chance: first, detection by the Japanese; second, non-payment for goods delivered. There were some internee dealers, however, who took no such chances. They were not smugglers, but hoarders who had bought sugar and other much sought-after foods to sell when prices soared high enough, or who sold part of their own Red Cross kits. A can of corned beef would bring one hundred dollars.

At least one internee sold his goods in lots. For 500 dollars, a starving fellow-internee could buy two tins of meat, several cakes of soap, some bouillon powder, firewood and assorted non-essentials. No substitutions or deletions: he could take the lot or leave it. Dealers in hoarded goods had one thing in common: they sold only for spot cash in Philippine pesos or American currency. No losses, no risks, unless the Japanese discovered their illegal money.

One day Japanese guards arrested the Meztizo smuggler Brooksey and locked him up in our camp jail. Mrs Brooks, forewarned by a friend that soldiers were on their way to search her shanty, quickly passed kilos of beans, rice and sugar out the window to a helpful neighbor. Then in clomped the soldiers. While attractive, pretty Mrs Brooks sat demurely on the bed, holding her attractive, pretty three-year-old daughter on her lap, Japanese guards ransacked the shanty, poking into every cupboard, every box, every jar, every crack behind the braces. They lifted the mattress of Mrs Brook's bed at both ends. Still Mrs Brooks sat quietly in the middle of the bed. Satisfied at last that the shanty concealed no evidence, the soldiers chatted with Mrs Brooks and played a while with her little girl.

Just after they had clomped away, Van stopped to ask Mrs Brooks if he could do anything to help. "I'm glad you've come," she replied. Rising from the bed, she reached under the mattress cover and pulled out a composition book. "If you want to do something for me," she continued, "take this out and hide it until Brooksey gets back. I didn't have time to get rid of it before the soldiers came."

Thumbing through the leaves, Van discovered that the book was a record of Brooksey's smuggling deals, past and pending, complete with customers' names and all relevant data. Between the pages were signed U.S. dollar notes, including the one that Van signed for Walter Stevenson. "My God!" was all that he could say.

"I don't know how I kept so cool while they were searching." Mrs Brooks trembled at the memory. "I think you'd better go now. Don't come back unless I send someone for you. The Japanese will probably watch the shanty, and they'll be suspicious of anyone who comes here."

In the evening, a messenger from Mrs Brooks told Van that the Japanese had found a notebook in Brooksey's pocket which listed names of internees who had given him articles to trade. Since the Japanese had forbidden trading for profit, Brooksey white-lied that he negotiated trades only for personal friends, who sometimes gave him a box of matches for his trouble, or sometimes nothing at all. An internee interpreter who had seen the book in the Japanese office named as many of Brooksey's customers as he could remember, among them Van.

Mrs Brooks suggested, as a precaution in case of a Japanese check up, that Van entrust her husband's important papers to someone whose name did not appear in the notebook. With a sense of relief, he turned over the vital evidence to a mutual friend for safekeeping.

Brooksey, an amiable and generally popular young man, had an enemy in camp who threatened a few days before his arrest to inform on him to the Japanese. Although there was no proof,

300

it was generally believed that the man had carried out his threat.

Knowing that jailed internees were allowed only line food, Mrs Brooks schemed with the jailer, who agreed to slip in to her husband a can of corned beef, providing that she paid him a can in commission. However, when Brooksey was released a week later (for lack of evidence), he told his wife that he had never even heard of the corned beef, much less seen or eaten it. Mrs Brooks then paid the jailer another visit. Normally a mild-mannered, gentle girl, she bristled now with the fury of a tigress, so cowing the tough internee jail-keeper that he handed back both tins without a whimper.

News of abuse to another prisoner outraged and dismayed the camp. A group of internees had been smuggling food, so they thought, to the valiant Chinese-American who was jailed rather than sign an oath to the Japanese. Their plan, to conceal regularly beneath the line chow some canned food from his own Red Cross kit, seemed to be working — until they learned that someone, presumably the jailer, was carefully removing the canned food before it ever reached he prisoner.

However weakened in body by long privation, the Chinese prisoner's spirit, at least, was as strong as ever: when the Japanese again offered to release him if only he would sign their oath, he still resolutely refused to sign. We saluted the courageous independence that led him to risk starvation for convictions and principles, but we greatly feared that he would never live to receive a hero's welcome.

Treachery and injustice of prisoners toward their fellow prisoners appalled us far more than mistreatment by the enemy, whose inhumanity we believed to have been inculcated by the traditional cruelty of the war-minded clique which long had dominated Japan. But among our own people there was no such explanation, and against them we had no recourse: any protest would have invited investigation and retaliation by the Japanese. Our dilemma had been shared the world over by those unfortunate enough to have fallen, whether by martial or political means, into the power of men who rule by force rather than by justice.

It is good to reflect on the words from our Pledge of Allegiance: "... with liberty and justice for all." And let none of us ever forget that with the death of a people's liberty, justice inevitably perishes, also.

Chapter Twelve

Dramatic activity on the part of the Japanese led us to believe on the morning of January 7th that they were about to abandon Santo Tomás. All through the night of the 6th, they had been feverishly burning documents and packing their belongings. Before morning, many soldiers already had left camp. Later in the day, Japanese consular liaison officer Hirose called on Fred Hagedorn, a shanty-neighbor of ours who had known Hirose well when he was Japanese consul in Manila some years before. Hirose confided to Fred that the Japanese planned to evacuate Santo Tomás on a moment's notice, and requested him to write after the war was over to his Brazilian wife and their two children, whom Hirose never expected to see again.

Knowing that Hirose had repeatedly taken our part against the Japanese Military, and had even gone so far as to risk his own neck by smuggling messages from outsiders and by bringing in food to pregnant women and mothers with infants, Hagedorn urged him to stay behind and surrender to the Americans. "There's no doubt that you will be well-treated by our army," Fred assured him. Hirose replied sadly that for the Japanese there was no surrender; that the army would not allow him to remain in Santo Tomás, but would force him to accompany them to the hills.

A startling conference took place during the day between Japanese officials from Los Baños and the Santo Tomás staff, who met to discuss a most unlikely topic: voluntary liberation of all prison camps. Los Baños internees, for the time being, were already on their own, as were also the few military prisoners (most of them left behind because of illness) who still remained at Cabanatuan. Earl Carroll, internee representative at the conference, vigorously opposed the Japanese proposal to abandon our camp, demanding to know where we were to obtain food, and who would protect us from Japanese soldiers outside.

On January 9, the following notice was posted on our bulletin boards:

> This morning, immediately after roll call, the Commandant summoned the internee committee and instructed them to make the following announcement to all internees:
>
> So that this camp may not become the scene of bloodshed endangering the lives of internees, the Commandant and his staff had planned to move to another place. Since such a condition has not yet arisen the Commandant and his staff are remaining. His anxiety for the welfare of the internees leads him to make public the following:
>
> 1. The Commandant's immediate concern is primarily in connection with food. It is also impossible to find any food in the city of Manila, but the Commandant and his staff will make every effort to secure food which can be found.
>
> 2. It is essential that we should make the fullest use of facilities within the Camp, and every effort must be made to keep the gardens going at full capacity.
>
> *The Internee Committee*

The Commandant and other officials from Los Baños returned to their "liberated" camp, Earl Carroll meanwhile claiming credit for having persuaded them to change their minds. Many internees censured Earl for his insistence that the Japanese remain, but whether he was right or wrong no one will ever know. We did not even know for sure that it was his opposition to their departure that had kept the Japanese in Santo Tomás. On January 6 an American task force had made a feint at Manila bay, then had continued northward. If, as Hirose had said, the Japanese planned to withdraw before the Americans took over, they may well have concluded that the time had come; then, when the task force sailed on, they perhaps realized that the danger of attack was not as imminent as they had feared.

Between the 6th and the 11th, American plane activity was almost continuous, and the Japanese accelerated the pace of their demolition program: the well-known "scorched earth" policy of destruction before enemy advance. Countless times, night and day, our shanties rocked with the concussion of colossal explosions that rustled our nipa walls like bursts of hurricane wind.

War news kept our hopes glowing. Allegedly, there was concealed in camp a radio, heard by a select few who passed on the news. We depended less however, on these word-of-mouth reports than on official Manila broadcasts beamed to us from radios in three houses situated at different location near our wall. The owners apparently worked in concert, because at each news period — and at no other time — one, and only one, of the three radios was turned on full blast. Sometimes the broadcasts came through as distinctly as a voice in the same room; again, we might catch only garbled words and broken phrases, the clarity depending on wind direction and relative street noise.

Soon we knew by heart the morning, noon and evening hours when news came over the air, and during those moments one could have heard a cat's footsteps in the shanty areas. If anyone chanced to forget, prompt shushings from all directions sounded a quick reminder of the all-important time of day. Through windows and doorways, as unobtrusively as possible to avoid attracting the sentries' attention, we strained our ears to catch every word, then compared notes on what we had heard and

305

passed the news along to others. The Japanese eventually discovered what our unknown Filipino friends were up to, and they succeeded in locating one of the radios, which they smashed. The owners of the two remaining radios managed to elude detection and, after a few days' silence, began again cautiously and intermittently to aim news broadcasts our way.

On January 11th, the radio confirmed a rumor that Americans had landed at Lingayen Gulf. We learned of task forces and convoys around Negros, Batangas and Manila Bay. The Japanese announcer disparaged American victories, quoting once from an article in the *New York Times* which warned readers not to be "too optimistic" about the Philippine campaign. Again he proudly read puppet-president Laurel's statement that Filipinos would "fight to the last man with the Japanese." In the same broadcast, he remarked that Americans were using Filipinos in their front lines, and that, although the Japanese so far had done nothing, they would soon "annihilate the enemy."

After the Lingayen landings on January 6th, we lived under permanent air raid status, which meant that we were permitted to walk across the campus only at periods announced over the loudspeaker. When internees disregarded this regulation, the Japanese served notice that unless movement between buildings and shanty areas ceased entirely, our shanties would be taken away.

Those who performed "essential" camp work were allowed to go to their jobs, but many non-essential activities were considerably slowed or brought to a halt by the order, which, for example, prevented me from reporting to the special activities committee in the main building. Mr Nolting, pained that his work was piling up, urged me somehow to sneak over to my job.

I recalled with amusement a recent discussion with my missionary boss about the moral right or wrong of disobeying the Japanese. Mr Nolting had then maintained that we should always follow Japanese regulations because a single violation, if discovered, could bring reprisal against the entire camp. I thought differently: smuggling food was forbidden, yet the risk, even of mass punishment, was well worthwhile to save internee lives. Mr Nolting rather vehemently disapproved of my moral outlook. His convictions now had undergone a remarkable turnabout: disobeying Japanese orders for the sake of special activities schedules appeared not only permissible but admirable, even though such defiance might cost shanty owners their homes. Mr Nolting had no shanty.

I declined to attempt anything so rash, but suggested instead that he arrange the release of my impounded typewriter so that I could do his work in the shanty. To this he readily agreed; we met at meal hours, when freedom of movement was permitted, and the schedules continued.

In justice to Mr Nolting, I must add that at this time he was recovering from a siege of beriberi, which may as grossly have altered his moral concepts as it had temporarily distorted his features. Only after days of hospitalization and vitamin B injections did his badly swollen face, mumps-jowled and slit-eyed, gradually resume its natural contours.

As cases of beriberi became ever more prevalent, it was no uncommon occurrence to pass without recognition a friend whom one had only seen the day before, so swift and disfiguring was the swelling stage of this disease. Van one day walked by a balloon-faced internee, not realizing until he spoke that this was a man he had known well for years.

"For God's sake, when did this happen?" Van asked.

"Started yesterday," the young man replied. "I'm taking vitamin B shots, but the doc says I ought to have food. We've been out about a month. I've got no money. I don't know what I'm going to do."

Van, knowing that his company would get credit, asked him why he did not sign a note to buy rice and beans.

"I tried, Van, but the dealers won't accept my note unless the boss signs for the company. A couple of us went to him several weeks ago and asked him to countersign our notes. He hemmed and hawed, and said he didn't want to do it unless it was a matter of life or death. He was afraid the Japs would find the note and get him for his signature. How does anyone know whether it's a matter of life or death? We said the hell with him. We'd sooner starve to death than ask him for help again."

"You need food in a hurry," Van replied. "I'll countersign your note."

Brooksey, back again in the smuggling trade, brought in rice and beans for this internee and three others for whom Van countersigned notes because their company manager refused. One of these was a woman whose husband had died at Cabanatuan Military Prison Camp, whose father had been killed by the Japanese, and whose infant son had died in Santo Tomás; she, who had no one else to turn to for advice, assistance or comfort, might have joined her beloved dead for all the company manager had done to keep her among the living.

It occurred to us to buy rice, beans, and sugar for ourselves. Rice we had never had, beans we had no longer, and our sugar was running very low — so low that when Edgar Kneedler asked us (as I had requested him to do when he brought us alcohol months before) if we could spare some meat and sugar, we gave him two tins of meat but could only offer half a cup of sugar. Yet, when we thought of the scarcity of smuggled goods, and the desperate need of many, greater than our own, we could not in conscience buy anything for ourselves.

On January 21st, the Japanese issued an order that worked grave hardship on the many whom chronic illness and hunger had weakened almost, but not quite, to the point of invalidism. The order stipulated that everyone not actually bedridden must attend roll call. Heretofore, a certain flexibility had been allowed semi-invalids; Van, for example, had seldom of late attended morning roll call. In the mornings he made up a little of the sleep lost during prolonged nightly asthma attacks, and was reported on the roll call list "sick in shanty." Now he, along with many others whose strength was ebbing daily but who were not yet bedridden all the time, had to forego badly needed rest in order to walk three blocks to report for roll call, where we stood in line from twenty minutes to an hour until reports were completed. When internees fainted, which happened not infrequently, they were carried quietly away to the nearest first aid office, while roll call routine continued as usual.

It is interesting to note in passing that, for all their meticulousness, the Japanese never once made a complete personal count of the camp population. Frequently they spot-checked a single group; yet potentially an internee might have climbed the wall and not have been missed for days.

During one morning roll call, a Japanese sergeant marched four soldiers out to change the guard. As they shuffled toward our line-up, the sergeant grunted an order which produced a memorable sight: instantly, the small group drew itself up to full, five-foot, round-shouldered height and strutted into a goosestep. If the sergeant had intended to amaze us, he succeeded admirably. All down the line, our titters swelled to rollicking laughter which not even the dread of another penalty ration cut could restrain.

Seldom enough in those grim days was there cause for laughter. The Japanese unleashed a fresh scare by demanding a list of all male internees between the ages of eighteen and forty-five, which brought visions of some sinister plan they might have evolved for our men of military age. Would they use them, perhaps, as a shield to their own front lines, or massacre them before the horrified eyes of wives, mothers and children? Or was the list merely a subtle torture to haunt our imaginations with fearful fantasies?

Apprehension and hunger reacted ineluctably on internee dispositions. In the close quarters of shanty areas, one could not avoid hearing words that never should have been spoken: a mother berating her children for wetting the bed; a husband cursing his wife for eating an extra spoonful of rice; a wife swearing at her husband because she was pregnant.

Yet many of our neighbors retained their equanimity throughout. Phil Shaouy, still boasting that he could lick his weight in wildcats, looked rapacious enough to have tossed into the pot any stray wildcat within reach; but he remained cheerful and optimistic.

Pop Phillip's wife, Ann, ill with a kidney infection, had returned, thin and weak, to her job on the meal-serving line as soon as she was able to be out of bed. After many months of faithful work, she now badly needed a rest, but to those who urged her to take one, she replied, "They need me."

Marie Pratt, five feet six-and-a-half inches tall and now a frail ninety-seven pounds, remained as poised and gracious as in pre-war days of luxurious plenty. Although weakness caused frequent fainting, she never spoke of her health. When we met in the air raid shelter, we exchanged news reports, dreamed of liberation, discussed plans for the future when the war was ended; we spoke also of music, of poets and philosophers, of history, of places far away that we had known and loved.

Tommy Pratt, who had lost pounds rapidly in recent months, still worked ungrudgingly at his food processing job. His face wore a drawn look, yet his courage and kindness never failed.

We tried to cheer one another as much as we could, and each day our hopes seemed about to be realized. Late in January, two American planes flew so low over Santo Tomás that we could see not only the stars and bars on the wings, but even the pilots' faces. Our hearts leapt as we cheered and waved to "our boys." Surely, surely the wait could not be much longer — but *how* long?

The night of February 2nd was clear and starlit. A tall tree that stood by the path near our shanty attracted fireflies by the thousands, their tiny lights dancing upward and whirling in clusters among the treetops like myriad sparks from a wood fire. It seemed almost that the great branches had gathered armfuls of stars from the sky above. Here, at least, were lights that no blackout could quench, lights that were gay and heartwarming to us who now had little of joy and beauty, that brought dreams of homeside fireplaces, of festive days, of shimmering lights along broad, American boulevards; each sparkling flash a symbol of freedom we had cherished so long in memory as we awaited the blessed day of its return.

PART FIVE : DAWN BREAKS THROUGH

Chapter One

All through the day of February 3rd, 1945, groups of low-flying planes swooped in from the north, wheeling at the northeast corner of camp (the corner nearest our shanty), then circling northward again. No bombing, no strafing, at least within earshot. Someone remarked that the planes looked like troop escorts. That evening we clearly heard every word of the news broadcast: our troops were twenty miles north of Manila. Perhaps the curious maneuvers we had witnessed all day indicated detailed reconnaissance before the big push. Another two weeks at most, we elatedly assured one another: then freedom at last!

Around seven p.m. we heard shots outside the wall, but paid little attention. Often before, the sharp staccato of rifle fire had broken the night's stillness: sentries signalling for tardy reliefs, or shooting to frighten some luckless stroller. Soon the shots intensified. We heard machine guns spluttering in the distance. Could it be that guerillas were staging an uprising in the city? The machine gun fire moved in closer, and outside the walls tanks rumbled by at top speed — Japanese tanks mustering for a counterattack? Keyed up as we were, the suspense was unbearable. Internees dashed hither and yon, swapping rumors and guesses. Suddenly a flare zoomed up over the front of our campus. That was too much for Van.

"Wait in the shanty," he told me. "I'm going to find out what the hell this is all about."

Above the gunfire, waves of shooting drifted through the night air. "The Japs are leaving, the Japs are leaving." Then, to my incredulous ears, another chorus, "The Americans are here!"

I could wait behind no longer. I did not quite believe the hysterical cries, but I had to find out for myself. When I rounded the corner by the Education building, I saw Van speeding toward me. We fairly ran into each other's arms. "I've just talked to my first American soldier!" he cried.

For a moment I was speechless. "Then it's true!" I managed to gasp at last.

"Sure. Let's go." His eyes were dancing, and he held tightly to my hand as we ran toward the main building plaza. One the way, he told me of watching our first tank charge into camp down the road from the main gate; of looking up and discovering amongst the soldiers Frank Hewlett, a former Manila news correspondent, now in uniform, who had yelled down to him, "Hello! I know you but I can't think of your name."

"Van Sickle."

The newsman jumped down and the two men flung their arms around each other. Then Frank asked about his wife, who was interned with us. Learning that she was in the camp hospital, he dashed off to find her.

As we pressed through crowds of internees on the plaza, we came suddenly face-to-face with our soldiers: twice as big as life to our starvation-ridden eyes, those husky young giants of the First Cavalry Division. Our joyful thoughts were too turbulent for articulation. We were stunned by the very suddenness of liberation, awe-stricken that so minute a force could have achieved instant victory — for our entire first-wave liberating army rode into camp in three tanks and a few jeeps.

At the moment, we had little time even to marvel at the miracle that had befallen us. Fresh excitement surged through the crowd. Someone cried, "Abiko's been shot!" We hastened toward the entrance of the main building, where swaggering Abiko, captain of the guards, lay prostrate. I turned aside before we reached the spot. To me, there was no joy in gloating over a dying man's body, however great the satisfaction in knowing that the world will forever be rid of a foul blot that once defiled it.

Many who did not share my squeamishness jammed around the limp form. Some hacked at Abiko's body with knives, slashing his throat from ear to ear before he was hauled away. Perhaps their efforts helped, for Abiko, still breathing when an internee doctor examined him, died during the night. Even death did not free Abiko from the internees' hatred. Men, women and children filed past his rigid mangled body, spitting in his face, taunting his corpse with grimaces and obscene gestures.

Again the Neolithic monster that hovers just beneath the civilized surface of our minds had sprung forth, club in hand, at the elemental call of vengeance. Each blow of that club smashes into a thousand bits the bright veneer, so carefully polished, layer on layer, throughout the centuries; and the brute of our primordial ancestor leers out at the chaos he has wreaked upon our enlightened entities. But few stopped to ponder the wreckage, or to wonder that man, who is capable of soaring to splendid heights, could sink so swiftly into the depths of degradation.

Things happened fast that night. Abiko had rushed out to the plaza, arms held high as if to surrender. Then he had grabbed for his belt, and one of our soldiers shot him. The doctor found a hand grenade concealed beneath his belt.

Consular officer Hirose, release man Ohashi and two other Japanese surrendered. I was glad that Hirose had his chance, and had taken it.

All the rest of the Japanese — sixty-three of them — made a dive for the Education building, barricading stairways and holing up on the second floor among internees. Our soldiers fired several rounds into the building. After an internee had been injured, however, there came a cease-fire order; our army did not want more casualties among us. Consequently, Japanese and Americans were at an impasse within the camp. Two hundred and sixty-seven internees were caught in the Education building, some who lived there, others who had merely wandered in to look down on what was happening outside.

Fearing treachery from the trapped Japanese, our soldiers ordered us all under cover. Just before we cleared the plaza, the camp jail was thrown open, and along with other liberated prisoners came our resolute Chinese American — thin, but determined as ever. The crowd gave a lusty cheer for the comrade whom neither Japanese threats nor internee treachery could daunt.

When we reached our shanty, we looked on amazed at our soldiers, in groups of three or four, digging foxholes along the wall. Naively, I offered mattresses, blankets, pillows and mosquito nets to make them more comfortable. The soldiers grinned like schoolkids whose teacher had fallen for an old gag.

"Naw, ma'am," drawled one of them, a strapping Texas lad, "Thanks just the same. We're so used to foxholes we couldn't sleep with all that stuff."

"Not even a mosquito net?" I persisted.

"No thanks, ma'am. It'd get in the way if we have to shoot down snipers."

We scarcely tried to sleep that night. The realization of our sudden freedom flooded away all weariness, and we lay in the darkness talking of our wonderful soldiers. Such calmness and courage, such self-assurance. No wonder Americans made the best soldiers in the world.

At five a.m., shanty dwellers were ordered into the main building for safety. The Japanese Education building still refused to come to terms, and our army feared some dastardly trick when daylight came. In the main building, hallways and patios were so jammed that we could scarcely find space to unfold our canvas chairs. Bathroom lines extended far down corridors; overworked toilets broke down, predictably, and had to be flushed with buckets. We washed grimy hands and faces in a thin trickle of water. Dishwashing was all but impossible.

During our tiresome ten-hour wait, we caught up on all that

had eventuated since the night before. Women with husbands and children in the Education building, still frantic with anxiety, were slightly reassured when the "magnanimous" Japanese permitted their hostages to receive food sent over from the central kitchen.

Since army rations had not yet reached Santo Tomás, we ate what rice and beans could be found in camp. Our portions were considerably amplified by supplies seized the night before from the Japanese warehouse and from trucks loaded for departure. Several internees had broken into a warehouse to scrounge cigarettes, tobacco, Japanese dried beef and whatever else they could lay hands on. Some who had seen the trucks swore they were laden with American canned goods. Red Cross supplies intended for us?

When the announcement came at three p.m. that we could return to our shanties, we made a dash for fresh air and the wide open spaces. Our little shanty looked almost like home; and when we talked with our splendid, bronzed soldiers of the First Cavalry Division, we could have closed our eyes and imagined, almost, that we *were* home. They were still standing guard around their foxholes, casual, easy, alert as panthers whose languid grace belies steely muscles poised for the spring.

They spoke of their homes, of their mothers and dads, their sisters and kid brothers; of what they had done before the war started; sometimes of what they hoped to do afterwards. Nothing much about the war, except when they had landed at Lingayen four days earlier, they were given road maps to Santo Tomás and were told to take the place as fast as they could. They had skirted the main army and headed straight for camp. We learned with astonishment that Santo Tomás was an isolated island of freedom, held in the heart of enemy territory by some 2000 troops that had come in during the night.

The soldiers told us that General MacArthur had been tipped off about a Japanese army plan to massacre every internee in our camp. Hence the urgency to liberate us first of all, a maneuver that caught the Japanese off balance; those outside still did not know what was happening. "It went off like clockwork," one of them declared. "MacArthur out-thinks the Japs every time. He'll be in here himself — he's always right at the front with us. I'm looking for him to come in about tomorrow."

Half-a-dozen internee children hung around to hear the soldiers' tales and to admire the bazookas, Tommy guns and other strange equipment from the faraway homeland that some of them had yet to see. The soldiers passed out chocolate bars from their own small combat rations. "It sure is good to see kids again," one of them said. "And American women. It makes me feel almost like I'm home again."

During the 4th and 5th of February, the Japanese set fire to a great part of Manila. Flames that stained the night sky a glowering red swept up to the very walls of Santo Tomás, gravely endangering the camp. While internees stood watch with the soldiers to stamp out burning debris that floated earthward among our shanties, the army alerted drivers of all vehicles in the area to be ready to evacuate us instantly, should the need arise. For a time it was touch and go; then the threat subsided as buildings nearby collapsed in charred ash heaps.

On the afternoon of the 5th, the Japanese who had barricaded themselves in the Education building agreed to leave peaceably. Retaining only their side arms, they were escorted by our soldiers to a spot several kilometers away. As soon as we heard the news, we rushed to the Education building to talk to the newly liberated internees, who told us that Japanese soldiers had shared candy and cigarettes with their prisoners, but that the officers, true to form, had remained insolently aloof. Everyone said, "They got off too easy." But how else could our army free the hostages?

Subsequently we heard that guerillas had killed the Santo Tomás Japanese, picking them off easily as soon as our soldiers turned back. Many thought sudden death too light a penalty for the High Command; for fat, ration-doler Shuraji especially, some had wished slow starvation before he received a ticket to join his ancestors. Nevertheless, in death our jailors could do no more harm; and what vengeful punishment could have restored life to those who had died of sickness, starvation and torture at the hand of the Japanese?

That same afternoon, we missed the troops guarding our foxholes and wondered if they might have formed a part of the escort for the Santo Tomás Japanese. Later, some of them returned, but when we enquired about their absent companions, we learned almost at first hand some of the horrors of war.

"I guess they won't be coming back," a survivor replied sadly. "We really got into it today. They sent us out to take a bridge — said everything was clear on the way. Before we reached the bridge, we ran into an ambush — Japs hiding in buildings that were supposed to be empty. They started pouring machine gun fire on us. I rolled off the tank into the gutter — they couldn't train the guns that low. I popped off a few of them when I could, and just lay there till things got under control. I think they got all the rest of the boys on my tank. We were trapped on that narrow street. I sure don't want to get into anything like that again."

Van wandered to the main building in the evening to pick up what news he could, and there he ran into a former internee, Russ Brines, the Associated Press representative who had gone to Shanghai in 1942. Repatriated in 1943, he had returned to camp with the Army. Van asked him whether he could send a cable to our families. "I can't do that, Van," Russ replied, "but I'll send back your names in a news dispatch. Emily's father being the Army Judge Advocate General, the message will go straight to Washington — probably be in the paper tomorrow."

Thanks to Russ, our parents got the news that otherwise would have taken some days to reach them. Official dispatches jammed the cable lines for weeks, but we began getting letters from home the very next day: letters written in October, the month when Leyte was taken. We eagerly ripped them open and read news that seemed, after these years, to have been written only yesterday. The Red Cross (which had brought in our mail) furnished limited quantities of note paper and we started immediately to pen messages home.

During the day, we wandered freely over a campus which already wore a new look: uniforms everywhere, tanks, jeeps, scout cars, gun emplacements, hastily constructed latrines, canvas water bags, a soldiers' VD medical tent. Our men lost no time in converting the erstwhile concentration camp into a military establishment. The new mechanized equipment astounded us. Most incredible of all was a huge vehicle which was a truck, boat and complete radio station all in one. This, we learned, was called a Duck. We began quickly to acquire a new vocabulary: Ducks, Alligators, and such terms as "G.I.", which we had perplexedly called "G-One" when we first encountered the symbol on a bulletin.

Army food supplies now began to come through to us: bread and tinned butter, dehydrated eggs and potatoes, canned fruits and milk, corned beef and rich meat stews. Cigarettes, also, and candy and chewing gum. The old army chow that G.I.s loathed tasted to us like ambrosia.

And then on the 7th of February, General MacArthur returned, as he had promised to do. Watching the flag-raising ceremony, our hearts filled with gratitude and pride, mingled with sorrow for those who had given their lives that we might be free, and for those of our fellow-prisoners who had not lived to see freedom again.

Chapter Two

Liberation, which had broken the shackles of imprisonment, brought fresh trouble of its own, for Santo Tomás remained a solitary stronghold surrounded by an enemy determined to annihilate us. Almost as soon as the Japanese had left camp, artillery shells began to explode near our wall. The main building, thrusting upward like a skyscraper above the razed and fire-blackened land around us, made a perfect target, and we knew it could not be long before the enemy would find our range. By the following day, Japanese guns had zeroed in: a shell tore a gaping hole in the wall just beyond our shanty, killing a nearby soldier. On the evening of February 7th, the First Cavalry Division pulled out of Santo Tomás, leaving rear-guard replacements. There was no rest for the brave: the Battle of Manila was on.

All the following day and part of the night, the Japanese scored bull's-eyes on the main building, where internee casualties (totalling more than seventy) were especially heavy. A shell ripped through the front entrance, badly wounding several and blowing one unfortunate woman to a thousand bits. Shanty dwellers, defenseless in their straw-and-matchstick abodes, did not know which way to turn. The stone and steel structure of the main building offered by far the safest shelter available, yet Japanese artillery was pounding it into a death trap. At first, Van and I agreed that our mud and bamboo air raid tunnel seemed the least dangerous spot, for there we were safe at least from fragments. We sat tight, hoping that shells marked, "To Whom it May Concern," would not concern us.

We spent the greater part of several days in the shelter, and a number of the night hours as well. Spasmodic Japanese firing kept us on edge all the time. No sooner would we venture out, after a forty-five minute lull, than they would begin blasting again, forcing us back like moles into our hole-in-the-ground.

Night shelling was especially exhausting and nerve-shattering. After diving half a dozen times into the mud enclosure, where the air was so foul as to be scarcely breathable, we would give up and agree to get some sleep, regardless of shells. Often we dropped dead tired onto our beds, slept fifteen minutes, then awoke with a start. Was that another shell? Was it fired by Americans or Japanese? At first, it was hard to tell, but soon we learned to distinguish between the "Boo-oo-m Swi-i-i-sh-sh" of American guns to the north and the "Swi-i-sh *Boom!*" of Japanese artillery in the city. Straining ears in the darkness to catch sound rhythms of the next shell, we sometimes heard both sides fire simultaneously with a confusing irregularity of booms and swishes. Why take a chance? Weary and frightened, we huddled again into the shelter, stepping gingerly over internee forms prostrate on mattresses, blankets and pillows paving the narrow dirt passageway. Finally, after four or five nights of sweating it out, we decided to seek refuge in the main building.

Jarred out of uneasy slumber by an ominous "Swish-Boom!" we would jump into our clothes, grab folding stools and stumble in breathless haste across the night-shadowed garden. When we had reached safety inside, we would pick our way through masses of miserably tired men, women and children who were standing, sitting or lying in the crowded back corridor, which was protected by the building's depth from direct hits. Eventually we would find a niche to park our foot-high canvas stools, on which we would squat sometimes for an hour, sometimes for three or four hours at a stretch. Many shanty dwellers, seeking a night's unbroken rest, dragged mattresses with them and slept in the main building corridors.

American observation planes hovered constantly over the city, spotting Japanese gun positions so that our artillery could knock them out or force them to new locations. When they succeeded, we had a brief respite, until a shifted gun began once more to explore our range.

Constant shell bursts, whether our own or the enemy's, do not make soothing music. American long-range artillery spoke from far away: a soft pung-pung-pung, followed by screaming whew-whew-whews as the shells whistled overhead. One felt a curious compulsion to duck, even though there was not the slightest doubt that the shells were ours. Closer and louder were the cannons that boom-swished their shells over us; but most startling of all was the hollow staccato of nearby mortar guns. When their resounding bung-bung-bungs shattered the relative silence, we nearly jumped out of our skins, and could have sworn they were emplaced directly behind our backs.

During the bombardment I became ill, and, to my utter disgust, the doctor ordered a liquid diet. The reason: inability because of partial starvation to assimilate rich foods. I smiled, but wryly, at the irony of having more food than we could eat, yet — because of undernourishment — only broth and tea!

Nervous tension from being shelled had, I think, much to do with my stomach's perversity: nothing in our current experience had made for peace of mind or metabolism. The metabolism settled down in a few days; the peace of mind was harder to recapture.

Soon after Japanese shelling began, our Army had removed from camp their few small cannons, in the vain hope that the Japanese would cease to regard Santo Tomás as a military objective. About a week later, there was a lull so prolonged that we thought our artillery had knocked out the last Japanese gun. Then, after a two-day breathing spell, they struck again with renewed ferocity.

Van and I, with some dozen of our shanty neighbors, were

crouched inside the air raid shelter when shells began bursting on either side of us, three of them striking the wall. Our shelter appeared to be in direct line of fire. Several panic-stricken internees dashed out and, while I hesitated at the entrance, Van grabbed my hand, saying, "Let's head for the main building." I ran along with him, but most unhappily, shouting that I thought we should stay behind until the shelling let up.

We were passing Bill Andrews' shanty, on the far side of the Harrises', when we heard a sickening swish rocket toward us. At the same instant, we saw Bill and Lettie, his Spanish wife, rush from their shanty toward the shelter. We threw ourselves on the ground just as the shell exploded behind us, so close that we were plastered with flying earth from the impact. As we jumped up, hearts pounding, legs in fast motion, another shell crashed ahead of us near the wall.

When we reached the Education building, Van said, "Let's go through. We'll make better time."

The thin-roofed Education building, converted into a hospital for internees and for wounded civilians from outside, afforded no real protection from shells. Nevertheless, being under cover gave us a false sense of security, and we slowed our pace through the long corridor. No sooner had we reached the exit, a door opposite the main building, than a shell burst in the lobby, which we had crossed only seconds before. "They seem to be following us," Van observed. And they continued following us. The moment we entered the main building, shells began pinpointing it. I do not know how many shells struck the building that day, or how long we waited there. Time seemed endless.

Shellfire is truly a terrifying experience — far more so than bombing, for at least one can watch enemy planes approach and can attempt to flee from them; while shells are hurled by an invisible robot who marks his target with ineluctable precision. One is helplessly trapped in the path of a ruthless machine-monster.

As we waited out the long hours, we wondered how friends left behind were faring in the air raid shelter. A late arrival told us that Lettie and Bill Andrew had been struck by the shell that had sprayed us with dirt. However, when we finally returned to our shanty, the first person we met strolling down the path was Bill Andrews.

"Bill! Thank God you're alive," Van exclaimed.

Then, fearfully, I asked, "Where's Lettie?"

"She's in the shanty."

"We saw you running — then the shell exploded right beside you," I said. "Later, someone told us you both had been hit."

"It was mighty close, at that," Bill replied. "That little banana tree between Charlie's shanty and mine was the only thing that saved us. We flopped on the ground just in time. The tree diverted the fragments." Bill began chuckling.

"It doesn't sound funny to me," I remarked.

"I was just thinking of Lettie. While I was lying there, she called out something that sounded like, 'I'm dead, I'm dead.' 'No,' I told her, 'you're not dead, Lettie.' 'I didn't say I'm dead,' she yelled, 'I said I'm deaf!' I have to laugh every time I think of it. She's okay now."

When we went inside our shanty, we had reason to be thankful we had not stayed there. Half-a-dozen wicked-looking shell fragments lay on the floor, having ripped three holes in our roof, one directly over my bed. The nipa shingles that formed our back wall had been slashed from end to end, as though a giant pair of scissors had nipped a jagged seam. The metal handle of our frying pan was splayed in two, its front section twisted into a fanciful curlicue.

Yet no one in our area was hurt. The Education building had suffered, but most of the day's casualties, as before, were in the main building. There among the wounded was a minister's wife who had lost an arm. Soon after she had been carried to the hospital, her husband returned to her room for her clothes, and was instantly killed by a second shell which struck the same spot near her bed.

Several direct hits had shattered my old room 44 on the third floor. Minna Nance was wounded in the hip. Another of my former roommates, a pretty girl of about eighteen, was badly injured by shell fragment which had struck her face. The doctors feared that she might never see again.

One of the most lamented casualties occurred in the gymnasium, where our doctors had set up an emergency surgical room which they decided to evacuate when shells began exploding dangerously near them. Just as they were leaving, Dr Francis, one of the three military doctors sent by the Japanese from Cabanatuan, rushed back for vitally needed instruments that had been overlooked. As he stooped to gather them up, a shell ripped through the wall. Dr Francis was instantly blinded by the shell fragments. All the camp mourned that this young doctor, admired for his skill and beloved for his ready smile, should have been stricken.

It is not surprising that several internees became shell shock victims. Undernourished as we were, weakened in physical and nervous resources, we were fit subjects for shock. We felt a special sympathy for a lovely teen-age girl whose mind snapped completely under the strain. Throughout internment she had worked willingly and well for the camp; but during recent months we had watched her waste away and grow listless from hunger. Now she was no longer hungry, but whether the ravages of slow starvation could ever be counteracted, the doctors did not know. When repatriation became possible, she was flown home with the first group by personal order of General MacArthur, and in time, happily, she did regain her health completely.

Starvation, too, continued to claim victims. Some who had survived to witness liberation were nevertheless too far gone to respond to nourishment that now was on hand in abundance. One who succumbed was a widely respected and admired altruist who, in the early days, had gathered together into one room of the Education building the camp's "problem children" — a group of teenage boys who had run wild and were causing much trouble with their mischief. Kind but firm in his discipline, he had transformed those young hoodlums into fine boys, helpful to the camp and a credit to themselves and their sponsor. Now, too soon, a useful life was ended; cause of death, TB induced by malnutrition.

There were many others, old men and younger men, dying after we thought the danger was past. The sad truth was that February's deaths from malnutrition continued at a higher rate than January's toll: somehow it was more unbearable now that the dawn had come.

Chapter Three

The shellfire that had kept us constantly on edge had also increased our impatience to shake the dust of Santo Tomás forever off our feet. But even as the wait became more intolerable, we realized that before we could leave, Manila had to be cleared of Japanese; and bit by bit our soldiers were liberating the city. The suspense mounted as they fought their way toward Bilibid Prison, where we believed that hundreds of our military prisoners were confined. On the very morning that the Army announced it was going in, we talked to the Stevensons, who were beside themselves with excitement and joy. Not least of their blessings was that Walter Stevenson, though still ill, had managed to survive. Moreover, word had just reached them that a friend outside had been able to save their many trunks, laden with furs and other valuables. And now, to crown their happiness, they expected that very day to see their son-in-law, Jack Littig, liberated from Bilibid.

Their premature rejoicing ended with tragic abruptness when the Army came back. Bilibid was liberated — but few of our men were left. The others had been sent away on ships: there were lists of names and sailing dates. Jack Littig had gone in December, on an unmarked ship which our flyers had bombed and our Navy had torpedoed until it sank, with most of its human cargo trapped in the hold.

The news, a cruel shock to all, paralyzed those who had husbands or sons among the missing men. Van met an army nurse, wife of an old friend who was among the lost, wandering

329

aimlessly in a daze. When he greeted her, tears came to her eyes. "Tell me what to do," she pleaded. "I can't think — I'm numb. We've just been told that army nurses are to be flown home with the sick boys from Cabanatuan. I don't know what to do. Today I had counted on seeing —" Tears choked her.

"Of course you should go home," Van told her. "You can't do anything here. Maybe things will turn out all right. You can't do anything but wait and hope."

"Thanks, Van. I'm going to take your advice. I hardly know what I'm doing. I just can't believe —"

Bilibid — hundreds of men — friends, fathers, husbands, sweethearts, brothers, sons — so near, we had thought; and now they were gone, all gone. How *could* one believe, at first?

Shock followed shock. Reports reached us from outside of atrocities perpetrated on civilians by the Japanese army: Spaniards and Filipinos shot down in cold blood as they ran from burning homes; people cremated alive in air raid shelters which the Japanese steeped in gasoline, then ignited; men, women and children bayoneted, their only crime running through the streets in search of haven among the chaotic ruins of the battered city. Spaniards, Filipinos, Chinese, Swiss, even Germans. Friends of ours — one entire Spanish family wiped out by mad monsters in Japanese uniforms.

Mingled with our horror was the full realization of what we in Santo Tomás had escaped. But for the grace of God and the brave and brilliant action of our armed forces, we, too, might have been wantonly massacred.

Our soldiers found evidence of another grisly Japanese deed when they discovered four decapitated bodies positively identified as those of Grinnell, Duggleby and two other internees arrested with them. Funeral services for the ill-fated men were held at Santo Tomás and their bodies were interred near the camp hospital. No need now for bitterness against Grinnell: whatever harm he had done us — or whatever good — he had paid for with his life.

Through some miracle, the internee buyers who had been arrested and removed from camp nearly a year before came back alive to Santo Tomás. We thanked God that such reunions were possible, and we prayed for those whose fate was still unknown.

Gradually, as the army pushed farther into Manila, we learned of others. All were well at Santiago Hospital, which had been undamaged; Mother Superior, the sisters and the nurses were still there, faithfully caring for those who needed them. We marvelled that the hospital, bordering Nielson Airport, had escaped the crossfire of bombing and anti-aircraft guns: surely God watched over his own.

Dr Campa had joined the guerrillas in September, and we could glean no information as to his whereabouts or well-being. But in due time he returned, safe and well and buoyant-spirited as ever.

Philippine General Hospital was badly damaged, but the few internees remaining there had come through safely. San Juan de Dios, the tuberculosis hospital in the Walled City, where the Japanese had run amuck, was completely destroyed. Between our own heavy bombardment and Japanese buoyants, few civilians had survived.

Ada Aplin, a patient at San Juan de Dios after her persecution in camp, was among the unidentified dead. There was a story told of finding by the altar of the hospital chapel a kneeling figure robed in a pale blue negligée, which Marie Pratt, who knew her better than I did, believed might have been Ada. "She was a devout Catholic," Marie told me, "and she had a pale blue negligée. It would have been so like her to take refuge in the chapel." Amid carnage and destruction, there appeared the quiet vision of a friend kneeling in death before her God, bringing peace and solace to the bereft in lieu of the horror which otherwise would have overwhelmed the spirit with images too painful to bear.

While the Battle of Manila raged, civilians of all nationalities sought refuge at Santo Tomás. Those with relatives in camp were

331

allowed to move in, and others who were vouched for by internees received passes to come and go. One evening, Big Van came over to our shanty. "Emily, have you any old clothes you don't need?" he asked. "Elsa Black is at the gate. They won't let her in on account of being German, but I talked to her. The poor kid is in rags. She spent eight days getting through the city — slept in the gutter — ducked shells and dodged Japs all the way. She's been living in a nightmare. I tried to get her into camp, but the Army won't hear of it. All I can do is round up some food and clothes for her. If you have anything you can spare —"

Mentally checking off my half dozen still wearable garments, I replied apologetically, "I haven't much, Van — a skirt and I think a pair of shorts, if Elsa can use them."

"Of course she can. That's wonderful. I'll try to scrape up a few more things so she can make herself decent."

Feeling in camp ran high against the half-Spanish, half-German young woman I have referred to as "Elsa Black." Daughter of a leading Manila Nazi and wife of an American, she had disagreed openly with her father's views. When war started, she had tried to help the Red Cross, but was snubbed by Americans who wanted no part of German assistance. In January, 1942, Elsa and her husband were brought to Santo Tomás with the rest of us. A week later her mother died. Released to attend the funeral, the Blacks elected to remain outside through German influence. Elsa stayed quietly at home and tried to help the camp as much as possible by sending in supplies, which were often ungratefully rejected.

Her husband had conducted himself with less decorum, frequenting Manila bars and nightspots even after the red armband days. Internees in camp and outside not unnaturally resented his actions; as a ward of the Germans, he had betrayed his own nationality, and by making himself conspicuous to the Japanese he was jeopardizing the privileges of all. The Japanese re-interned him in the spring of 1943, and immediately he was sent to Los Baños — through no accident, I suspect.

Enough of the husband; Elsa shared the contempt and opprobrium that were his portion. Most internees though that she should have remained in camp, regardless of her German nationality. One could scarcely admire her for valuing personal comfort above principles, of for changing sides twice when the going was hard. However, the rebuffs and innuendoes of self-righteous Americans and Europeans had made the decision no easier for her; and if she lacked the courage of her convictions, she had harmed no one but herself. I felt sorry for her now. My Van said, " I hope no one recognizes your skirt and shorts on Elsa." And I replied, "I don't care if they do!"

The prejudice of nationality against nationality, or perhaps more accurately, of those inside the camp against those outside, was brought ironically to my attention one happy day when two Spanish friends from Nasugbu paid us a brief visit. These Spaniards, who had served as guides to our armed forces after they landed there, and had helped to liberate friends in a nearby town still occupied by the Japanese, brought welcome news of Edu Roxas and others who recently had sought refuge in and near Nasugbu, to the south of Manila. Edu sent word that my jewelry was safe; he had taken it with him. Clothing, books and other personal effects we had left with him were burned up, along with all his own possessions at his Manila home. We were sorry for Edu's losses, compared with which our own were nothing.

We asked of Juan Elizalde: there was no word. And his brother — his brother's wife and family — his mother? Nothing — no news at all. Fred Guettinger? Enrico Pirovano? No, nothing. Manila was bedlam. They might be safe, but who could tell? And then again —

After our Spanish friends had left, I walked across the garden, past the shanty of one of the camp's leading food sellers. His wife, discussing Japanese atrocities with a neighbor, made a remark that engraved itself on my memory: "The Spaniards — hah! I have no sympathy for them. While we starved in here, they've been living the life of Riley outside, coining money hand over fist.

333

What's happening now serves them right."

I thought of Juan Elizalde, who had sent money and food into Santo Tomás as long as he was free, who, if he was still alive, had languished for more than a year in a worse prison than ours, starving, probably tortured, because he, a neutral Spaniard, who had given his services unstintingly to internees. I thought of Edu, and the many others who had helped us personally to a greater or lesser degree.

Then I thought of this woman's husband, whose sale of canned goods to fellow internees had netted a tidy fortune, allegedly stashed away in a locked trunk to which she kept the key. When he played poker, he paid his debts in IOU's. Life of Riley? Coining money hand over fist? People who live in glass houses. . . .

Chapter Four

Life in camp gradually resumed a type of interim normality, not dissimilar, in the sense that it was a normality of waiting, to our long period of internment. The routine necessary for existence re-established itself, with the difference that now we had food and friends and news from home, and even domestic help from Filipinos, screened by the Army, who were willing to wash dishes and sweep floors for a share of our ample rations. Thus, our day-to-day existence became easier in the physical sense; yet, because we were restive after our years of imprisonment and almost frantic with longing to escape the horror of death around us, we seemed at times to be riding a Ferris wheel, rolling over and over and getting nowhere.

Van had gained not a single pound since liberation and still suffered severely with asthma. I kept remembering that day in May, 1944, when he had hovered near death. Then late in February, an attack of vomiting and diarrhea laid him low. So violent were the seizures that I feared cholera. However, far from burning with fever, his hands and face were cold, clammy and grey. He lost consciousness every few moments, only to regain it in an agony of cramps. Frightened out of my wits, I called our neighbors Charlie Harris and Don Keiffer, who came over immediately.

While they stayed with Van, I ran to the Education building to find a doctor, only to be told that all patients must be brought into the hospital for treatment. I searched in vain for Dr Fletcher

335

and for two army doctors whom I knew: all were outside camp on special sanitation work. Leaving a message with Mrs Fletcher, I hurried back to the shanty, where I found Van still convulsively ill and so weak that Charlie and Don had to brace him in their arms to prevent him from collapsing while he used the pot beside his bed. But he refused to go to the hospital.

My thoughts raced in furious circles. If only we knew what was wrong....

Charlie and Don suggested a stimulant: Van refused whisky but tried to drink some coffee. Swathed in blankets, he continued to shake with cold.

Gradually — I do not know who first thought of it — we concluded that he might be suffering from heat exhaustion: he had stood bareheaded in the morning sun, waiting several hours for a friend from outside. I remembered that he had had similar attacks in the past, though never before so exacerbated. Anything was worth a try, and we began to give him salt water as prescribed for heat exhaustion.

All afternoon the paroxysms continued. When Dr Fletcher finally returned to camp at about four-thirty, he came immediately to our shanty, and after a careful examination, confirmed our diagnosis. "I can't do anymore for you than your wife and friends have already done," he told Van. "You'll start feeling better in two or three hours. Be sure not to stand in the sun without a hat anymore."

It was a blessed relief to know that, sick as he still was, Van's ailment was not critical. Nevertheless, that sudden attack made me more than ever anxious that he leave Manila quickly. Had it been only three weeks since liberation? What a lifetime it seemed!

While we waited, more friends came in: Spaniards, old army friends, officers of my father's corps, some of whom I had known, some who were strangers to me. No one could have shown greater kindness than those army men, who gave us the best of all they had. Among the Spaniards, we rejoiced to see Dr

Aboitiz, thinner by some thirty pounds, but safe and healthy. And at last, when we had all but given up hope for him, we heard a shout outside our shanty, "Anybody home?"— and there was Fred Guettinger!

Fred had had a bad time making his way through Manila. Every building he had chosen for shelter was either shelled by Americans or burned by the Japanese. He had narrowly escaped trouble with Japanese soldiers, especially on one occasion when they had almost discovered records he was carrying of money borrowed for internees — auditor that he was, he could not bring himself to destroy those incriminating records. He had been hauling knapsacks over his shoulders when two guards halted him. As Fred looked on, a cold sweat pouring from his brow, they meticulously examined the innocent contents of the first sack. Then one soldier turned away while the second, evidently believing that both sacks had been inspected, picked up the account-filled case and helped Fred throw it over his shoulder.

"The Japs didn't seem to know what they were doing anywhere," Fred remarked. "In some parts of Manila, they actually helped civilians. In others, they killed them on sight. A Swiss chap who is staying at the same house with me was wounded by shell fragments, and he lay in the street with a dozen injured Filipinos until a Japanese civilian took him into his house and dressed his wounds. When he mentioned the Filipinos who lay wounded beside him, the Jap said, 'Oh, Filipinos? No. Can't help.' Yet it was the Filipino they tried to make friends with, not the European. You just can't figure them out."

When we asked about friends at the Swiss Club, Fred told us that some had survived; however, his closest friend, who had left the Club with him after the fighting started, had been killed because he turned back to help his wounded servant girl. He had dragged the girl into the German Club air raid shelter just before Japanese soldiers had drenched it with gasoline and set a torch to it.

After more than three years' knowledge of Japanese cruelty —

337

the Death March of Battaan; the abuse and starvation of military prisoners; the beating and execution of civilian internees; the starvation of interned men, women and children; the bayoneting and burning of innocent neutrals — it was not surprising that we in Santo Tomás abominated all that pertained to Japanese militarism. However, it sickened me to read in an overseas copy of a New York newspaper that American "Patriots" harbored such violent hatred toward the Japanese as a race that they kicked and spat in the faces of wounded Nisei heroes who had fought with exceptional valor in Italy. What were we fighting for, I wondered, if not to wipe out tyranny and race prejudice? Was this Americanism, to abuse men who believed so strongly in our ideals that they offered their lives to save our country and our necks? If so, neither country or necks were worth saving.

In camp there were Nisei soldiers among our liberators, whom we saw bring in Japanese snipers for questioning. We owed our lives to those brave men, men of varied backrounds and racial origins who had fought gallantly for us. Yet I heard internees express feelings of loathing and abhorrence for our Nisei soldiers. Undoubtedly, had they dared, they would have spat in each face that bore Japanese features.

I have never understood those who condemn a race or a nation because some of its members are reprehensible. If we encounter a score of mad dogs, we do not jump to the conclusion that all dogs are mad. Should we be less intelligent in our assessment of human beings? The imponderable hatreds caused by the war grow like cataracts until our spiritual vision becomes dimmed and distorted, like the sight of some child peering through darkness at harmless shadows which his frightened fancy conceives to be goblins or ghosts or other fearful phantoms of the night.

"If the light that is in thee is darkness, how great is the darkness itself." We had come through the external darkness of imprisonment into the light of freedom; but to guard that light, to keep it burning brightly as a beacon for all the world, there must be light within: the light of justice and love. "When we reach home," I thought, "we can help to keep that light burning!"

Home! The day came at last. An army friend, Colonel C.C. Young, burst in on us at about noon of March 9th. "Hey, folks, you better get packed. You're going home!"

"What? Who told you? Are you sure?" Van and I exclaimed in breathless unison.

"Sure I'm sure. One of your pals in Administration asked me to tell you. They're flying you to Leyte in about an hour, so you better pitch in!"

Van hurried to the office for details, while I tore suitcases apart and threw things helter-skelter back into them. We had been packed for days, but not to go by plane, having been told that no more internees would be flown out. Now it was necessary to cut down weight, still keeping clothes enough for the boat home from Leyte.

When Van returned, the loudspeaker boomed out the names of repatriates, and friends began pouring in to say goodbye. I hated most of all to leave behind Marie Pratt, still so thin and wan that I wondered whether she would ever again be really strong. However, like Van, she had somehow survived the worst, and now it was just a matter of time.

Van and Colonel Young carried our bags to the front of the Education building, where army trucks were waiting to take us out. After a few words with the officer in charge, the Colonel came back beaming.

"It's all fixed up. You're going with me. I just got permission to drive you to the airfield."

We whipped along in the middle of the truck convoy: across a pontoon bridge; past shattered façades that once had been building fronts; through the Walled City where, although parts of the south and west walls were intact, there remained not even a trace of stone to indicate walls sixteen feet high and twenty feet thick that had risen from level land to the east and from the river on the north. In the rubble-strewn port area we were ordered to speed up because of snipers. Bumping along the shellpocked streets through the ruins of a once-lovely city, we saw little that was familiar: the gutted shell of the Bay View Hotel, here and there a crumbling fragment of some unidentifiable building, and of course Manila Bay, whose beauty even war had not marred.

Soon we reached Nichols Field, where our bucket-seated C-46s were warming up.

"Goodbye, Colonel. Thanks for everything. Take care of yourself."

"Happy landings!"

As we boarded the plane, two soldiers helped us don lifebelts. Then we roared off the field, up over the city, and circled back across Santo Tomás: one more goodbye to the camp, and to friends we had left behind; one last look at the city we had loved, the city that had brought death and destruction to so many, the city that held the secret of Juan's fate, and Enrico's — a fate that we learned, only months later, with deep sorrow, when their graves were identified by Japanese war prisoners who had sent them, and many others, to their deaths.

We who had survived imprisonment in Santo Tomás had much to be thankful for: that loyal friends had been permitted for many months to help us; that women had never been isolated in separate camps and had been treated, if not with consideration, at least with indifference; that we had never had to contend with the discomfort of cold, which, added to other hardships, undoubtedly would have caused many more deaths. Although several dozen internees had been beaten and tortured, and more than thirty had been executed or had died from brutal punishment, most of us had escaped corporal punishment in any form. Numbers had died of starvation, and all of us had been hungry; yet the vast majority had lived to see dawn break over our twilight world.

For more than three years, some four thousand of us had lived together, worked together, hoped together, hungered together, sorrowed together and rejoiced together. If those dreary years of captivity had taught us anything, surely it was this: that no nation or race holds a monopoly on virtue; that all individuals of all races and nations can be valiant or cowardly, kind or cruel, just or grossly unjust; that evil triumphs when just men grow weak and complacent; that therefore, seekers of true and lasting peace, which springs only from justice, must be strong: not with the strength of a bully to torment and terrify the weak, but with the strength of men who, knowing that they *are* their brother's keeper against ruthless forces of tyranny, "seek first the kingdom of God and His justice" to protect the rights of the weak as well as the strong. Such men seek peace through reason, self-sacrifice, education, and consultation with their fellow men of all nations and beliefs; but if those means fail, they have the courage and intelligence to stand firm, united in battle against all who would crush freedom and justice.

We in Santo Tomás learned to exist without the freedom that we had taken for granted before the war, and we learned that its loss means suspension into a trance-like nightmare, waiting for a re-awakening to life itself. Having been restored to the living, may we who regained our priceless freedom be ever vigilant in guarding it, not only for ourselves but for, and with, all our fellow human beings, against any who would deny the just rights of others, whoever they are, wherever they may be: that the whole world may some day truly live in peace. Dawn had come for us; how far the dawn for all?